Understanding Local Area Networks
Second Edition

Stan Schatt

HOWARD W. SAMS & COMPANY

A Division of Macmillan, Inc.

11711 North College, Suite 141, Carmel, IN 46032 USA

*This second edition is dedicated to my wife Jane,
who I hope will always understand
why all of my books are dedicated to her.*

©1990 by Howard W. Sams & Company

SECOND EDITION
FIRST PRINTING—1990

International Standard Book Number: 0-672-27303-9
Library of Congress Catalog Card Number: 89-64340

Acquisitions Editor: *James S. Hill*
Development Editor: *James Rounds*
Manuscript Editor: *John E. Spence*
Illustrator: *T. R. Emrick*
Cover Art: *DGS & D Advertising*
Cover Photo: *Cassell Productions*
Indexer: *Hilary Adams*
Compositor: *Shepard Poorman Communications Corp.*

Printed in the United States of America

Contents

Preface

Since the birth of the IBM PC, the microcomputer has become a common sight. Until recently we lacked the technology to connect these units so that companies could share expensive resources and ensure data integrity. This situation changed, however, with the release a few years ago of MS-DOS 3.1, which comes with network features, and with the development of faster microprocessors such as the Intel 80386 and 80486 to serve as the workhorses of network file servers. Today we have both the necessary software and hardware to implement cost-effective, efficient local area networks (LANs). Although we use companies in our examples for convenience, the use of LANs is certainly not limited to them but also includes such organizations as universities and hospitals.

In order to understand the benefits of a local area network and what greater connectivity can mean for a company, we need to understand the basic building blocks of a LAN. The first three chapters of this book cover the hardware and software fundamentals of a LAN and the requirements for a network to communicate with other networks and with mainframe computers and minicomputers. The connection between microcomputers and mainframes is increasingly important because we now have the software to transfer mainframe data to a LAN and to manipulate this data within the programs. Advances in the telecommunications industry also relate to LANs, since it is now possible to transmit voice and data signals simultaneously. Therefore, we will also examine how some companies are using their telephone system as LANs.

The next five chapters apply this network theory to major LANs from IBM, Novell, 3Com, and AT&T as well as to several different LANs running on Macintosh computers. The Macintosh has often been shortchanged in LAN books, so this book tries to balance its coverage by providing an in-depth look at NetWare, 3+Share, and AppleShare and AppleTalk networks.

Chapter 9 covers three networks that are becoming increasingly popular: VINES, 10Net, and Arcnet. With VINES we can see how a universal naming service works to simplify internetwork connectivity. 10Net provides examples of peer-to-peer networks in which individual workstations have the opportunity to share resources with the network. And Arcnet represents a flexible topology network that provides economical performance.

The last three chapters examine some significant management issues associated with LANs. Chapter 10 takes an in-depth look at electronic mail on a network through "hands-on" tours of several major software packages and an examination of the theory behind the X.400 electronic mail standard. Chapter 11 presents some guidelines for networkable software, and Chapter 12 serves as a guide for selecting and managing a LAN.

This book is arranged somewhat like a textbook, with quizzes following each chapter. Each chapter builds on the previous chapter's information. Try to master a chapter before moving on. If you wish to explore the data communications topics in even more depth, a companion book in this series entitled *Understanding Data Communications* should prove useful. If you wish more information on Novell's NetWare, the LAN operating system with the largest share of the market, my *Understanding NetWare* will provide you with a much more detailed description. I hope this book will help you understand why local area networks are destined to become an important part of our lives. I also hope it will prove valuable if you are considering a local area network for your company or organization.

ACKNOWLEDGMENTS

I wish to acknowledge the technical expertise and generous help of Marc Covitt of Hewlett Packard; Steven Fox, David Guerro, and Randy Sprinkle of AT&T; Orval Luckey of IBM; and Bob Schulte of 3Com. I also want to thank a few students—Jo Conley, Steve Leopold, and Ken Robinson—who made teaching local area networks fun. I want to thank Howard W. Sams for permission to reprint portions of *Understanding NetWare*.

Trademarks

All terms mentioned in this book that are known to be trademarks or service marks are listed below. In addition, terms suspected of being trademarks or service marks have been appropriately capitalized. Howard W. Sams & Company. cannot attest to the accuracy of this information. Use of a term in this book should not be regarded as affecting the validity of any trademark or service mark.

AppleShare, AppleTalk, and Macintosh are registered trademarks of Apple Computer Corporation.
Arcnet is a registered trademark of Datapoint Corporation.
cc:Mail is a trademark of CC:Mail.
COMPAQ is a registered trademark of Compaq Computer Corporation.
The Coordinator is a trademark of Action Technologies.
dBASE III Plus and dBASE IV are registered trademarks of Ashton-Tate.
DEC is a registered trademark of Digital Equipment Corporation.
Ethernet is a registered trademark of Xerox Corporation.
Hewlett Packard and HP LaserJet Plus are registered trademarks of Hewlett Packard.
IBM is a registered trademark and IBM PC, AT, XT, PS/2, Systems Network Architecture, NetView, PC LAN Program, PC LAN, Token Ring Network, and LAN Server are trademarks of IBM Corporation.
Intel is a registered trademark of Intel Corporation.
Lotus 1-2-3 is a trademark of the Lotus Development Corporation.
Microsoft is a registered trademark and WORD, Multiplan, MS-DOS, and OS/2 are trademarks of Microsoft Corporation.
Multimate is a trademark of Ashton-Tate.
The Network Courier is a trademark of Consumer Software.

Microcomputers and Local Area Networks: A Survey

ABOUT THIS BOOK

This book is intended to explain how local area networks and their various
hardware and software components work. Throughout it tries to strike a
balance between theory and practice. On the one hand, it examines the theory
behind the various kinds of network architecture (the different forms
networks take) and the various methods of data transmission (how
information is sent through a network). On the other hand, it discusses the
major local area networks themselves and the degree of compatibility among
them.

In the course of this book you will learn about several of the major
issues facing local area network users today, including network security,
compatibility between network software and application software written
under DOS, and bridges between different local area networks. You will also
be introduced to some of the more innovative approaches to integrating voice
and data over a network, and you will examine the ways that local area
networks can now communicate with mainframe computers.

Since the first edition of this book, the Apple Macintosh has become
the workstation and file server of choice in many local area networks. This
edition therefore adds substantial material on Macintosh networks and
bridges between the Apple and IBM worlds. The main goal of the book
remains the same, however: to help you decide whether a local area network
is really a viable option for your office or organization.

ABOUT THIS CHAPTER

Before studying the theory behind contemporary local area networks, it is
important to examine the personal computer that serves as a network
workstation. This chapter provides a brief tutorial on the IBM microcomputer
environment. Some of the unique features of the Macintosh will be covered in
Chapter 7, which looks at the various Macintosh networks currently available.
If you are already familiar with this subject, you may wish to skip to the
second half of the chapter, which reviews the history of local area networks
and then describes a typical company that is using today's network
technology to handle a wide range of office functions. By the time you finish
reading this book, you should have a good understanding of how to achieve
the same level of network integration as the Widget Corporation illustrated in
this chapter.

THE IBM PERSONAL COMPUTER: A TUTORIAL

Because so many businesses have selected IBM personal computers or computers designed to run IBM PC programs (*compatibles*), these machines have become the building blocks of local area networks. Later in this book you will learn how dozens and, in some cases, even hundreds of these computers can be linked together by network software, network hardware, and cabling so that information and resources such as printers can be shared by a number of users. Although I will define local area networks in a much more precise fashion later in this chapter, at this point you must realize that each network user has his or her own personal computer and that often this unit is an IBM PC or compatible. Before looking at how a network actually functions, you need to understand how information is processed by a microcomputer such as the IBM PC. Figure 1-1 shows an IBM PS/2 Model 50, an example of the second generation of IBM's microcomputers.

**Figure 1-1.
An IBM PS/2 Model 50**
*(Courtesy of IBM
Corporation)*

Bits and Bytes

Computers can keep track of whether a wire has current flowing through it (1) or no current flowing through it (0). We refer to each of these binary digits of information as a *bit*. The American Standard Code for Information Interchange (ASCII) specifies that each character of the alphabet requires seven bits of information with an eighth *parity* bit as insurance that the information has not been garbled. To an IBM microcomputer the binary combination of 10000010 represents the letter *a*. This 8-bit unit of information is known as a *byte*.

The original IBM PC contains an Intel 8088 microprocessor, a microcomputer chip that serves as the *central processing unit* (CPU), or brains, of the computer. This particular chip can process 16 bits (2 bytes) of information at one time. The CPU has a clock speed of 4.77 megahertz (MHz). This means that the microprocessor produces 4.77 million pulses each second. It schedules its work based on these pulses. Some microprocessors have faster clock speeds and thus can perform tasks such as mathematical operations faster. The IBM AT (Advanced Technology), for example, uses an Intel 80286 microprocessor and has a clock speed of 8.0 MHz. The IBM PS/2 Model 80 uses a 32-bit Intel 80386 microprocessor and has a clock speed that can reach 25 MHz. The next generation Intel 80486 microprocessors are already approaching a speed of 50 MHz. Since a local area network generally will use its fastest, most powerful computer to service network workstations, clock speed becomes a significant factor in a local area network's overall efficiency. In addition to performing routine mathematical operations, a PC's CPU also processes information that comes to it from a variety of sources, including the keyboard. It needs a workspace in which to store some of its calculations temporarily, a need it satisfies by using some of the computer's memory.

RAM and ROM

There are two types of memory associated with microcomputers—random-access memory (RAM) and read-only memory (ROM). ROM is permanent memory that retains information even when the computer is turned off. Microcomputers store their most critical programs in this area, including a program to diagnose the computer when it is turned on to ensure that all components are working properly. A computer also stores its *bootstrap* program in ROM, the program that provides the computer with enough knowledge to load information from a disk.

Unlike ROM, random-access memory (RAM) is temporary memory that retains information only while the computer is on. It is measured in *kilobytes* (thousands of bytes of storage). The original IBM generally came standard with 256K (256 kilobytes) of RAM on its system board ("motherboard"), but it could be expanded to 640K by adding a memory circuit card to one of the expansion slots located on the motherboard. Using the original IBM PC as an example, Figure 1-2 illustrates the location of both ROM and RAM on its motherboard.

Expansion Slots

The expansion slots illustrated in Figure 1-2 are sometimes known as *peripheral slots* since they link the computer's CPU with external devices or *peripherals*. One slot might be used for a disk controller card that links the computer to a disk drive capable of reading information on disks. A second slot might contain a printer interface card that connects the computer to a printer. A third slot might contain a card with a built-in modem that can transmit information over a telephone line to a computer in another city.

Monitors and Video Adapters

Unlike today's second generation of IBM microcomputers, which have built-in video interfaces, the original IBM PC uses one of its expansion slots for a video adapter, a circuit card that sends video signals to a monochrome or color computer monitor. A monochrome monitor displays one color in addition to black, and generally amber, green, and white are the types of monochrome

Figure 1-2.
An IBM PC Motherboard

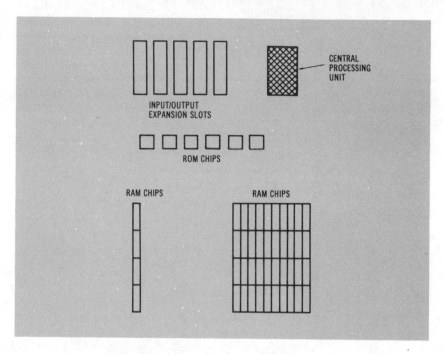

monitors used with an IBM PC. Because of its high resolution, a monochrome monitor is ideal for word processing, spreadsheet analysis, and database management, all tasks that do not require color. A monitor's screen contains a number of small blocklike picture elements (pixels) that are either lit or unlit to form characters. The number of pixels that can be displayed horizontally and vertically is a function of both the monitor and its video adapter card. For the original IBM PC, IBM offered the Monochrome Display Adapter, which could display 720 horizontal pixels × 350 vertical pixels. This is still considered to be very high resolution.

A monochrome monitor requires a monochrome adapter card in one of the PC's expansion slots and a cable connecting the card to the monitor. Many computer users with monochrome monitors want to see graphs displayed on their screens, which is possible only if the monochrome adapter card can also display graphics. Although IBM's own monochrome adapter card does not permit graphics to be displayed, several companies offer video adapters such as the Hercules Monochrome Graphics Card (from Hercules Technology) that can display graphics without diminishing resolution.

Users of the original IBM PC who wished to display color graphics usually selected a color graphics adapter (CGA) or an enhanced graphics adapter (EGA) along with a monitor capable of displaying the appropriate level of resolution. CGA cards, for example, provide a monitor with 640 × 200 resolution and can also display sixteen colors, though only four simultaneously. EGA cards, on the other hand, provide 640 × 350 resolution and can display sixty-four colors, sixteen of which can be displayed at any given time. Table 1-1 summarizes the different standards for monochrome, CGA, and EGA cards and the standards associated with IBM's second generation of microcomputers.

**Table 1-1.
IBM Video Adapter
Card Standards**

Standard	Resolution Pixels	Total Colors	Colors/Screen
Hercules MDA	720 × 348	N/A	N/A
CGA	640 × 200	16	4
EGA	640 × 350	64	16
PGA	640 × 480	4096	256
MCGA			
CGA Mode	640 × 200	4096	256
Text Mode	640 × 480	16	2
VGA			
CGA Mode	640 × 200	4096	256
Text Mode	720 × 400	16	2

Most programs require a user to indicate specifically which type of video adapter card will be used so that the program will send the proper signal to the card. As you will discover later in this book, this can present some problems when a program is used on a local area network, since different workstations may contain different video adapter cards.

Disk Drives and Disk Storage

Because the RAM retains information only while the computer is turned on, a disk drive serves as the standard storage device. A disk (Figure 1-3) must first be prepared to handle information sent from the IBM PC through a procedure called *formatting*. Today IBM's second generation of microcomputers uses high-density 3½" diskettes that hold more than a megabyte of storage. The majority of original IBM PCs and compatibles found on networks still use the standard 5¼" disk format that holds approximately 360,000 bytes of data. A formatted disk contains 40 concentric circles, or *tracks*, each of which contains a number of 512-byte *sectors* or blocks for storing data. The computer maps these sectors so it can keep track of precisely where on a disk specific information is stored. IBM PC and compatibles format a disk so that it is double-sided double-density (DSDD). There are 9 sectors per track and 40 tracks on each side of the disk. Simple mathematics reveals that each formatted DSDD disk can hold 40 tracks per side times 9 sectors per track times 512 bytes per sector times 2 sides per disk, for a total of 368,640 bytes per disk.

**Figure 1-3.
Floppy Disk for an IBM
PC or Compatible**

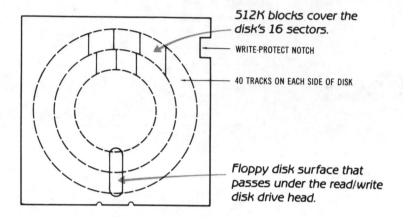

*512K blocks cover the
disk's 16 sectors.*

WRITE-PROTECT NOTCH

40 TRACKS ON EACH SIDE OF DISK

*Floppy disk surface that
passes under the read/write
disk drive head.*

Information is saved on these disks in the form of files. Most IBM PCs and compatibles have two disk drives (labeled A and B) so that information can be copied from a disk in one drive to a disk in the second drive. In much the same way that a record player functions, a *read/write* head on a disk drive moves across the tracks of a spinning disk until it locates a particular file of information. Then it stops the disk from spinning and copies the pattern of bits to RAM locations within the computer. The time it takes to accomplish this task (the *access time*) is measured in milliseconds (thousandths of a second) whereas tasks performed by the CPU are measured generally in nanoseconds (millionths of a second). Obviously, if several computers need information that is stored on a particular disk, this disk access procedure must be repeated a number of times, resulting in a measurable slowdown in computer operations. In later chapters we will discuss this problem and the methods several local area network manufacturers have developed for speeding up this procedure.

Hard Disk Drives

A user can work faster and more efficiently by loading all programs and data files onto one hard disk drive. Rather than using several dozen "floppy" disks, he or she can place all information on a single hard disk drive unit capable of holding anywhere from 10 megabytes (10 million bytes) to several hundred megabytes of information. As Figure 1-4 illustrates, a hard disk is actually a rigid platter coated with a metal oxide material that looks very much like a phonograph record. In the sealed hard disk unit, the read/write head travels rapidly (about 3600 revolutions per minute) on a very thin cushion of air that separates it from the magnetic surface of the hard disk. The distance between the read/write heads and the magnetic surface of the hard disk varies from 1 millionth of an inch to ½ millionth of an inch depending on the brand of hard disk. It might take approximately thirty milliseconds for the hard disk to locate and load a file compared to ninety milliseconds with a floppy disk drive. You will learn in the next chapter how hard disk drives can serve several different personal computers in a network environment.

Figure 1-4.
A Hard Disk *(Courtesy of Seagate Technology)*

The Disk Operating System (DOS)

For the IBM PC and compatibles a series of programs handles such "housekeeping" tasks as loading programs into the computer from a disk, saving information to disk, and translating typed keyboard characters into a number language the computer can understand. These programs collectively make up the Disk Operating System (DOS). The IBM PC version licensed from Microsoft Corporation is known as PC-DOS, and the identical programs used by IBM PC compatibles are known as MS-DOS (Microsoft Disk Operating System). Among other routine tasks, DOS helps users format a blank disk, copy a file from one disk to a second disk, and delete a file from a disk.

The most significant portions of DOS are the Supervisor, the Input/Output Manager, the File Manager, and the Command Processor. The Supervisor coordinates the activities of other programs and runs programs sequentially when necessary. The Input/Output Manager ensures that the computer can communicate effectively with a wide range of peripherals, including disk drives and printers. The File Manager keeps track of all information stored on disk so that data may be retrieved quickly. Finally, the Command Processor provides communication between the computer user and the computer itself. When the user types characters they are converted into a language the machine can understand.

Microsoft has published several different versions of PC-DOS and MS-DOS that, for the most part, are upwardly compatible. Although under most conditions it is not possible to mix different DOS versions of programs on the same disk, you will learn later in this book how some local area networks divide a hard disk into various sections, each of which can contain programs running under a different version of DOS.

Although DOS is designed specifically to coordinate the communication between a computer and the rest of its world, including disk drives, printers, and keyboard, some local area network programs superimpose a "shell" around the DOS programs and intercept commands normally handled by DOS. As you will see in Chapter 5 when you examine the Novell NetWare software, this approach is advantageous because several people can use a program that originally was designed for only one user without ruining the program or the information (data files) associated with it.

The MS-OS/2 Operating System

PC-DOS was designed for the original IBM PC at a time when hardware resources were far more limited than they are today. Since the IBM PC usually replaced a microcomputer that contained between 64K and 128K of RAM, the ability of PC-DOS to address a maximum of 640K of RAM seemed more than anyone could possibly ever need. Similarly, the operating system's ability to address up to 32 megabytes of secondary storage seemed more than enough in an era when 10-megabyte hard disk drives were a luxury.

Whereas PC-DOS was designed as a single-user, single-tasking operating system, OS/2 is a single-user, multitasking operating system that can address a maximum of 16 megabytes of RAM as well as manage a virtually unlimited amount of secondary storage. This powerful operating system has become the basis of two key local area networks that will be discussed in later chapters: 3Com's 3+ Open and IBM's LAN Server.

Parallel and Serial Transmission

As indicated earlier, a microcomputer's expansion slots allow it to communicate with peripherals such as disk drives and printers. A parallel printer adapter, also known simply as a printer interface, fits in an expansion slot and is connected by cable with a printer. Eight bits of data travel in parallel along eight separate wires from a PC to a printer. This method of transmission is relatively fast but of limited range (25 feet) before data is lost.

Some printers and virtually all modems require an asynchronous communications adapter, which usually is known as a *serial port*. This circuit card converts data from the parallel form found within the PC to the serial form in which the bits travel sequentially in single file along the same wire. Though often not as fast as parallel transmission, serial transmission can transmit data for longer distances. A serial cable contains twenty-five different wires. Normally the data is transmitted along one wire while other information is sent along other wires consistent with the Electronic Industries Association's (EIA) RS-232C standard for serial transmission. Parallel and serial printers as well as serial modems are critical elements of most local area networks.

Now that we have discussed the major features of the IBM PC and compatibles, let's take a brief look at the evolution of the PC before examining a company that has linked its PCs together to form a local area network with which to share information and printers. Virtually all the applications used in this example will be explained in much greater detail in subsequent chapters when we look more closely at specific brands of local area networks.

A BRIEF HISTORY OF DISTRIBUTED PROCESSING AND NETWORKS

In three decades the computer industry has gone from batch processing and time-sharing with mainframe computers to distributed processing with minicomputers to local area networks with microcomputers.

Although companies have been able to implement local area networks only with the arrival of the microcomputer, the concept of LANs is not new. In fact, it represents a logical development of computer technology. The first computers in the 1950s were mainframes that often occupied entire buildings. Not only were they expensive and reserved for a few select users, but they also used a batch approach instead of on-line response to a user's commands. Users submitted coded cards containing their data and program commands. Computer professionals fed these cards into the computer and usually sent the printed results to the users the next day. A miscoded card generally meant that the user would have to resubmit the entire program the following day.

At this time there was little need to share computer resources such as printers and modems because there were so few computers that the average office could not afford one. The solution to this expense problem was the concept of time-sharing. During the 1960s it became possible for an office to use a "dumb" terminal to connect through a telephone line with a mainframe computer. By leasing (or "sharing") time on this computer, the user was able to enjoy the benefits of computerization without massive capital expenditure.

The major problem with time-sharing was the slowness of sending information over telephone lines. The production of the minicomputer during the early 1970s avoided this problem by dramatically reducing prices, thus enabling departments to have their own computers. A new user simply needed a terminal and the cabling between it and the minicomputer to become operational. As Figure 1-5 illustrates, several users could use the same computer, and much higher speeds were possible than under time-sharing.

The concept of distributing the computer resources through a company by providing different departments with their own computers rather than using one central computer for everybody became known as "distributed processing." But, even though several different departments within a company had their own minicomputers, there was still a problem in providing communications among these computers. So companies began cabling these computers together and writing the software necessary for these different units to communicate.

As microcomputers became more and more powerful and less and less expensive during the 1980s, companies began to take a second look at their minicomputers. These larger computers cost hundreds of thousands of dollars and could not run the newer, more sophisticated business programs that were coming out for IBM PCs and compatibles.

By the mid-1980s, thousands of office workers began bringing their own personal computers to work in order to use the office productivity software available on microcomputers. Companies began to experience serious

Figure 1-5.
Distributed Processing
with a Minicomputer

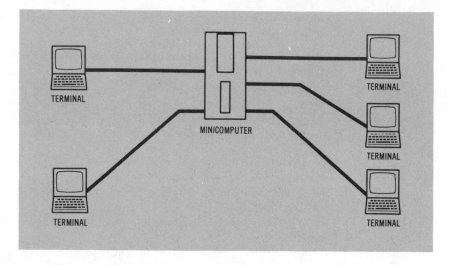

problems maintaining the integrity of data as employees began exchanging floppy disks and keeping their own databases. The answer to these problems was the local area network.

WHAT IS A LOCAL AREA NETWORK?

A local area network
covers a limited distance
and facilitates sharing of
information and resources.

Let's define a local area network in the broadest way possible. It is a communication network used by a single organization over a limited distance that permits users to share information and resources. The next chapter will survey the different physical configurations possible for a LAN. Whether PCs are arranged in the form of a star, a ring, or even a straight line, the speed of the network will depend to a great extent on the type of media used to connect all units together. The next chapter will return to this subject and examine the different types of cabling available for LANs.

Distributed processing taken to its logical conclusion means the linking together of microcomputers to share information and peripherals. The first local area networks were relatively primitive and were faced with a serious shortage of software designed for more than one user. At best, these first LANs used *file locking*, which allowed only one user at a time to use a certain program. Gradually, though, the software industry has become more sophisticated. Today local area networks can use sophisticated accounting and productivity programs that permit several users to work with the same programs at the same time (*record locking*). Let's take a close look at an actual local area network in operation at the Widget Corporation.

WIDGET'S LOCAL AREA NETWORK

A company such as
Widget can realize
staggering savings and
increased productivity by
sharing hardware and
software resources.

Widget's local area network enables company employees to share peripherals (hard disk drives, printers, plotters, etc.) and data. So instead of each personal computer workstation having its own dot matrix printer, the Widget network enables dozens of workstations to share a variety of printers, including laser, daisywheel (letter-quality), and dot matrix. Instead of buying dozens of copies of a word-processing program, Widget buys a special network version of the program that enables dozens of network users to share the program and, even more importantly, share each other's documents. A single computer's hard disk functions as a network file server, acting very much like a waiter in a busy restaurant, serving up the items requested by the customers. With its local area network Widget can keep dozens of varying standard contracts on its network disk server so that individual workstations can load these documents, make whatever changes are necessary to individualize the contracts, and then save them under appropriate names. The cost savings from these and other communal uses are staggering.

Using Word Processing, Graphics, and Electronic Mail on a LAN

Widget's LAN makes it easy to produce an annual report. Several people can write different sections and then revise and combine them using the network's electronic mail.

Every year Widget is required to produce an annual report that is printed and sent to stockholders. Ever since the company connected all departments with its LAN, the job has become much easier. The Accounting department's audited balance sheet is already available through the network since its general ledger, accounts payable, accounts receivable, inventory, purchase order and receiving, and payroll programs are already installed on the network. The corporate controller begins the job by printing a copy of the balance sheet to disk (rather than sending it to the printer). He or she then uses a word-processing program to comment on several aspects of the company's financial position before also saving the document on the company's file server.

Since many stockholders prefer to view financial information in graphic format, the president asks two graphic artists in the Marketing department to develop appropriate pie charts and bar charts to show the company's growth over the past few years. The artists use a graphics program designed for the Apple Macintosh to develop their charts and then send the information to a plotter that is part of the local area network. Widget's LAN contains a number of IBM PCs, IBM PS/2 models, and some Macintosh computers that can communicate with each other over the network. After the researchers receive the president's comments by electronic mail over the network, they revise the charts and then save the files on the file server.

Everyone at Widget with a workstation that is connected to the LAN can receive and send mail electronically. The network informs users as they are entering the network ("logging on") that they have mail, so Widget employees find that they no longer can use the excuse that they never saw a memo because it was lost in the mail. The electronic mail program lets the sender know when a message has been read. It even permits you to send blind copies (bcc) to other network users as well as to send letters and even reports to distribution lists. Secretaries who used to spend hours photocopying reports to distribute to managers now simply use the electronic mail to send a copy of each report to each manager's workstation.

Since Widget manufactures four different products designed for four different markets, the president asks each of the four product managers to write a description of their products' current status and plans for the future. Each product manager saves his or her comments in a word-processing file on the file server.

Meanwhile the president is busy writing a letter to the stockholders analyzing Widget's performance and indicating the direction the company would take for the following year. After the staff prints the requested material from the Marketing and Accounting departments, the president reads the documents and then sends electronic mail to other employees requesting material to fill in remaining gaps in the corporate report. After another round of revisions, the annual report is printed with a laser printer that provides letter-quality text and crisp graphics and is sent to the print shop for reproduction. The whole process is faster and far more efficient because the company's LAN permits almost instant sharing of information.

Connecting a LAN to the Rest of the World

By using a remote bridge to connect the local area network to the outside world, Widget salespeople can enter orders from remote customer locations, update current inventory levels on-line, and use the customer database to generate personalized sales letters.

This ability to share information is particularly valuable in a competitive sales environment. Each of Widget's outside salespeople has a portable computer with a built-in modem to access the LAN over a phone line. Widgets come in an assortment of colors and configurations, and the company used to lose several thousand dollars worth of orders each year through cancellations. A salesperson would take a large order, drive to Widget headquarters, and submit the order to the sales manager. Only after the order was input into Widget's mainframe computer would the salesperson learn that several of the items were backordered. When customers were informed that there would be a substantial delay before delivery, they usually cancelled the entire order.

Now the situation has changed dramatically. Widget's LAN contains a *remote bridge*, a communications link between the network and the outside world. The salespeople use their portable computers, which contain built-in modems and communications programs, to connect to the network using their customers' regular telephone lines. They enter an order while talking with the customer. If an item is backordered, the computer indicates a possible alternative: "The yellow widgets are backordered two weeks, but green is very popular this time of year and it is available immediately." Since the customer is in a buying mood and the salesperson is present and very persuasive, it is not surprising that many customers choose an alternative or agree to wait for a backordered item.

Whenever a customer's order is entered into the computer, a file is established for that customer. Salespeople find this information invaluable since they are able to determine buying trends and preferences. Frequently they will send out individualized form letters announcing new product releases or indicating that the old widget might need an overhaul.

Because the customer list is integrated with the company's accounting programs, including accounts receivable, the Accounting department occasionally will ask a salesperson to contact a delinquent customer about an overdue account. The receivables clerk simply sends the account information by electronic mail to the salesperson. Widget's accounting program on the LAN contains one useful safeguard to keep its receivables low. When a salesperson inputs an order from a customer site, the order entry program will flash a message on the screen indicating that the customer has an overdue account. Frequently the salesperson can collect a check and then override the message to enter the new order.

Sharing Database Information on a LAN

A common database is particularly valuable for marketing functions.

While Widget's salespeople are busy transmitting orders from customer locations, the Marketing department's researchers and analysts are busy sifting through sales reports to discover trends and develop market forecasts. The department's personnel share all their data on the LAN. Three analysts, for example, have used a Lotus 1-2-3 spreadsheet program to analyze the buying patterns of the company's major distributors. Traditionally, Widget has offered volume discounts to encourage large purchases, but now it is considering offering monthly sales specials to help balance its inventory. By identifying specific items and the month when major customers purchase them, the marketing analysts will develop a twelve-month sales plan.

Because the analysts are using the same Lotus 1-2-3 program and then saving their spreadsheet data on the network file server, the information can be shared among them. This means that after the researchers develop an item-by-item sales analysis, one researcher can access all three spreadsheets to develop a composite report that summarizes information by product group. Using the Lotus 1-2-3 spreadsheet, the researcher sends a command over the LAN to the six-pen plotter in the sales department to print a series of detailed graphs.

Accounting on a LAN

The Accounting department can use the flexibility of record locking on a LAN to have several employees run the same program during peak periods.

The Widget Corporation's accounting information is on the LAN, but many of the programs have password security beyond the usual network level of security. Only a few employees in the Accounting and Personnel departments, for example, have access to payroll records. The information on customer orders and inventory usage is available to certain employees in Marketing, Sales, and Manufacturing. The marketing analysts can use a special interface program to take sales orders and customer information from the accounting programs and convert this data into a form that can be used in a Lotus 1-2-3 program. Although a copy of this valuable accounting information can be moved to another program, the original accounting data is protected from tampering or change. This is necessary to ensure that the Accounting department maintains a clear audit trail, which means that all changes and additions to accounting program data must originate in the Accounting department and be recorded in a journal entry. This method leaves a permanent record that can be traced to answer future questions.

The controller has been delighted with the advantages of having all accounting programs available on the company LAN. During peak periods, accounting clerks can be shifted from doing accounts payable to accounts receivable. Each workstation in the department can access any accounting program, assuming the user has the proper level of password security. Most of the clerks have only the network security level that permits them to perform routine tasks. Payroll clerks, for example, cannot change employee salaries, although they can print monthly salary checks.

The controller must consult with the LAN administrator before providing newly hired accounting clerks with new workstations. Every LAN requires a network administrator, who is responsible for the network's overall management. Among the administrator's tasks are adding new users and providing them with new passwords. If a department wants to add a new program to the LAN, the network administrator will analyze the effect of the program on the network as a whole and make sure that the program will integrate completely with the other programs already present.

Using Printers on a LAN

Word processing on a LAN provides the user with a number of advantages, including print spooling and the choice of several different kinds of printers.

Perhaps the major use of the LAN requires the least amount of the network administrator's time. Every day secretaries, administrative assistants, and managers use the network's powerful word-processing program. All of Widget's form letters are word-processed, including direct sales solicitations, requests for additional warranty information, notification that service contracts are about to expire, and the actual service contracts. The LAN contains a couple of laser printers with triple-bin cut-sheet feeders. This means that it is possible automatically to print a cover letter on Widget Corporation stationery, a second sheet on normal bond paper, and the corresponding envelope.

The company LAN has what is known as "print-spooling" software, which enables a user to specify a specific printer for a job and then "spool" the file to a storage area where it will be held until its turn to be printed. The president can specify that a job requiring immediate attention exchange places with another file in the spooler in order to be printed immediately. The LAN can print several documents simultaneously on its various letter-quality and dot matrix printers without slowing down network performance.

The most sophisticated word processing is handled by the Technical Publications department, which supports sales, marketing, and service as well as working on special projects for the president's office. Four technical writers use many of the more advanced features of the word-processing program, such as the ability to create multiple columns and the ability to create indexes and tables of contents automatically. These materials require feedback from several individuals, including engineers, programmers, and trainers. The technical writers use the LAN's electronic mail to send their rough drafts to appropriate departments for comments before beginning revisions. By not having to take the time to mail copies of the manuscript to the various departments and then wait for their return, the technical writers have increased their productivity substantially. Now when the writers receive electronic mail informing them that a section has been read and revised for technical accuracy by an engineer, they simply load the revised section from the engineering department and then proofread for correct grammar and spelling.

A technical writer and illustrator are assigned to support the Marketing department. They develop brochures and other sales materials. Since it is absolutely necessary for all sales materials to reflect the products accurately, the two send manuscript sections and illustration files to appropriate technical personnel for comments and corrections before moving on to the finished product.

Communications between a LAN and a Mainframe Computer

The Manufacturing
department can use a
LAN to share information
with a mainframe
computer.

The Manufacturing department was the only department not to leave its mainframe environment. Located at the manufacturing facility, the mainframe computer runs a sophisticated manufacturing resource planning program. This program controls manufacturing costs by making sure that the plant runs at maximum efficiency. The computer makes sure that the assembly line will not run out of key raw materials and that all standing orders will be filled on time.

Since the Accounting department now runs all its programs on microcomputers as part of the LAN, Manufacturing needs to have access to all sales order data at company headquarters. It needs to know what has been sold in order to update its inventory file and revise its forecasts. This communication is accomplished using the same gateway to the local area network that salespeople used when communicating from customer sites.

There is one critical difference, however. Whereas the salespeople were using microcomputers to communicate with the company's microcomputer local area network, the Manufacturing department needs to establish communications between a microcomputer and a mainframe computer, two machines that do not even speak the same language. Widget's network administrator uses the LAN software interface to the accounting programs to convert the appropriate data into a form that can be sent over a telephone line. The administrator uses another program to emulate an IBM 3270 terminal and convert the information into the synchronous form that the mainframe can understand.

Every evening the LAN sends the day's sales information over a telephone line to the company's mainframe computer, which digests the data and produces a revised schedule for the next day's assembly-line work. When supervisory personnel arrive in the morning, they can use their terminals to read this information from the mainframe, where it has been stored.

All the LAN activities of the Widget Corporation described here are available today. In the next few chapters we will learn how a LAN's hardware and software work together to produce this kind of integrated information. We will also survey the leading LANs currently available and highlight differences that could prove significant in helping you determine which kind of local area network is in your future.

WHAT HAVE YOU LEARNED?

1. A local area network is a communications network used by a single organization over a limited distance that permits users to share information and resources.
2. Time-sharing with terminals and modems enabled companies to share resources.
3. Minicomputers were the first computers to permit cost-effective distributive processing.
4. A dedicated file server is not used as a workstation.
5. Electronic mail is a major feature of many local area networks.

6. Outside computers can use a remote bridge to communicate with computers within the local area network.
7. Print-spooling software permits users to designate which printer they wish to use to print their files.
8. Record-locking software permits more than one user to use the same program at the same time.

Quiz for Chapter 1

1. Handing in program cards and receiving the results the next day is characteristic of
   a. batch processing
   b. on-line processing
   c. distributed processing
   d. remote processing

2. Time-sharing was not a very effective way for a company to do its data processing because
   a. it required a computer at every station
   b. communication over a phone line with a modem was too slow
   c. computers were constantly breaking down
   d. computers do not like to share

3. Distributed processing means
   a. computers distributed to different users and departments
   b. computer cards distributed to different departments
   c. a mainframe computer doing all the work
   d. a computer doing nothing but computing

4. The person who provides passwords for new computer users on the local area network is called
   a. the chief of security
   b. the network administrator
   c. the department manager
   d. the president of the network user's group

5. A byte is composed of
   a. 2 bits
   b. 4 bits
   c. 6 bits
   d. 8 bits

6. A 5¼" double-sided double-density disk formatted for the IBM PC can hold approximately
   a. 360K
   b. 180K
   c. 256K
   d. 512K

7. To attach a modem to an IBM PC or compatible, its expansion slot must contain a(n)
   a. parallel interface
   b. synchronous communications adapter
   c. asynchronous communications adapter
   d. monochrome video adapter

8. Memory which retains information even after the computer is turned off is called
   a. RAM
   b. ROM
   o. RIM
   d. REM

The Basics of a Local Area Network

ABOUT THIS CHAPTER

This chapter describes the building blocks of a local area network using as examples the IBM PC, the second generation PS/2 models, and various compatibles. (Macintosh networks are treated in Chapter 7.) We will explore how computer workstations are cabled together and how they share resources. Then we'll take a close look at the rules that all local area networks follow to ensure that information is not garbled or lost. Finally, we'll look at a number of standards that have begun to establish some order to what has been a very chaotic field.

THE CHANGING FOCUS OF LOCAL AREA NETWORKS

As indicated in Chapter 1, a local area network enables microcomputers to share information and resources within a limited (local) area, generally less than one mile. A LAN requires that the individual workstations (microcomputers) be physically tied together by cabling (usually coaxial or twisted-pair) and that some network software reside on a hard disk to permit users to share peripherals, data, and application programs.

Until recently, the major use of LANs was to share peripheral equipment such as printers, hard disk drives, and plotters. Since hardware equipment represented the major microcomputer cost in most offices, these early, primitive networks more than justified their cost by ensuring that valuable equipment did not remain idle. Today, some networks (such as Novell's) further increase office savings by allowing for a workstation that does not have a hard disk. A special "autoboot" ROM chip inserted in the network workstation permits the computer to become part of the network and use the network's disk drive when it is turned on.

It is difficult to generalize about microcomputer networks because of a lack of compatibility that has plagued the industry, this despite the efforts by the Institute for Electrical and Electronics Engineers (IEEE) to standardize the ways that information can be transmitted within a network. In this chapter we will look at the components that all networks require and at the various forms they can take.

2

THE INDIVIDUAL NETWORK WORKSTATION

The individual network workstation can work independently as a personal computer or share network information and resources.

Most companies decide to install a local area network because they already have a major investment in microcomputers, peripherals, and software. Rather than scrap everything and start over again with a minicomputer, these companies opt to tie their existing equipment together to share hardware and software resources.

Each microcomputer attached to the network can work both as an independent personal computer running its own software and as a network workstation capable of accessing information on the network disk server. As Figure 2-1 illustrates, this ability to function as a network station requires network software for communicating with the network server and other network workstations as well as a special interface (almost always a circuit board) that plugs into one of the microcomputer's expansion slots.

The workstations in Figure 2-1 are IBM PCs containing network interface cards. The network program they are using works in conjunction with PC-DOS version 4.1. A cable connects the workstation (through its network interface card) to the network disk server or file server. As indicated earlier, the workstation's user can choose whether to treat the microcomputer as an independent unit working on his or her own programs or as part of the network. By simply running the network software program and "logging on" (identifying oneself with a password as an authorized user), the user becomes an active part of the network.

**Figure 2-1.
Workstations
Connected with
Network Interface
Cards and Cabling to a
Disk Server**

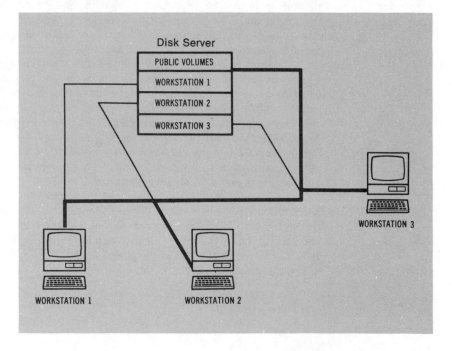

UNDERSTANDING LOCAL AREA NETWORKS

NETWORK DISK SERVERS

Some networks use a disk server to store files and to provide workstations with files upon request.

Some local area networks use a *disk server*, a hard disk containing information that can be shared by the various workstations on the network. To the individual workstations, this disk server simply looks like another hard disk drive. If this disk server were designated as drive E, for example, Frank Jones would save his business expense spreadsheet as E:busexp. The E tells Jones's DOS software to send the data to the network hard disk for storage.

A file allocation table (FAT) helps the disk server keep track of where a particular file is located.

This procedure is a bit more complex, however, when a workstation wants a particular file residing on the disk server. IBM PCs and compatibles use a file allocation table (FAT) to keep track of exactly where a file is stored. The network disk server keeps its own FAT. An individual workstation has no idea of exactly where one of its files is stored without seeing a copy of this valuable table. The disk server sends a copy of this table to the workstation, which stores it in its RAM, the workspace used when running programs. Using the FAT under DOS, the workstation can access its files on the disk server.

Imagine what would happen, though, if dozens of workstations were to receive copies of the FAT and begin saving documents back to the disk server. Each copy of the FAT saved back on the disk server would overwrite (and thus erase) the FAT file existing prior to the new copy's arrival. It would prove almost impossible to determine which was the original FAT without a safeguard for this important table's integrity.

Disk servers partition their hard disk drives into separate volumes for each user.

With a simple disk server, the integrity of its FAT is maintained by dividing up (partitioning) the hard disk drive into several user volumes. Each volume is reserved for one workstation's exclusive use, thus preserving the integrity of the FAT for that volume. Certain volumes might be established as *public volumes*, but they are usually safeguarded by being classified as "read-only," which means that the individual workstations can view this information but cannot change it. An example of a typical public volume is the large customer database file of the Widget Corporation described in Chapter 1. Several different departments might need to view this information, but the network administrator has declared the file read-only so that no one inadvertently changes or destroys the data.

FILE SERVERS

A file server uses software to form a shell around the computer's normal DOS.

File servers are far more efficient and sophisticated than disk servers. A file server contains special software that forms a shell around the computer's normal disk operating system. This shell software filters out commands to the file server before DOS can receive them. The file server maintains its own FAT so that when a workstation demands a specific file it already knows where the file is and can send the file directly to the workstation. Note that the individual workstation does not designate the file server as another disk drive, as is the case with a disk server. It simply requests a file, and the file server responds.

The file server is much more efficient than the disk server because there is no need to send copies of the FAT to each workstation requesting a file. Also, there is no need to partition the network hard disk drive into volumes since the individual workstations no longer have to worry about where a particular file resides. In short, a file server makes for greater efficiency in a local area network, as Figure 2-2 illustrates.

**Figure 2-2.
Workstations
Connected to a File
Server**

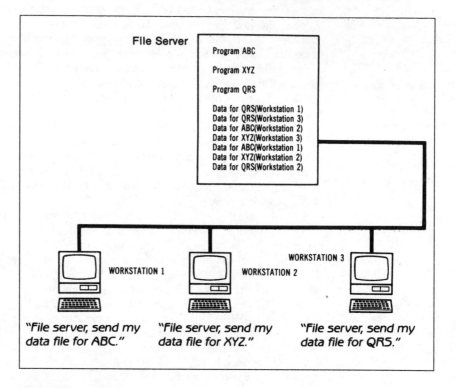

File Server

Program ABC

Program XYZ

Program QRS

Data for QRS(Workstation 1)
Data for QRS(Workstation 3)
Data for ABC(Workstation 2)
Data for XYZ(Workstation 3)
Data for ABC(Workstation 1)
Data for XYZ(Workstation 2)
Data for QRS(Workstation 2)

WORKSTATION 1   WORKSTATION 2   WORKSTATION 3

*"File server, send my
data file for ABC."*   *"File server, send my
data file for XYZ."*   *"File server, send my
data file for QRS."*

Distributed File Servers

A network may contain
one centralized file server
or several distributed file
servers.

For most office networks, a single file server, or "centralized server," is more than adequate. It functions very much like a minicomputer since the one unit handles all file serving and each workstation waits its turn. If the LAN is designed to connect several different departments, as is the Widget Corporation LAN described in Chapter 1, then it is usually more efficient to add additional file servers.

These additional units are known as "distributed file servers" because they divide up or distribute the file serving duties for the entire network. Since all Accounting department workstations use the same accounting programs and access the same data, it is inefficient to send this information to a file server several hundred feet away. A distributed file server right in the Accounting department can speed access time and also reduce the load on the rest of the network, thus maintaining optimum speed for other users. With such a system, accounting personnel no longer have to request files from a central file server that also services other network users' requests. Also, the file server itself operates more efficiently and quickly, since it has fewer files to search in order to locate the requested information and since it sends files over a shorter distance to the requesting workstations.

There is one other advantage of distributed file servers. If one file server becomes inoperative, the LAN is not shut down. With sufficient disk space, this distributed file server can be used to service the entire LAN temporarily.

Despite these advantages, distributed file servers can make security more difficult. The network administrator must now ensure that both hard disk drives are protected from unauthorized entry. Chapter 12 will address this major issue of network security.

Dedicated and Nondedicated File Servers

A dedicated file server is used only for that function whereas a nondedicated file server also serves as a workstation.

In the business world, ironically, dedication is not always prized because it can be very expensive. Some LAN manufacturers extol the price savings they offer because their file servers need not be dedicated. A *dedicated* file server is a microcomputer with a hard disk drive used exclusively as a file server. By dedicating all its memory and processing resources to file serving, the particular computer usually provides increased network speed and efficiency. When a file server is *nondedicated*, it is used as a workstation in addition to its file-serving functions. This means that RAM must be partitioned so that some of it is available for running programs. It also means that a network workstation might have to wait for a file to be sent while the file server loads a program from memory. Because file servers generally are the fastest and most expensive computers in the network, deciding whether to dedicate the unit can be difficult. Yet the money initially saved by opting for a nondedicated file server would most likely be lost several fold by the degradation of the entire LAN. The time lost by users of all the other workstations in the network would soon show the folly of trying to economize on this critical network element.

PRINT SERVERS

Network print servers enable workstations to share several different printers.

Just as a network file server permits users to share a single network hard drive, eliminating the need for each of several personal computers to have its own hard disk drive, a network print server can enable dozens of workstations to share various types of printers. A manager might need a letter-quality printer for his daily correspondence, but once a month he or she might need a wide-carriage dot matrix printer in order to print a critical spreadsheet. An accountant on the very same network might use a wide-carriage dot matrix printer daily to produce balance sheets, financial reports, and charts. Once or twice a month he or she might need to write a business letter using a letter-quality printer. With a LAN and print-server software, the manager and the accountant both may choose any printer on the network.

Printers can be limited to certain users on a network. These local printers usually perform very specific tasks.

Print-server software does not prevent a network station from having its own dedicated printer. Let's say that a marketing analyst uses a color dot matrix printer almost exclusively to print transparencies of charts for presentations. This printer, connected by a parallel interface and cable to the analyst's workstation, can remain a dedicated *local* printer and not a network printer should that serve the best interests of the office. If the analyst needs to produce a letter-quality report, he or she can send a word-processing file over the network to a letter-quality printer.

A second major reason for dedicating a printer to a particular workstation is the need to print special preprinted continuous-feed forms. A purchasing agent, for example, might need to print dozens of purchase order forms, and likewise an accounts payable clerk might need to print continuous-feed company checks. For both these individuals to have to remove the continuous-feed forms in order to print an occasional letter would be troublesome indeed.

The network administrator usually ensures that a program is installed on the network with a default printer driver. This means that normally the program's files will be printed on a particular printer. Word-processing programs, for example, might routinely send files to the office letter-quality printer or to a laser printer whereas spreadsheet programs would send files to a wide-carriage dot matrix printer.

Print-server software contains a *print spooler*, software that creates a buffer where files can be stored until it is their turn to be printed. Think of this as a list of print jobs. As each file is printed, the next file in line takes its place. Sophisticated print spoolers have additional capabilities, such as moving a job to the front of the line if it requires immediate printing. On a large office network, time-consuming printing jobs such as daily reports are often placed in the print spooler for printing during the evening so as not to tie up a printer during peak hours.

> Print-spooler software enables network users to place files in a buffer for printing at a later time.

One problem that occasionally occurs with print-server software is that some software defaults to a certain type of printer even though there may be times when you require a different printer—a letter-quality rather than a dot matrix printer, for example. The network administrator can solve this problem by creating a special *batch file* that automatically loads the program version with the appropriate printer driver.

A GUIDE TO LAN CABLING

The local area network must have cabling to link the individual workstations together with the file server and other peripherals. If there were only one type of cabling available, then the decision would be simple. Unfortunately, there are a number of different types of cabling, each with its own vocal supporters. Since there is a considerable range in cost and in capability, this is not a trivial issue. This section will examine the advantages and disadvantages of twisted-pair cable, baseband and broadband coaxial cable, and fiber-optic cabling.

Twisted-Pair Cable

> Twisted-pair cable is inexpensive and easy to install—an ideal selection when interference is not a major consideration.

Twisted-pair cable is by far the least expensive type of network media. As Figure 2-3 illustrates, this cabling consists of two insulated wires twisted together so that each wire faces the same amount of interference from the environment. This "noise" in the environment becomes part of the signal being transmitted. Twisting the wires together reduces but does not eliminate this noise. Twisted-pair wire comes in a wide range of pairs and gauges. Wires have an American Wire Gauge number (AWG) based on their diameter.

A 26-gauge wire, for example, has a diameter of 0.01594 inch. For network purposes 22- and 24-gauge cabling are the two most common types of twisted-pair media used. Twisted-pair cable is bundled in groups ranging from 4 to 3000 twisted pairs, although 25 pairs is standard in many local area networks. Some LANs use the very same inexpensive unshielded twisted-pair cable found in telephone wire whereas others require higher quality data-grade cable. As one option for its Token Ring Network, IBM supports Type 3 unshielded twisted-pair cable (telephone wire) but does require that it be 22- or 24-gauge with a minimum of two twists per linear foot and with two spare pairs that can be dedicated to the network. When installing new wire, IBM recommends four twisted pairs.

**Figure 2-3.
Twisted-Pair Wire (two pair)**

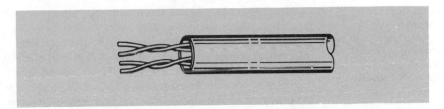

On the other hand, AT&T's StarLan requires data-grade cable. AT&T specifies that its network requires *shielded* 24-gauge wire with two twists per foot, one pair of wires to transmit data and one pair of wires to receive data. Because of AT&T's higher grade twisted-pair standard, its workstations may be up to 990 feet from a wiring closet whereas IBM workstations must be within 330 feet.

The major limitations of twisted-pair wiring are its limited range and its sensitivity to electrical interference. When standards were first proposed for twisted-pair networks, the medium was able to handle transmission speeds of approximately one megabit per second (mbps) over several hundred feet. Today a new industry standard known as 10 base T reflects the technological advances that make it possible to transmit information at 10 mbps over twisted-pair wire.

Coaxial Cable

Coaxial cable is used in both baseband and broadband networks. Although more expensive than twisted pair, it can transmit data significantly faster over a much longer distance.

Coaxial cable is almost as easy to install as twisted-pair, and it is the medium of choice of many of the major local area networks. As Figure 2-4 illustrates, coax is composed of a copper conductor surrounded by insulation. An outer jacket of copper or aluminum acts as a conductor and also provides protection. This type of cable is commonly found in the home as an integral part of cable television.

Figure 2-4.
Coaxial Cable

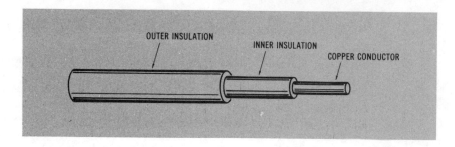

OUTER INSULATION

INNER INSULATION

COPPER CONDUCTOR

Baseband Networks

Although baseband networks are very fast (between 10 mbps and 80 mbps), they are limited to a single channel and cannot carry integrated voice, data, and video signals.

Baseband coaxial cable has one channel that carries a single message at a time at very high speed. Its carrier wire is surrounded by a copper mesh, and usually the diameter of the entire cable is approximately ⅜ inch. Digital information is sent across a baseband cable's bandwidth in serial fashion, one bit at a time. Depending on the LAN, baseband coaxial cable can handle a data rate of between 10 mbps and 80 mbps. Ethernet, the first major local area network with nonproprietary communications interfaces and protocols, uses baseband coaxial cable. The Ethernet standard has in turn been supported by both Xerox Corporation and Digital Equipment Corporation, making baseband cabling a popular choice for LANs. A further advantage is that it is easy to tap into this cable to connect or disconnect workstations without disturbing network operations. Baseband's single-channel limitation, however, means that it cannot accommodate integrated voice, data, and video signals. Also, although the maximum recommended distance for a baseband LAN is approximately 1.8 miles (3 kilometers), 1500 feet (500 meters) might prove to be a more realistic figure if the network is heavily used. These disadvantages to baseband cable must, of course, be considered when configuring a network, but they may not be significant if the primary criteria in media selection are speed of data transmission and cost.

Broadband Networks

Broadband networks can carry integrated voice, data, and even video signals. Because amplifiers are used, broadband has a greater range than baseband.

Unlike baseband, broadband systems have the capacity to carry several different signals broadcast at different frequencies at the same time. This is the approach cable television companies have taken using 75-ohm broadband coaxial cable. Subscribers can select from several different stations, each broadcasting on its own designated frequency. All broadband systems can use either a single cable with bidirectional amplifiers, as depicted in Figure 2-5, or a dual cable. In either case, carrier signals are sent to a central translating and broadcast device known as the *head end*, from which they are retransmitted to all points on the network.

The single-cable approach splits a cable by frequency in order to transmit data bidirectionally. Commercial cable companies use 6-MHz channels for each communication path. Even with some frequencies designed as "guard bands" between the different channels, it is possible to allocate 346 MHz for forward communications (6 MHz per channel times 56 channels) and 25 MHz for the return data path (6 MHz per channel times 4 channels).

Figure 2-5.
Single Broadband
Coaxial Cable with
Bidirectional Amplifiers

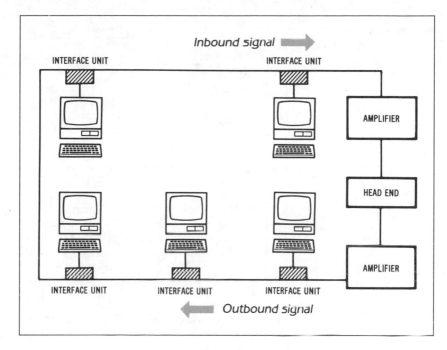

This 25 MHz devoted to returning data can be used for several narrow band channels.

Dual-broadband cable uses one cable for inbound data moving toward the head end and a second cable looped at the head end for the outbound carriers. The full frequency spectrum is available for both inbound and outbound signals. This duplication of cabling, amplifiers, and hardware makes dual-broadband cable much more expensive than single cable but also provides twice as many usable channels, which some networks may require. Let's take a closer look at this particular broadband approach.

With a dual-cable configuration, coaxial cable forms a two-way highway composed of two bands, each containing several channels. Since standard television channels transmit at 6 MHz and a band has a range of approximately 300 MHz, as many as 50 channels can broadcast at a data rate of 5 mbps. The *inbound band* carries data from the local area network's *nodes* (individual workstations) to the head end, and the *outbound band* carries data to the network's nodes, as illustrated in Figure 2-6.

Broadband cable installation requires far more planning than baseband. Because broadband signals are broadcast, amplifiers need to be installed to maintain the strength of the signals. In a company with several departments such as the Widget Corporation described in Chapter 1, each department would have a *drop line* with *tap lines* coming off this line to each node. These taps contain resistors to ensure that all workstations receive signals at the same strength. If the Widget Corporation were planning to add an additional building in the near future, it would want to add a *splitter*, as

**Figure 2-6.
Dual-Broadband Cable
Configuration**

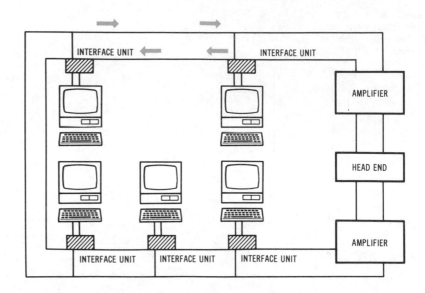

shown in Figure 2-7. This divides the signal into two paths. Since a splitter would be added to ensure future LAN growth, the unused port would be sealed until needed. Because splitters affect transmission quality across the entire network, splitters for future, anticipated growth should be added in the LAN's initial plan.

Fiber-Optic Cable

Fiber-optic technology offers immunity from electromagnetic interference and error-free transmission for several miles with the highest level of network security.

One of the most exciting media advances in recent years has been the use of fiber optics in local area networks. This new type of data transmission has a number of advantages over twisted-pair and coaxial cable. Besides possessing superior data transmission rates, fiber-optic cabling is immune to electromagnetic and radio-frequency interference and can send signals several miles without loss. This mode of transmission is virtually immune to unauthorized reception. The cable is made of pure glass drawn into very thin fiber to form a core. As Figure 2-8 illustrates, these fibers are surrounded by *cladding*, a layer of glass with a lower refractive index than the glass in the core.

A fiber-optic network uses a laser or light-emitting diode (LED) to send a signal through the core portion of the cable. Optical repeaters are often used along the path to amplify the signal so that it arrives at its destination at full strength. At the receiving end of the cable, the message is translated back into a digital or analog signal by a photodiode. The cabling can consist of a single fiber (*monomode*), several fibers (*multimode fiber*), or a variation of multimode fiber (*graded-index*) in which the index of refraction drops slowly from the center of the fiber toward the outside. Monomode fiber has a very wide bandwidth, but its small core makes it extremely difficult to splice. It also requires a laser as a signaling source, which is more expensive than an LED. Multimode fiber has a smaller bandwidth but is much easier to

**Figure 2-7.
Coaxial Cable
Configuration with
Splitters**

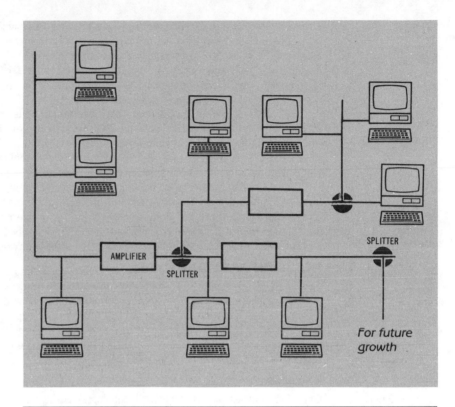

**Figure 2-8.
Fiber-Optic Cabling**

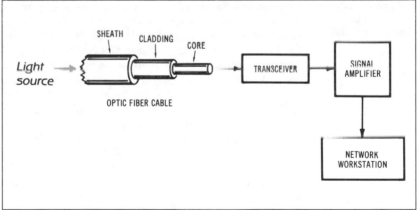

splice. Graded-index multimode fiber is the most expensive medium, but it does provide the highest transmission rate over the greatest distance of the three.

Multimode fiber optics for network cabling comes in groups from two to twenty-four fibers, with groups of two to four fibers the norm. Each fiber is unidirectional, since a beam of light is transmitted in only one direction. Two-way communications require another fiber within the cable so that light can travel in the opposite direction. The American National Standards Institute has established a standard for the physical media-dependent (PMD) layer of the fiber data-distributed interface (FDDI) to work in conjunction with data transmission at 100 mbps, although it is possible to achieve rates up to 1 gigabit per second (gbps).

Most importantly, this new fiber-optic standard is consistent with AT&T's Premises Distribution Scheme (PDS) in its ratio of cladding to core (62.5/125 multimode fiber). Therefore, companies that have installed AT&T fiber-optic equipment for voice transmission are already cabled for data transmission by local area networks that use fiber-optic technology.

At present, fiber-optic cabling is too expensive for most installations, and its sophisticated technology makes it difficult to add new workstations after initial installation. If a company has a serious problem with interference, a need for absolute network security, or a need to send signals several miles, fiber optics might be the only solution at present.

NETWORK ARCHITECTURE

Just as there are several different ways to cable a local area network, there are also several different forms a network can take. These different shapes are known as "network architecture" or "topology." Keep in mind that the form of the LAN does not limit the media of transmission. Twisted-pair wire, coaxial cable, and fiber-optics all lend themselves to these different topologies.

The Star

The star topology makes it easy to add new workstations and to provide detailed network analysis.

One of the earliest types of network topologies is the *star*, which uses the same approach to sending and receiving messages as the telephone system. Just as telephone calls from one customer (workstation) to another customer (workstation) are handled by a central switching station, all messages in a LAN star topology must go through a central computer that controls the flow of data. AT&T's STARLAN (discussed in Chapter 7) is an example of a network that uses this approach. As Figure 2-9 illustrates, this architecture makes it easy to add new workstations, requiring only that you connect a cable from the central computer to the workstation and that you install a network interface card in the microcomputer.

Another advantage of the star topology is that the network administrator can give certain nodes higher status than other nodes. The central computer will then look for signals from these higher priority workstations before recognizing other nodes. For networks where a few key users require immediate response from on-line inquiries, for example, this feature of star topology can be crucial. Finally, a star architecture permits centralized diagnostics of all network functions. Since all messages come through the central computer, it is easy to analyze all workstation messages and produce reports listing the files used by each node. This particular type of report can prove valuable in ensuring that network security is not breached.

**Figure 2-9.
A Star Network
Topology**

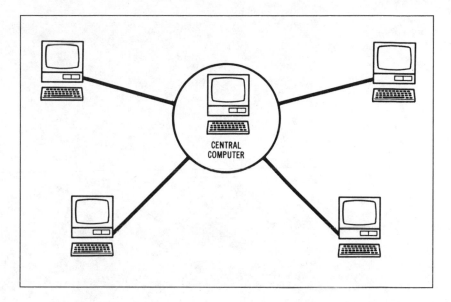

CENTRAL
COMPUTER

The failure of the central
computer results in the
entire network's failure.

The major weakness of a star architecture is that the entire local
area network fails if anything happens to the central computer. This is
precisely the same weakness of multiuser minicomputer systems that rely on
a central processor.

The Bus

A bus topology is like a
data highway. It is easy to
add new workstations but
difficult to maintain
network security.

A second major network topology is the *bus*, which, as Figure 2-10 reveals, is
like a data highway that connects together several LAN workstations. In
many such networks, the workstations check whether a message is coming
down the highway before sending their messages. Since all workstations
share this bus, all messages pass other workstations on the way to their
destination. Each workstation checks the address on the message to see if it
matches its own address.

Unlike the star topology, where dozens of cables can congregate
near the central computer, causing logistical problems, bus cabling is simple.
Many of the low-cost LANs use a bus architecture and twisted-pair wire
cabling. Another advantage is that the failure of a single workstation will not
cripple the rest of the network. 3Com's 3+Share LAN is an example of a
network that uses the bus approach.

A disadvantage of the bus topology is that generally there must be a
minimum distance between taps for workstations to avoid signal interference.
Also, there is no easy way for a system administrator to run diagnostics on
the entire network. Finally, a bus architecture does not have the network
security features inherent in a star topology. Since all messages are sent
along a common data highway, security can be compromised by an
unauthorized network user.

**Figure 2-10.
A Bus Network
Topology**

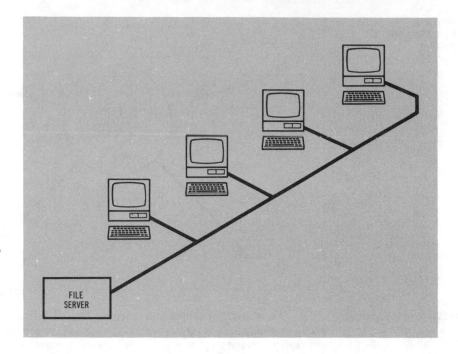

The Ring

The ring topology
combines advantages of
the star and the bus.

Figure 2-11 illustrates a third major type of network architecture: the *ring*. A ring topology consists of several nodes joined together to form a circle. Messages proceed from node to node in one direction only. (Some ring networks are capable of sending messages bidirectionally, but they can still send a message in only one direction at a time.) The ring topology permits verification that a message has been received. When a node receives a message addressed to itself, it copies the message and then sends the message back to the sender.

One of the major issues in a ring topology is the necessity of ensuring that all workstations have equal access to the network. In a *token ring* LAN, a data packet known as a *token* is sent from the transmitting workstation throughout the network. The token contains the address of the sender and the address of the node to receive the message. When the receiving station has copied its message, it returns the token to the originating workstation, which then sends the token on to the next workstation in the ring.

The intricacies of how a token is designed will be discussed in Chapter 4, which examines IBM's Token Ring Network. It is important to note, however, that in order to administer the system one workstation is designated as the monitoring node in the network. This workstation handles all diagnostic functions. Should it fail, the network itself is protected since another workstation can be designated for this task. There are many advantages to a ring topology. With bypass software, it is possible for the

**Figure 2-11.
A Ring Network
Topology**

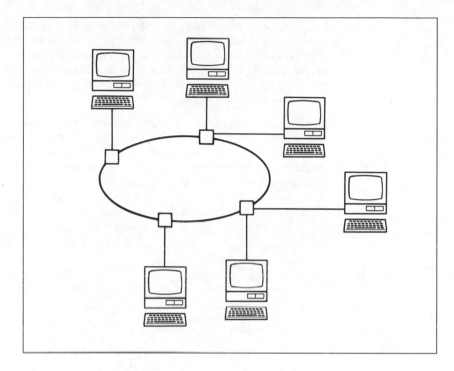

network to withstand the failure of various workstations by bypassing them while maintaining the network's integrity. Additional ring networks can be linked together through *bridges* that switch data from one ring to another.

If several workstations are cabled together to form a ring topology, it is extremely difficult to add new workstations. The entire network would have to be shut down while a new node is added and the cabling reattached. There is a simple solution, however. Most token ring networks now come with *wire centers*. These connectors, displayed in Figure 2-11, enable network administrators to add and remove workstations by connecting and disconnecting them from the appropriate wire centers while the network remains intact and in operation.

NETWORK STANDARDS AND PROTOCOLS

Over the past few years some governing organizations within this field have developed standards and designed protocols, which are rules that ensure compatibility for different vendors' network hardware and software.

So far in this chapter we have examined the major components of a local area network. If the computers, application software, network software, and cabling were all manufactured by the same vendor, there would be little problem in making everything work together smoothly. In reality, however, network software from one LAN manufacturer usually will not work on a competitor's network, and application programs and even cabling must be selected for a specific local area network.

To provide some level of uniformity among network vendors the International Standards Organization (ISO) has developed Open Systems Interconnection (OSI) standards. Different computers networked together need to know in what form they will receive information. When will a particular word begin and when will it end and the next word begin? Is there a way for one computer to check whether its message was garbled in transmission? The OSI model answers these questions and more with a set of standards that in the future may allow you to buy network products from different vendors with some assurance that they will work together.

The OSI Model

The Open Systems Interconnection (OSI) standards constitute a seven-layer model that ensures efficient communication within a local area network and between different networks.

As Figure 2-12 illustrates, the OSI model consists of seven layers of standards. Each of these layers is designed so that it provides a service for the layer immediately above it. To illustrate the principle behind this model, think of using a citizen's band radio (CB). Whenever you communicate with another person by CB, you are using a set of agreed-upon standards very much like the OSI model. Let's look more closely at how a call from Frank to Betty follows a series of uniform standards.

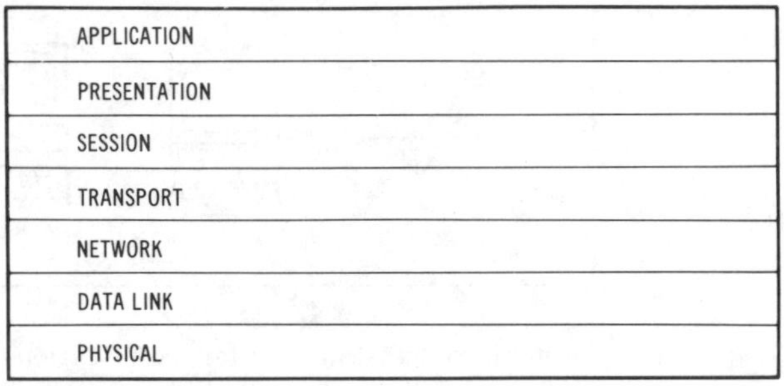

**Figure 2-12.
The OSI Model**

| APPLICATION |
| PRESENTATION |
| SESSION |
| TRANSPORT |
| NETWORK |
| DATA LINK |
| PHYSICAL |

By pressing his send button and announcing "breaker, breaker," Frank indicates he wishes to send a message. He then uses his commonly agreed-upon nickname to identify himself before asking for his friend Betty by her nickname: "This is Happy Hacker, can you read me PC Woman?" After making contact with Betty, Frank tells her to "switch over to channel 25 because it's clearer." Betty acknowledges that she understands the message by replying, "That's 10-4, Happy Hacker."

At the physical level, Frank had to press certain buttons to broadcast a message using radio hardware equipment including transistors. His use of nicknames established a concrete address for the recipient of his message and identified himself as the sender. He then determined the quality of transmission, and, after switching to an error-free channel of communication, he began talking to Betty (in his slight Brooklyn accent) about his new communications program. Betty was kept very busy translating Frank's technical jargon and his Brooklyn slang into standard American English. She was able to do this because Frank followed certain generally accepted rules—he used American English grammatical patterns.

Likewise, the OSI layers of standards work only when all vendors adhere to them and do not bypass any for "shortcuts." By dividing the complex procedures necessary for data communications along a network into seven different layers, the OSI model is designed to make it easier to achieve agreement initially on the lower layers and ultimately on the entire seven layers.

The Physical Layer

The physical layer outlines the hardware standards for network compatibility.

The first layer is really a set of rules regarding the hardware used to transmit data. Among the items covered at this level are the voltages used, the timing of the data transmission, and the rules for establishing the initial "handshaking" communication connection. The physical layer establishes whether bits are going to be sent half or full duplex. Half-duplex transmission is very similar to the way data is sent across a CB. A message is sent and then an answer is received. Full-duplex transmission requires that data be sent and received simultaneously. We will look at this process more closely in the next chapter when we examine communications between local area networks and mainframe computers.

The physical layer standards also include descriptions of the acceptable connectors and interfaces to media. At this layer, the OSI model is really concerned with electrical considerations and bits (1s and 0s). The bits do not really have any meaning here—that is the responsibility of the next OSI layer.

The Data Link Layer

The data link layer is concerned with packaging data into data frames for transmission.

Earlier you saw that the OSI model has been developed so that each layer provides the layer above it with a key element. The physical layer provides the data link layer with bits. Now it is time to give these raw bits some meaning. At this point we no longer deal with bits but with *data frames*. The data link adds flags to indicate the beginning and ending of messages. At this layer the standards ensure that data is not mistaken for flags and check for errors within the data frame. This error checking can take the form of sending information about a data frame to the receiving machine and getting an acknowledgment if everything has been received correctly.

The Network Layer

The network layer is concerned with packet switching.

This third layer of the OSI model is concerned with packet switching. It establishes virtual circuits (paths between two computers or terminals) for data communications. The network layer takes messages from the fourth layer and repackages them as data packets before sending them to the lower two layers where they are transmitted. The corresponding data link layer of the receiving computer layer then reassembles the message. To understand this use of data packets, it is necessary to look at an industry standard found at the lower three OSI model layers, the X.25 standard.

CCITT X.25 Standard

The CCITT X.25 standard establishes rules for data packets that are sent to public switched networks.

The Consultative Committee for International Telephony and Telegraphy (CCITT) has developed a set of international telecommunications standards. As Figure 2-13 illustrates, the X.25 standard's three layers (physical, frame, and packet) correspond to the first three layers of the OSI model, the physical, data link, and network layers. X.25's physical layer uses the CCITT's X.21 recommendation to define the RS-232 standard for asynchronous data transmission as well as full-duplex point-to-point synchronous transmission between the data termination equipment (DTE) and a public switched network. At the frame layer data is actually exchanged between a DTE and the network. At the packet layer data is in packet form, which is a requirement for public switched networks. The X.25 standard ensures that information sent from a DTE can be understood when received by a public packet network.

Figure 2-13.
X.25 Standards and the OSI Model

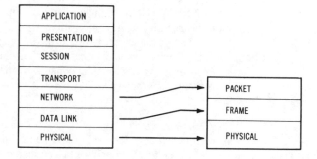

These packets contain several discrete types of information that distinguish one message from another. A packet contains an address field indicating where it is being transmitted. A control field provides several different kinds of information, including indications that a message is beginning or ending, that a message has been received successfully, or that an error has occurred.

The X.25 standard is designed for packet switching. When using this convention, the network layer of the OSI model functions very much like a gigantic mail room. Messages from a host computer are placed in packets, addressed, and sent to the bottom two layers for transmission. Since there may be several different ways (circuits) to route a message to a particular workstation, special routing tables keep track of traffic in order to balance the work load. In general this standard is used in conjunction with mainframe communications and public switched networks, a subject covered in Chapter 3, which looks at communications between local area networks and mainframe computers.

The network layer contains other conventions besides X.25, including procedures for recognizing message priorities and sending messages in proper order. Finally, this layer also controls network congestion by preventing one computer from sending information faster than it can be received or stored.

High-Level Data Link Control Procedure (HDLC)

A High-Level Data Link Control procedure (HDLC) defines the standards for linking a DTE with data communications equipment (DCE).

The X.25 standard found particularly at the data link and network layers of the OSI model defines the standards for linking a DTE and data communications equipment (DCE) by using a High-Level Data Link Control procedure (HDLC). Under HDLC all information is sent in frames. A frame consists of six fields with flags composing the beginning and ending fields. As Figure 2-14 illustrates, the flags are identical bit patterns characterized by six straight one-bits. The address field consists of the destination address if the frame is a command and a source address if the frame is a response. The control field contains information indicating whether the frame carries a command or a response. The information field usually contains integral multiples of 8-bit characters except in a few cases. As we will see shortly, this is a significant difference between HDLC and a subset of it used by IBM called SDLC.

**Figure 2-14.
The HDLC Standard**

01111110	ADDRESS	CONTROL	INFORMATION	FRAME-CHECK SEQUENCE	0111110

The frame-check sequence field ensures that the receiving station can distinguish information from garbage. In particular, this field handles situations in which information contains more than five straight one-bits. In such instances the receiving station needs to determine whether the data is really information or simply a flag indicating the end of a frame.

Bit stuffing ensures that data in a packet will not be mistaken for control bits.

The solution to this problem is called *bit stuffing*. The HDLC protocol ensures that a zero-bit is inserted in any word that contains more than five straight one-bits. The information contained in the frame check sequence field tells the receiving station where to eliminate the zero-bits that have been stuffed into the frame before reading the information.

The HDLC protocol is designed to handle data exchange between a central computer that controls communications and its secondary stations. The central computer is responsible for error checking as well as for polling the secondary stations at designated times. When it receives a signal that a station has a message to send, it sends a poll bit that permits a response from that station. This mode of operation is called "Normal Response Mode" (NRM).

A second mode of operation permits all secondary stations to send messages whenever they desire without waiting for a poll bit from the central computer. This method is called "Asynchronous Response Mode" (ARM).

Synchronous Data Link Control (SDLC)

Synchronous Data Link Control (SDLC) data packets contain some control codes unique to IBM.

IBM's computers running under its Systems Network Architecture use Synchronous Data Link Control (SDLC), a subset of HDLC. Although SDLC contains the basic HDLC frame, with beginning and ending flags and the same HDLC bit pattern, there are some differences. SDLC's information field contains data that can only be integral multiples of 8-bit characters. Also, SDLC contains several commands and responses not found under HDLC. In

Chapter 3 we will return to SDLC when we examine the link between local area networks and the IBM mainframe world of Systems Network Architecture.

More About OSI

The Transport Layer

The transport layer is primarily concerned with error recognition and recovery.

The transport layer has many functions, including several orders of error recognition and recovery. At the highest order, the transport layer can detect and even correct errors as well as identify packets that have been sent in incorrect order and rearrange them in correct order. This layer also multiplexes several messages together onto one circuit and then writes a header to indicate which message belongs to which circuit. Finally, it regulates the flow of information by controlling the movement of messages.

The Session Layer

The session layer is concerned with network management.

So far, we've seen that the OSI model is concerned with bits and data messages. However, it also recognizes particular users on the network through its session layer. Users communicate directly with this layer, which can verify a password, enable a user to switch from half-duplex to full-duplex transmission, and determine who speaks for how long and how often.

Think of the session layer as the layer concerned with network management. It can abort a session and so controls the orderly termination of a session. It controls data transfers and even handles recovery from a system crash. Finally, it can monitor system usage and bill users for their time.

The Presentation Layer

Network security, file transfers, and format functions are dealt with at the presentation layer.

The presentation layer of the OSI model is concerned with network security, file transfers, and formatting functions. At the bit level, the presentation layer encodes data in a variety of forms, including ASCII and EBCDIC. ASCII is the most universal convention, but many of the larger IBM computers use Extended Binary-Coded Decimal Interchange Code (EBCDIC), so the presentation layer must handle this second standard for data transmission as well. For accurate communication, the presentation layers of both communicating computers must contain the same protocols. This layer also handles protocol conversion between different computers using different formats and most of the word-processing functions we associate with the formatting of text, including pagination, the number of lines per screen, and even cursor movement across the screen.

In addition to these functions, the presentation layer deals with the proliferation of terminals with incompatible codes. A terminal protocol resolves these differences by enabling each data terminal to map the same virtual terminal. In effect, this procedure means that a set of translation tables exists between a local terminal and a remote terminal. The local terminal sends a data structure that defines its current screen in terms of how many characters will be displayed per line. This number can vary considerably. Many terminals routinely display 132 characters per line, but other formats are readily available. The data structure goes to the remote terminal's corresponding control object, which translates this number into a code that its terminal can understand and implement.

The Application Layer

Network programs found at the application layer include electronic mail, database managers, file-server software, and print-server software.

For the most part, the functions performed in the application layer are user specified. It is difficult to generalize about the protocols found here since different user programs establish different needs. Certain industries such as banking have developed sets of standards for this layer, which handles messages, remote logins, and network management statistics. At this level of the OSI model you will find database management programs, electronic mail, file-server and print-server programs, and the command-and-response language of the operating system.

IEEE Network Standards

IEEE has developed standards for a bus LAN (802.3), a token bus LAN (802.4), and a token ring LAN (802.5).

Using the OSI standards as a foundation, several IEEE committees have worked to develop a set of standards for local area network topologies and access methods. The committees developed three IEEE 802 standards of particular interest to us: 802.3—the CSMA/CD bus standard; 802.4—the token bus standard; and 802.5—the token ring standard. A fourth standard, 802.6, is concerned with standards for a metropolitan area network, a subject beyond the scope of this book. The complete set of 802 standards may be ordered directly from the IEEE, whose address is listed in the bibliography.

Why develop four different and even contradictory standards? The reason is that by 1980, when the 802 subcommittees first met, a wide range of incompatible local area network products already existed. Some vendors had opted for bus topologies whereas others had chosen token rings or even stars. Vendors had also adopted widely differing methods to handle a significant problem facing LANs, that of avoiding data collisions caused by network nodes sending information. So many different kinds of local area networks had proliferated because no one topology or data-access method proved best for all LAN applications. IBM has recognized this diversity by offering both a bus topology (PC Network) and a token ring topology (Token Ring Network), each of which was designed to meet the needs of a different set of customers. Chapter 4 will discuss IBM's networks.

The major advantage of the IEEE 802 standards for the network end user is that they'll eventually result in the standardization of the OSI model's physical and data link layers so that hardware from different manufacturers that complies with these standards will work together. For network software to work, however, vendors will have to follow the standards established by the higher layers of the OSI model. This may take some time.

IEEE 802.3 and Ethernet

When the IEEE 802 committees began their deliberations, they were faced with a de facto standard, Xerox's Ethernet local area network. By 1980, Intel and Digital Equipment Corporation had joined Xerox in indicating that all their products would be Ethernet-compatible. Rather than requiring that all local area networks follow the Ethernet standard, a subcommittee provided 802.3 as an acceptable Ethernet-like standard.

As we indicated, the IEEE 802 subcommittees developed standards based on the first three layers of the OSI model. They developed the data link layer into two sublayers: a logical link control sublayer (LLC) and a media access control sublayer (MAC). The LLC standard is much like the HDLC standard we described earlier, whereas the MAC sublayer is concerned with detecting data collisions.

The Ethernet Data Packet

The IEEE 802.3
committee defined an
Ethernet data packet's
format, the cabling to be
used, and the maximum
distance for the network.

The IEEE 802.3 standard describes a LAN using a bus topology. This network uses 50-ohm coaxial baseband cable that can send data at 10 mbps. As Figure 2-15 illustrates, the committee specified exactly how a frame should be composed. Notice the similarity between this frame and the HDLC protocol discussed earlier in this chapter.

Figure 2-15.
An Ethernet Frame

PREAMBLE	DESTINATION ADDRESS	SOURCE ADDRESS	TYPE	DATA	FRAME-CHECK SEQUENCE

The Ethernet packet begins with a preamble consisting of 8 bytes used for synchronization. The destination address can be a single workstation, a group of workstations, or even several groups of workstations. The source address enables the workstation receiving the message to recognize where it came from. The type field is important because there must be a way of designating the format the data is using. Without this information, it is impossible to decipher the packet when it arrives. The data field is strictly limited; it can hold a minimum of 46 bytes and a maximum of 1500 bytes of information. Finally, the frame check sequence field ensures that the data in the other fields arrives safely. In addition to specifying the type of data frames that can be packed in a packet and the type of cable that can be used to send this information, the committee also specified the maximum length of a single cable (1500 feet) and the ways that repeaters can be used to boost the signal throughout the network.

CSMA/CD Protocol

Carrier-Sense Multiple
Access with Collision
Detection (CSMA/CD) is a
protocol for defining the
ways that networks will
avoid data collisions.

The IEEE 802.3 subcommittee specified the way that a local area network using the bus topology should construct its frames of information and send them over the network to avoid collisions. The protocol is known as Carrier-Sense Multiple Access with Collision Detection (CSMA/CD). The CSMA portion of this protocol can be visualized by imagining a network user who wishes to send a message. The physical layer of the user's workstation generates a carrier-sense signal and then listens to detect a carrier-sense signal from another user who is about to send a message. If no other signal is detected, the user sends his or her message.

There are problems with this seemingly tidy solution to traffic control on a network. What happens if two network users are located fairly far apart? It is possible for them to issue a carrier-sense signal, listen and hear nothing, and then send their messages only to have the data collide. To avoid this type of accident, the committee added Collision Detection (CD) to the Carrier-Sense Multiple Access approach. What this means is that two users listen while they transmit a message. If a user detects a collision, he or she listens for the other workstation to repeat the transmission and then transmits his or her message again.

There is still another problem with this approach. Imagine two drivers arriving at an intersection with four-way stop signs. Both drivers arrive simultaneously, come to a complete stop, wait a reasonable time, and then begin to move again only to have to slam on their brakes to avoid a collision. Embarrassed by the near collision, the two drivers pause before starting again. Unfortunately, they start again at precisely the same time and once again narrowly avoid a collision.

While the two drivers' adventure at an intersection sounds like a scene from a silent movie comedy, the reality of collision after collision is certainly not funny to network administrators. To avoid this possibility, network planners have designed their CSMA/CD approach so that each workstation waits a different random amount of time after a data collision before once again transmitting a message. After a collision, a special signal called a *jam* is sent through the network. This signal ensures that all workstations know that there has been a collision, no matter how far apart they are on the network.

After repeated collisions, the network will double its random delays before permitting stations to transmit once again. This approach does not totally eliminate collisions since it is theoretically possible for two workstations well separated to wait different amounts of time and still transmit messages that collide. These accidents, however, are infrequent and thus manageable.

Despite the ingenuity of this approach to collision avoidance, there is one additional consideration. A heavily used bus network with CSMA/CD can begin to look very much like a Los Angeles freeway during rush hour. Even though data is supposed to move at 10 mbps, the doubling and redoubling of the delay duration after a few collisions could reduce the network's throughput to between 1 mbps and 3 mbps.

IEEE 802.4 Token Bus

IEEE 802.4 defines a bus topology using a data packet "token" that is passed from workstation to workstation.

The IEEE 802.4 subcommittee developed a standard for a different type of bus network that does not have the contention approach of the 802.3 model. This type of network is desirable if it is absolutely necessary that there be no data collisions.

To understand how this token approach contrasts sharply with the CSMA/CD bus approach, imagine a public forum on a controversial issue. Under the CSMA/CD method, several people might try to speak simultaneously only to stop politely when they heard another speaker begin. With dozens of speakers trying to speak yet not wanting to interrupt each other, the process would become very chaotic and inefficient. With the token approach, a token would be accepted as a symbol of authority giving a person the right to speak. Whoever held the token would stand and make a speech.

When finished, he or she would pass this symbol of authority to the next person who desired to speak. No one would attempt to speak without physically possessing the token.

Figure 2-16 illustrates the token bus frame format under IEEE 802.4. The preamble field primarily synchronizes the signal. The start frame delimiter and end frame delimiter fields define the limits of the frame. The control frame carries information from either the logical link control (LLC) or media access control (MAC) sublayers. Both the destination address and source address fields function identically with those found in the 802.3 Ethernet frame. The destination address field can contain a specific workstation's address, a group address for several workstations, or addresses for several different groups (a *broadcast* address). The information field and the frame check sequence fields are both identical with those discussed under the 802.3 model.

Figure 2-16.
A Token Bus Format

PREAMBLE	START FRAME DELIMITER	FRAME CONTROL	DESTINATION ADDRESS	SOURCE ADDRESS	INFORMATION	FRAME-CHECK SEQUENCE	END FRAME DELIMITER

The token is actually a data packet. A workstation sends the token to the address of the workstation designated to receive it. This station copies the message and then returns the token to the sending station. Figure 2-17 illustrates how a token is actually passed in a bus topology. The network maintains a table composed of addresses for each workstation. These addresses may bear no resemblance to where the station is physically located on the bus network, but they are an indication of the order in which stations will receive the token. A workstation that requires the token frequently because it needs to use the network more than other workstations can be listed several times in the network table of addresses so that it will receive the token more often. The token is passed to the station with the next lowest address. For example, the station at address 100 sends the token to address 75 and then listens to make sure that the token was received satisfactorily.

Remember that the token is really a bit pattern. If a station does not receive a reply from the station it sent a token to, it sends a second token. If there is still no reply, the sending station requests the address of the next station to receive the token by directing what is called a "who follows" frame down the network. If this fails to invoke a response, it sends a general request through the network asking any station that wants to send a message to respond in order to receive the token. This is known as a "solicit successor" frame. The sending workstation then changes the token's address to match this address and sends the token.

Notice that the topology of this 802.4 standard is a bus, yet the token is passed in the form of a logical ring. The lowest address workstation to receive the token will send it back to begin the process all over again. In a smoothly working token bus, each workstation receives the token, inserts the

Figure 2-17.
A Token Bus Network

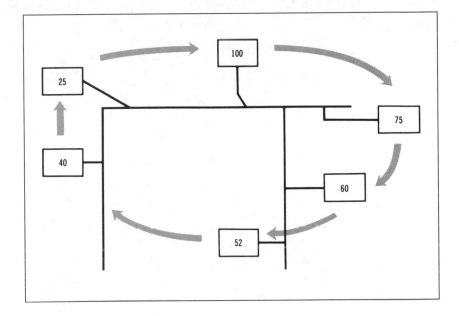

information it wishes to send, and then sends it to its destination where another workstation repeats the process.

Problems can occur with this approach, however, the most serious of which are caused by malfunctioning hardware that can result in missing tokens or even multiple tokens. The network controller assumes responsibility for monitoring and error checking to keep such a situation from crippling the network. Other weaknesses inherent in this token bus approach include some specific distance limitations as well as limitations on how many new workstations can be "tapped" into the bus. Ethernet, for example, defines minimum distances required between individual workstations and also sets limitations on how many new workstations can be added to the bus, because each new workstation creates a certain amount of signal distortion.

IEEE 802.5 Token Ring Network

IEEE 802.5 defines a token ring network in which workstations pass a token around a physical and logical ring. The token ring uses amplifiers to boost signals so it has a greater range than bus networks.

The IEEE 802.5 standard was developed to cover local area networks with ring topologies that use a token to pass information from one workstation to another. At this point, we will examine the theory behind this set of standards and reserve a later chapter to take a closer look at IBM's Token Ring Network. As Figure 2-18 illustrates, in a token ring network the sending workstation places a message on the token and directs it to its destination address. The receiving workstation copies the message and then sends the token back on the ring where it continues its journey until it reaches the originating workstation. This unit removes its message and then passes the token to the next station for its use.

Because it is crucial that an originating station know whether or not its message has been received, the frame format differs slightly in the 802.5 standard to allow for this information. As depicted in Figure 2-19, an access-

Figure 2-18.
A Token Ring Network

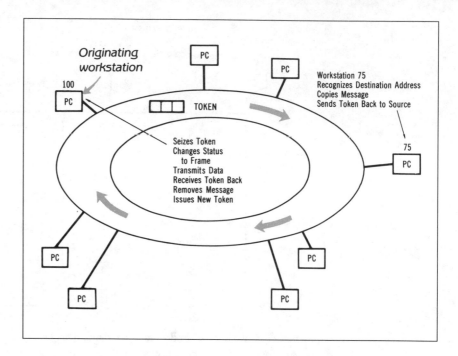

control field is added to the format to control the actual passing of the token. The ending frame delimiter field also contains a new wrinkle. Two bits in this frame are used to indicate whether the station receiving a message recognized the address and whether it actually copied the message successfully.

Figure 2-19.
Format for a Token

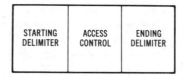

In a smoothly running token ring network, each station receives the token and checks to see if the message is addressed to it. If its address matches, it copies the message and sends the token on by repeating the signal. If the message is for another workstation, it repeats the signal and sends it on. The network also has to have a provision for dealing with an inactive or defective workstation; otherwise, the entire network would fail. One way to address this situation is to use hardware that enables the network to bypass a nontransmitting workstation. As we discussed earlier, for example, wire centers can be used to keep the token moving past inactive stations.

A major advantage of a token ring network is that it can cover a greater distance than a token bus without loss of signal since each workstation repeats the signal. On the other hand, a token ring is vulnerable to a malfunctioning station and requires significantly more cable for large installations than a corresponding bus topology. In a very large network, however, there may not be another viable alternative. Because of IBM's Token Ring Network, this topology is expected to gain at least 70 percent of the local area network market within the next few years.

WHAT HAVE YOU LEARNED?

1. File servers offer many advantages over disk servers in a local area network.
2. The major LAN media include twisted-pair wire, coaxial cable, and fiber optics.
3. Broadband coaxial cable can transmit several different messages simultaneously using different frequencies.
4. In a star topology, the entire local area network fails if the central computer fails.
5. CSMA/CD is a method for detecting and avoiding data collisions on a local area network.
6. X.25 is a standard for packet switching with layers of standards corresponding to the first three layers of the OSI model.
7. The OSI model consists of seven layers of standards designed to ensure local area network compatibility of hardware and software.
8. HDLC consists of protocols for placing a message in a packet for transmission.

Quiz for Chapter 2

1. The X.25 set of standards covers how many layers of the OSI model?
  a. one
  b. two
  c. three
  d. four

2. Which OSI model layer concerns itself with hardware specifications?
  a. data link
  b. network
  c. physical
  d. presentation

3. Bit stuffing is used to
  a. pad insufficient information
  b. distinguish beginning and ending flags from information
  c. convert 8-bit words into 16-bit words
  d. fill a data turkey

4. When a central computer polls a station to see if it has a message to send, this is an example of
  a. Asynchronous Response Mode (ARM)
  b. Normal Response Mode (NRM)
  c. Infrequent Polling Procedure (IPP)
  d. Polling by Authorization (PBA)

5. A protocol is really
  a. a set of demands
  b. a set of rules
  c. a translation book for diplomats
  d. a call with very high authorization

6. A CB radio call is very much like
  a. full-duplex transmission
  b. half-duplex transmission
  c. quarter-duplex transmission
  d. no duplex transmission

7. In the OSI model, error recognition and recovery is really the responsibility of
  a. the physical layer
  b. the application layer
  c. the session layer
  d. the transport layer

8. In the OSI model, password verification is the responsibility of
  a. the session layer
  b. the physical layer
  c. the data link layer
  d. the network layer

9. Distributed file servers are
  a. special file servers designed for LANs
  b. multiple file servers designed to speed up the network
  c. inexpensive file servers
  d. file servers also used as work stations

10. A dedicated file server is
  a. a hardworking file server
  b. a file server used as a workstation and as a file server
  c. a file server used only for serving files to workstations in a local area network
  d. a file server that never breaks down

11. A print spooler is really a
  a. buffer used to store files for printing
  b. the central processing unit
  c. a printer's spooling mechanism
  d. a place for assembling and disassembling printer material

12. To send simultaneous voice and data signals, a LAN should use
  a. twisted-pair wire
  b. baseband coaxial cable
  c. broadband coaxial cable
  d. two coffee cans with lots of string

13. A data highway is a good description of which network topology?
  a. A bus
  b. A star
  c. A ring
  d. A token ring

14. A dead workstation on a token ring network can cripple the network without
  a. special software
  b. wire centers or special bypass hardware
  c. extra tokens
  d. a dead-station token (DST)

15. A broadcast address enables a message to go to
  a. a single workstation
  b. a single group of workstations
  c. several groups of workstations
  d. a selected peripheral

16. A jam signal sent through a network means
  a. the network traffic is too congested
  b. there has been a data collision
  c. it's time to go
  d. the printer's paper feeder is jammed

17. The IEEE 802.3 standard is closest to
  a. IBM's Token Ring Network
  b. Xerox's Ethernet local area network
  c. a generic star network
  d. a generic token ring network

18. For a relatively large network covering a long distance, probably the best network topology would be
  a. a bus
  b. a token ring
  c. a token bus
  d. a superbus

19. If interference is a major problem, a network designer should consider
  a. baseband coaxial cable
  b. broadband coaxial cable
  c. twisted-pair wire
  d. fiber optics

20. Database management software and electronic mail software would be found in which layer of the OSI model?
  a. The application layer
  b. The presentation layer
  c. The data link layer
  d. The network layer

Gateways

ABOUT THIS CHAPTER

Microcomputers linked together in a local area network and mainframe
computers belong to two completely different worlds. In this chapter we will
examine how microcomputers can communicate over LANs with mainframes
and minicomputers by using communications gateways, and we will look
closely at the way mainframes handle information and their most common
protocols.

 We will also discuss the emerging standards for microcomputer
communications with mainframes and minicomputers and the different levels
of communications possible between microcomputer networks and
minicomputers and mainframes. Finally, we will examine how some
companies are using their private branch exchange (PBX) phone systems as
limited local area networks.

THE WORLD OF SYSTEMS NETWORK ARCHITECTURE (SNA)

IBM's SNA contains
several layers of protocols
similar to the OSI model
discussed in the last
chapter. SNA uses SDLC,
a subset of HDLC.

Any discussion of mainframes has to begin with IBM's specifications for
distributed data-processing networks. As Figure 3-1 illustrates, Systems
Network Architecture (SNA) provides a model of network layers much like
the OSI model we examined in Chapter 2. Data flows through SNA almost
exactly as in the OSI model, except that the frames use the Synchronous
Data Link Control format (SDLC) rather than the High-Level Data Link
Control procedure (HDLC). As was pointed out in the last chapter, the SDLC
frames contain some frames that are transmitted from one node to another
throughout an SNA network.

**Figure 3-1.
Systems Network
Architecture**

TRANSACTION SERVICES	controls document exchange distributed database access
PRESENTATION SERVICES	formats data
DATA FLOW CONTROL	synchronous exchange of data
TRANSMISSION CONTROL	matches data exchange rate
PATH CONTROL	routes data packets between source and destination
DATA LINK CONTROL	transmits data between nodes
PHYSICAL	provides physical connections

 Recently IBM has replaced five network management programs in
SNA with a single new program, NetView. NetView is a centralized

management system that performs diagnostics on SNA protocols, establishes communication sessions, carries out network accounting procedures, displays network diagnostic alerts, and determines network component failures. NetView also can monitor X.25 traffic in the SNA environment. An IBM program, X.25 SNA Interconnection, allows SNA networks to carry data under X.25 packet-switching protocols.

SYNCHRONOUS VERSUS ASYNCHRONOUS DATA TRANSMISSION

Data transmission in the microcomputer world long has taken the form of asynchronous transmission. Serial printers and modems are everyday reminders of how common this form of data communications really is. The SNA mainframe world, however, uses the SDLC protocol discussed briefly in Chapter 2, which is a synchronous method of data transmission. As Figure 3-2 illustrates, asynchronous transmission sends characters a byte at a time, whereas the synchronous approach sends continuous information until the transmission is concluded.

> Whereas asynchronous transmission sends data one byte at a time, synchronous transmission uses frames that permit a stream of data.

**Figure 3-2.
Asynchronous versus
Synchronous
Transmission**

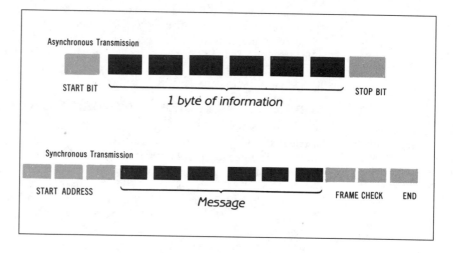

Some older IBM mainframes use Binary Synchronous Communication (BSC), a synchronous protocol that is character-oriented (with 8-bit characters) rather than bit-oriented (as is SDLC). Several companies, including IBM, market a Binary Synchronous Communication Adapter card and Binary Synchronous 3270 Emulation program, the keys to tying a microcomputer local area network to an older IBM using the BSC protocol. This chapter, however, will focus on SDLC protocol machines.

Logical Units (LUs)

> Logical units (LUs) can represent end users or application programs.

Communication in an SNA network takes place between logical units (LUs). Logical units can represent end users (such as the firmware associated with IBM 3270 terminals, for example) or application programs. Application programs recognize only a terminal's network name, not its physical location. SNA translates the network name into a corresponding address.

Network-Addressable Units (NAUs)

Network-addressable units (NAUs) consist of logical units (LUs), physical units (PUs), and system services control points (SSCPs).

SNA uses network-addressable units (NAUs) to handle the communications portions of application programs and provide network control. There are three types of network-addressable units: logical units, physical units (PUs), and system services control points (SSCPs). A PU is not actually a physical device but something tangible (a terminal or an intelligent controller, for example). In effect, SNA deals with the PU rather than with the device itself. An SSCP serves as the network manager for a single SNA domain, coordinating communications between network elements, making sure that the corresponding physical devices are active when two logical units wish to converse, and providing error-checking information.

The Path Control Network

The path control network identifies the addresses of devices that wish to converse and establishes a network path for their conversation.

Under SNA the path control network contains a path control layer and a data link control layer, which handle traffic flow, transmission priorities, and error recovery. Remember, under SNA, all LUs, PUs, and even SSCPs have different network addresses. The path control network identifies the correct addresses of units that wish to converse and then establishes a network path for their conversation.

Sessions

A session consists of a logical and physical path connecting two NAUs for data transmission. NAUs can have multiple sessions.

A session under SNA is a logical and physical path connecting two NAUs for data transmission. SNA thinks of its terminals, controllers, and front-end communication processors as nodes, each having a corresponding PU. If a terminal wishes to communicate with a front-end communication processor, for example, the SSCP establishes a session between the two nodes; in the case of two end users, the SSCP establishes an LU-LU session.

The SSCP also controls the activating and deactivating of a session. An application program can maintain several different sessions with different terminals simultaneously under SNA. Figure 3-3 illustrates the NAU elements found under SNA.

LU 6.2

LU 6.2 contains specifications that ultimately will enable programs written in different languages under different operating systems to communicate with each other.

IBM recently added Advanced Program-to-Program Communications (APPC) to SNA, resulting in the development of two new protocols (LU 6.2 and PU 2.1). Earlier we saw how it was possible to have a session between a program and a terminal; likewise, two programs can communicate with each other.

Ultimately LU 6.2 will enable a microcomputer running a program under one operating system (such as DOS) to communicate with a mainframe computer while retaining its full processing capabilities. Underpinning the protocol is the revolutionary concept that different computers running different programs written in different languages under different operating systems can interact with each other.

For years corporations have longed for the ability to download information directly into an IBM personal computer running Lotus 1-2-3. Similarly, there is a real need to upload customer files under a DOS program such as dBase III directly into a mainframe database.

**Figure 3-3.
The NAU Elements
Found under SNA**

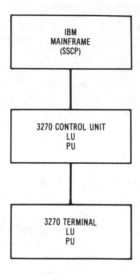

IBM developed SNA before personal computers were popular. As a result, the concept of distributed processing incorporated under SNA is a master-slave relationship: all communication goes through the main computer. For example, two end users who wish to send information to each other can do so only by going through the mainframe computer. Under LU 6.2 true peer-to-peer communications will theoretically be possible. A personal computer that is part of an SNA network would be able to address a second personal computer directly without going through the mainframe. Such a path might be particularly valuable if the mainframe should fail.

LU 6.2 overcomes many of the limitations of SNA because it provides a true generic applications programming interface (API). Since this interface includes hardware specifications, the network can be thought of as machine independent as long as all vendors adhere to these requirements. Rather than the traditional master-slave relationship that historically has been the norm under SNA, LU 6.2 allows either node in a network session to initiate the session.

IBM has begun to provide tools that will help implement LU 6.2. The Server/Requester Programming Interface (SRPI) is a protocol that allows PC applications to issue requests for services and receive replies from IBM mainframe computers. SRPI permits program-to-program communications under terminal emulation conditions and is a subset of IBM's APPC programming interface. IBM has upgraded its mainframe operating systems to work in conjunction with LU 6.2. TSO/E Release 3 is an operating environment upgrade for mainframes running under the MVS/XA TSO/E environment, which implements SRPI and allows it to handle requests for data and services from PCs. IBM has also developed IBM PC Requesters, a product that runs under the new SRPI interface. With this product, an IBM PC will have a DOS menu with which to access data from databases. The workstation will be able to request data on a record-by-record basis if necessary.

The major problem with LU 6.2 is that existing software packages and hardware do not follow the API guidelines. It will take some time before enough programs are available to make this new protocol a major force in the SNA world.

MICRO-MAINFRAME COMMUNICATIONS

Until the software and hardware that follows LU 6.2 comes along, the main method for micro-mainframe communications will continue to be IBM terminal emulation.

Despite the exciting possibilities of LU 6.2, the dearth of software written for the interface means that microcomputers will have to continue to communicate with the mainframe world by emulating various IBM terminals. Let's examine several different ways, both local and remote, to tie the two worlds together.

327X Terminal Emulation via Cluster Controller

An IBM mainframe computer can communicate with various peripherals through a 3274 or 3276 cluster controller. The 3274 controller can connect up to thirty-two terminals or printers to the mainframe, whereas the 3276 can accommodate only seven devices. As Figure 3-4 illustrates, an IBM PC can be connected directly to the mainframe through the cluster controller using coaxial cable and special 3278 terminal emulation software and hardware. A terminal emulation card usually contains RAM, ROM, a 3270 coaxial interface, and a high-speed processor that can handle up to four million instructions per second. By pressing the PC's two shift keys simultaneously, a user can shift between a DOS application and 3270 terminal emulation.

**Figure 3-4.
An IBM PC Connected
to a Cluster Controller**

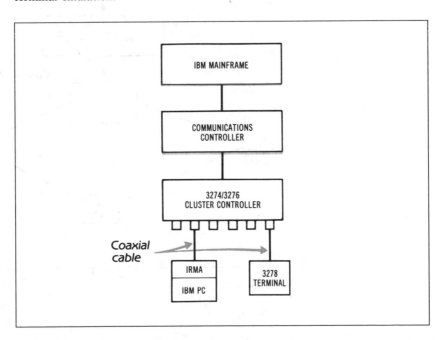

The keyboard and screen are both far different on an IBM 3278 terminal than on an IBM PC. The terminal emulation software allows the PC user to press keys and have the equivalent keystrokes of a 3278 sent to the cluster controller. Similarly, the software "paints" the IBM monitor's screen with what appears to be an IBM 3278 display. Although the 3278 monochrome terminal is the most common form of terminal emulation, there is also software to emulate the 3279 color terminal. IBM even offers a 3270-PC, which is really the IBM PC with a built-in 3270 terminal emulation board and a hybrid keyboard that combines the best features of the two very different keyboards.

Local LAN Gateways

A LAN gateway can be attached by coaxial cable to a 3274 cluster controller to provide a local micro-mainframe connection.

A major limitation of using a single IBM PC in 3278 terminal emulation that is connected directly to the cluster controller by coaxial cable is that the PC uses one of the controller's ports. Several PCs connected in this way would severely limit the mainframe's ability to serve all company users. But, as shown in Figure 3-5, it is possible to connect an entire microcomputer local area network to an IBM cluster controller with a gateway and coaxial cable. Any PC in this network has access to 3270 terminal emulation.

**Figure 3-5.
An IBM PC with 3270
Terminal Emulation**

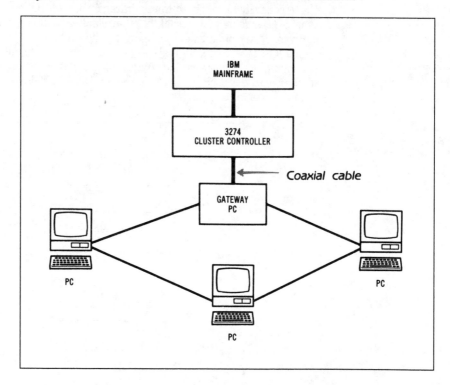

Remote Gateways

Remote gateways enable local area network users to communicate with a mainframe computer by using 3278 terminal emulation on a gateway PC.

The more likely scenario for micro-mainframe communications, however, is illustrated by the Widget Corporation in the first chapter. Many companies have their local area microcomputer network at one location and their mainframe facilities at another. In this situation LAN gateways prove particularly valuable.

At the remote site, the designated "gateway" PC is equipped with a gateway interface board and special gateway software to emulate a cluster controller. As Figure 3-6 illustrates, each remote PC can emulate a 3278 terminal and use its synchronous modem to communicate over a phone line with a mainframe computer. This one gateway server can run as many as sixty-four 3270 emulation sessions. Some gateways permit sixty-four concurrent host sessions and a data rate as fast as 56 kilobits per second (kbps) via synchronous modems attached to an IBM 3705 or 3725 controller. IBM's 3720 communications controller links the mainframe with local area networks. IBM currently offers a special token ring interface to its 3720 controller. It is important to remember from our discussion of the SNA world and the nature of SNA sessions that one user can find himself needing three or four editing sessions simultaneously. Often the network administrator will establish some order of priority for these valuable mainframe sessions.

Figure 3-6.
Remote 3270 Emulation
with a Gateway PC

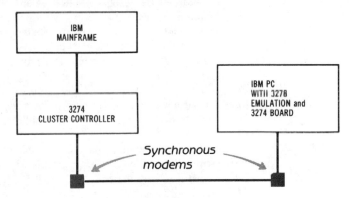

Although in theory all network users can emulate a 3278 terminal and communicate with a mainframe through a gateway PC, in practice such demand would quickly cause a traffic jam.

There are a number of ways of alleviating this problem. If the gateway PC is also being used as a workstation, it can be designated as a *dedicated gateway* and used only for that purpose.

If the processing speed of the dedicated gateway PC is still not adequate to handle the communications workload, a second gateway file server can be installed. Remember, though, that these two servers will be sharing a single modem and telephone line. If this remedy proves inadequate, the only solution is to install a second network complete with PC workstations, gateway PC, modem, and a second telephone line. Both networks can in turn be connected together using a bridge, which we'll explore more fully when we look at some specific local area networks.

Micro-Mainframe File Transfers

Many of the micro-mainframe file-transfer programs permit only bulk transfer of files and do not allow the microcomputer user to select key fields from a mainframe database and retrieve specific information.

We have seen that it is possible to link workstations in a local area network to a mainframe computer using 3270 terminal emulation and a gateway. The major limitation of this emulation is that an intelligent PC is forced to assume the role of a "dumb" terminal. The terminal-emulation software normally permits on-line inquiry using the mainframe programs and the ability to save each screen of 3270 terminal information.

Yet users want to be able to download and upload selected information and not merely dump screenfuls of information. File transfers in both directions create enormous problems since microcomputers and mainframes run different programs under different operating systems. Likewise, the file structures of microcomputer and mainframe application programs usually do not correspond—IBM mainframes use an EBCDIC format whereas microcomputers use an ASCII format. The size limitations of a microcomputer pose even more serious problems. Mainframe files may not be downloadable simply because the microcomputer does not have enough disk space to handle them. And microcomputer software may not be able to handle the number of records found within a mainframe file.

Many of the leaders in micro-mainframe communications offer file-transfer programs with their 3270 terminal emulation products. These programs do not permit a user to manipulate the data within a mainframe's application program or select certain fields but only to download or upload complete files. With the necessary hardware and software a user can transfer files between an appropriately equipped PC and an IBM mainframe running under CICS, VM/CMS, or MVS/TSO. For example, AST offers the AST-3270/FTS-R advanced file-transfer system for the MVS/TSO and VM/CMS environments, which basically provides bidirectional transfer of binary or text files.

Several companies have developed *intelligent links* that tie together their own mainframe computer programs with major microcomputer software. Information Builders, for one, offers FOCUS for the IBM mainframe and PC/FOCUS for microcomputers, which make it possible to use a mainframe database for distributed processing. PCs tied to a local area network can thus be used as transaction workstations to enter data. Management Science of America markets Executive Peachpack II, which ties together data from its mainframe MSA application programs with Lotus 1-2-3 formats running on a PC. Several vendors offer links to spreadsheets that will accept Data Interchange Format (DIF). The lack of uniformity in microcomputer and mainframe software means that until now users have had to purchase separate interfaces (if even available) for each vendor's programs. On-Line Software's OMNILINK addresses this problem by including software for both the microcomputer and the mainframe. Its file reformat utility program automatically converts downloaded data into formats used by Lotus 1-2-3, dBASE IV, and several other leading programs. A user can select criteria and then download only those records within a file that meet these standards.

A few vendors have begun to address the possibilities of LU 6.2 and its potential for facilitating data transfer from microcomputer to mainframe. Network Software Associates' AdaptSNA LU6.2/APPC is just what the name implies, an implementation of LU 6.2 and PU 2.1. This software enables a PC-DOS program to communicate directly with a partner program running on a mainframe or minicomputer, thus doing away with the traditional SNA master-slave relationship. PCs can be configured to participate in IBM's Distributed Office Support System (DIOSS) or other host-based APPC system. Rabbit Software has developed a Program Interface Module (PIM) that permits direct transfer of data. Microcomputer users find this process transparent, which means they do not have to learn mainframe computer procedures in order to use a microcomputer program.

Remote Job Entry (RJE)

There are many times when remote PCs need to send information in batch form to unattended mainframe computers.

Often, micro-mainframe communications are needed primarily for uploading data after business hours. A company with several retail outlets might require each branch to upload sales figures during the evening so that the mainframe computer can digest the information and update its accounting files. IBM originally designed the 3270 terminal emulation protocol for on-line inquiry and remote job entry (RJE) for transferring large amounts of data. RJE contains such features as data compression and compaction to minimize line charges for data transmission.

Network Software Associates' AdaptSNA RJE is a good example of an RJE SNA communications emulator. This hardware and software package emulates an IBM 3770 RJE workstation and includes a number of powerful features such as an applications programming interface, which permits unattended operation as well as automatic error recovery, support for LU-LU and SSCP-LU sessions, conversion tables between EBCDIC and ASCII formats, "on-the-fly" processing, and automatic reformatting of data received from the host computer.

Clearly, despite the inherent limitations of 3270 terminal emulation, particularly its method of dumping one screenful of information at a time, RJE is a useful form of micro-mainframe communications.

MICRO-MINI COMMUNICATIONS

Terminal emulation allows microcomputers to communicate individually or as part of a local area network with minicomputers such as IBM's System 34, 36, 38, and AS/400 computers.

Many microcomputer users prefer to communicate with their departmental minicomputer than with a corporate mainframe computer. This process is similar to 3270 terminal emulation except that microcomputers need to be equipped with 5250 emulator boards and file-transfer software in order to communicate with IBM minis and with other appropriate software and hardware in order to communicate with minis from DEC, Hewlett-Packard, and other vendors.

Several major vendors offer this combination of hardware and software. AST, for example, offers the AST-5250/Local Cluster, which enables a PC to function as a local cluster controller and provides 5250 terminal emulation for up to four clusters of PCs attached serially to a "master" controller PC. As Figure 3-7 illustrates, this controller is connected by standard twinax cable to a host System 34, 36, 38, or AS/400 minicomputer. This "master" PC can also be connected via synchronous modems with remote PCs, which then can also use 5250 terminal emulation. Significantly, these modems can support speeds of up to 9600 bits per second (bps).

**Figure 3-7.
Local Microcomputers
Linked to an IBM
Minicomputer**

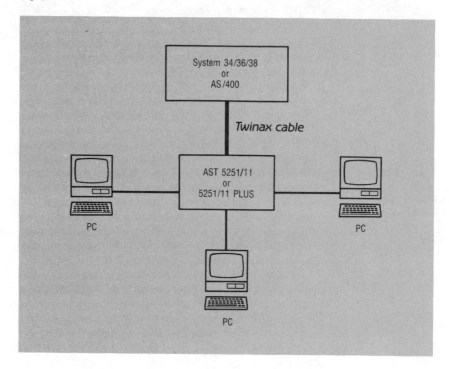

Clustered PCs operate in a background mode to the master PC. This means that one or more clustered PCs operate in 5250 emulation mode while the master PC operates in DOS mode. It is also possible to have concurrent PC-DOS and host sessions.

Many of the same file-transfer limitations found in micro-mainframe communications are also present in micro-mini communications. Techland System's Blue Lynx hardware and software address many of these problems. With this board and DecisionLink's file-transfer software the microcomputer user can perform bidirectional file transfers and support four concurrent host sessions. On-Line's OMNILINK functions in much the same way as for micro-mainframe file transfers, permitting the selection of key fields within a minicomputer database for downloading to a microcomputer. Companies such as Fusion offer even more sophisticated software that permits the transfer of selected data from as many as eight different files on an IBM minicomputer.

VIRTUAL NETWORKING SYSTEMS

Banyan Systems has developed VINES software, which permits sharing of resources on a virtual network.

Banyan Systems has developed VINES software in conjunction with its family of network file servers. As Figure 3-8 illustrates, VINES permits the accessing and sharing of resources, applications, and information wherever they are located on a virtual network. In a virtual network the differences between microcomputers, minicomputers, and even mainframes are of limited importance to the end user. A microcomputer user can access files from a mainframe as easily as if this information were on his or her PC. The microcomputer can save information onto the "virtual disk" of the mainframe or minicomputer while also being attached to the Banyan file server. Since the software supports LU 6.2, it is extremely easy to communicate with other users even if you do not know precisely where they are on the network. The software keeps track of users' addresses and permits electronic mail transfer simply by indicating the receiver's name.

**Figure 3-8.
Banyan's Virtual
Networking System**
*(Courtesy of Banyan
Systems, Inc.)*

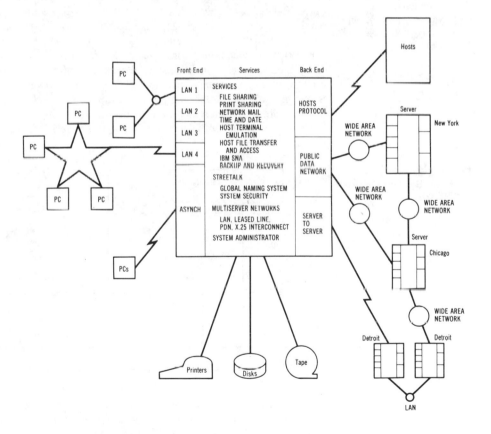

THE PBX

One of the major capabilities offered by Banyan's virtual network is that it enables the user to transmit and receive information from different networks without becoming too concerned with the mechanics of the process. To the end user, who uses only the common DOS commands, this complex system really seems simple because the complexities are handled by the VINES software. For several years data-processing professionals and telecommunication managers have speculated about the possibility of using an office's telephone system—its PBX—to accomplish not only what Banyan has done but also the integration of voice and data.

PBX History

The PBX has been in use for approximately eighty years. Newer units are completely digital and are distributed most commonly with twisted-pair wire but also with coaxial cable and fiber optics.

The PBX has a long history. To understand the concept of a public branch exchange, imagine an office before the PBX. As Figure 3-9 illustrates, each phone was directly connected into the trunk cable that carried the signals back to the central office exchange. The PBX simplified this situation. As Figure 3-10 shows, only a few wires are required to connect the PBX to the trunk. A first-generation PBX phone system was in operation as early as the late 1800s. Bell's 701 family of PBXs launched in 1929 represents the second generation, in which operators were no longer needed to handle outgoing calls. A third-generation PBX arrived around 1980 and featured distributed architecture, nonblocking operation, and integrated voice and data.

Sometimes we use the phrase *private automatic branch exchange* (PABX) to differentiate a PBX in which all in-house and outgoing calls are automatically switched. To avoid confusion, we will use the generic PBX term to mean the newer PABXs as well.

**Figure 3-9.
A Phone System before the PBX**

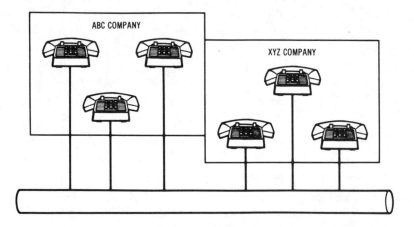

"Distributed architecture" simply means that switching modules are distributed over coaxial cable or fiber-optic media. The nonblocking operation is more a promise than a reality. The new systems promised that their additional channel capacity made it impossible for them to become overloaded and unable to access a call. AT&T allows users the opportunity to select a

**Figure 3-10.
A PBX Phone System**

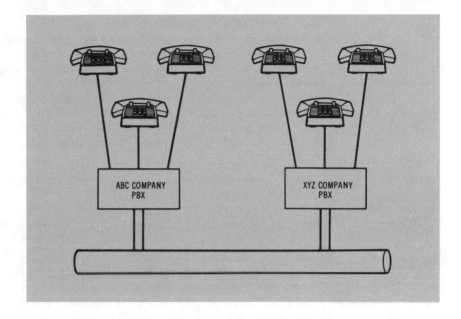

configuration that can be blocking, nonblocking, or essentially nonblocking. An "essentially nonblocking" configuration means that one in one million attempts to access a call will be blocked.

Today there is some debate over whether we now have a fourth generation of PBX. AT&T points with pride to its System 85's high-speed data bus that can handle voice and data simultaneously over the same wire. Other vendors insist that their digital switches are just as sophisticated. But for our purposes this debate really does not matter. What does matter is how the new PBXs work and why they are becoming increasingly popular as alternatives to local area networks.

The coder-decoder is essential to a PBX since it converts a digital signal to analog and an analog signal to digital.

To understand how a PBX digital switch works, it is important to remember that our telephone system sends analog signals over phone lines. A device called a coder-decoder, or CODEC, converts the voice analog signals into digital form. Many of the newer PBX systems place this CODEC in the telephone headset. As Figure 3-11 illustrates, this means that all communication to and from the PBX is digital.

**Figure 3-11.
A Digital PBX with the
CODEC in the
Telephone Handset**

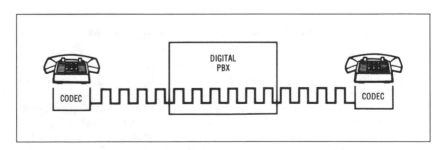

Data Switching within the PBX

The analog transmission of voice signals is really the transmission of audio frequency sine waves that are equal in frequency and amplitude to the original voice tones. Using *Pulse Amplitude Modulation* (PAM), a telephone system samples the analog voice signal 8000 times per second. This sampling produces pulses of varying amplitude that represent the original signal. As Figure 3-12 illustrates, the switch amplifies the voice call to regenerate this original signal. This type of signal transmission can lead to noise, however, which can be enhanced as it is regenerated, causing distortion of the original signal.

**Figure 3-12.
Regeneration of a
Sampled Sine Wave as
a PAM Stream**

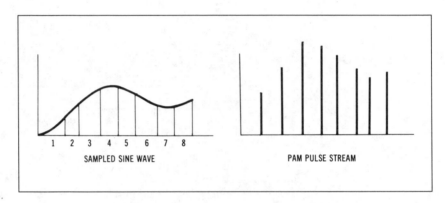

SAMPLED SINE WAVE   PAM PULSE STREAM

Today digital PBXs have moved a step beyond Pulse Amplitude Modulation (PAM) to Pulse Code Modulation (PCM), in which they measure the sampled signals and then digitally encode them. Since these signals are sampled at 8000 times per second and then translated into 8-bit words, PCM produces a bit stream of 64,000 bps (64 kbps). As Figure 3-13 illustrates, this process reproduces the voice signal very clearly.

**Figure 3-13.
PCM Bit Stream**

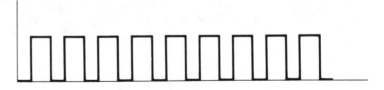

Transmitting the PCM Data Stream

A PBX transmits the PCM data stream along a coaxial cable data bus. This data highway assigns the conversations to time slots using Time-Division Multiplexing (TDM).

A PBX uses a high-speed data bus to transmit the PCM data stream. The digital switch's network controller is responsible for monitoring this data highway. Since the coaxial cable used in the data bus can transmit data much faster than the PCM voice signal of 64 kbps, the same path can carry several messages simultaneously through multiplexing. Each conversation multiplexed onto the bus is given a time slot. This technique is known as Time-Division Multiplexing (TDM), and the data bus is sometimes called the

"TDM bus." AT&T's System 75 PBX has two TDM buses with 512 available time slots. Since two time slots are required for a conversation and some are lost owing to overhead considerations, it is possible to have 236 simultaneous voice conversations. A data conversation, however, takes up three time slots and even more slots on some other PBXs.

Connecting the PBX to Other PBXs and Computer Networks

PBXs can communicate over high-speed T1 lines at 1.544 mbps. The data is multiplexed using either TDM or Frequency-Division Multiplexing (FDM).

There are several different ways to connect digital PBXs to other PBXs as well as to other computer networks. Most PBXs contain digital multiplex interfaces that enable them to send data to host computers or PBXs over high-speed (1.544 mbps) T1 links provided by common carriers. Each of the twenty-four T1 channels can support one asynchronous connection of up to 19.2 kbps or a synchronous connection of up to 56 kbps. As we have learned, TDM is one of the ways data is moved through T1 lines. Rather than assigning data specific time slots along the data highway, a second method, Frequency-Division Multiplexing (FDM), divides the T1 channels into subchannels by frequency. Voice and data can then be sent simultaneously over different frequencies. Figure 3-14 illustrates the difference between these two approaches to transmitting data.

In Chapter 2 we discussed the significance of the CCITT's X.25 protocol for communication between a computer (a DTE) and a public data network. We saw that X.25 provided a standard for the packets of information that are transmitted synchronously over a network. In this case, we want to transmit information from a PBX in X.25 packet form to such public data networks as GTE-TYMNET and TELENET. Let's assume that a microcomputer tied to a digital PBX wished to send a message to a public data network (PDN). Several different CCITT standards would have to be observed for this to work:

X.3 Packet Assembly/Disassembly Facility (PAD) in a PDN
X.25 Interface between DTE and DCE for terminals operating in the packet mode on PDNs
X.28 DTE/DCE interface for a start-stop mode DTE assessing the PAD in a PDN situated in the same country
X.29 Procedures for the exchange of control information and user data between a PAD and a packet mode DTE or another PAD

The PBX functioning as a local area network contains an X.25 gateway. A microcomputer tied to the PBX sends an asynchronous transmission (over RS 232 cable) to a PBX serial port. The PBX X.25 gateway places this information into X.25 packets and transmits them to the public data network. Packet messages received from the PDN are stripped of headers and trailers before being transmitted to the microcomputer in asynchronous form.

One particular case we have not considered is the communication between two PDNs. The CCITT's X.75 protocol handles this situation:

X.75 Terminal and transit call control procedures and data transfer system
on international circuits between packet-switched data networks

**Figure 3-14.
Frequency-Division
Multiplexing and Time-
Division Multiplexing**

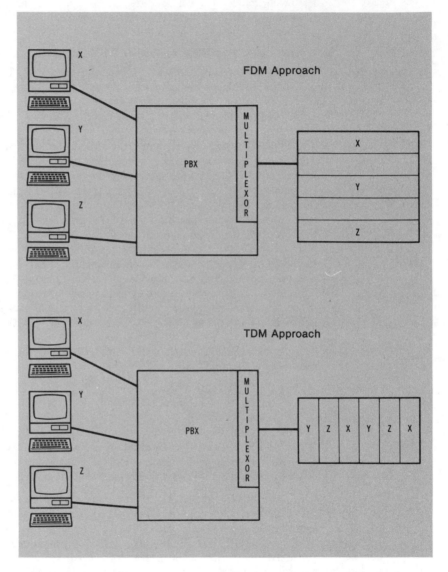

Figure 3-15 illustrates how the CCITT standards work together to ensure
effective data communications among network components as well as
between dissimilar networks.

**Figure 3-15.
The CCITT Standards**

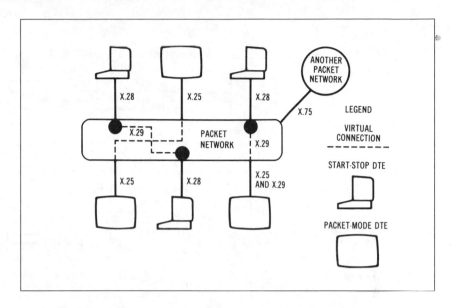

PBX Communication with IBM Mainframe Computers

A PBX offers substantial savings for companies using it for micro-mainframe communications.

A principal cost normally associated with 3270 terminal emulation communication with IBM mainframe computers is the coaxial cabling required. A great advantage of using a PBX as a gateway to an IBM mainframe is that the terminals or microcomputers using 3270 terminal emulation can be connected to the PBX by twisted-pair wire. As Figure 3-16 illustrates, data from a 3270 terminal can be transmitted to the PBX by a special data module that converts this coaxial stream of data traveling at 2.36 mbps to the 64-kbps speed that twisted-pair wire can handle.

Figure 3-16 also illustrates the way that a PBX can transmit data to an IBM mainframe. Using 3270 circuit packs and a 3270 data module, a System 75 PBX communicates with an IBM cluster controller. Let's assume that the real need for many of the microcomputers linked to a PBX is not so much for on-line inquiry and communication with an IBM mainframe as for the uploading and downloading of data. The microcomputers can connect to the PBX asynchronously through its asynchronous RS-232C ports. The PBX can provide protocol conversions from the micro's ASCII data to IBM EBCDIC-coded 3270 BSC or 3270 synchronous data by using the SDLC format.

PBX resource management tools such as modem pooling, station message detail reporting (SMDR), and automatic route selection (ARS) provide useful controls for cost-effective management.

If the PBX is situated at a remote site from the mainframe, it offers several advantages as a micro-mainframe communications gateway, most notably, modem pooling. Modems can be accessed through hardware (by dialing a specific number for a specific modem) or software. The software approach automatically selects the fastest modem that the connection between terminal and host can support.

One area in particular where PBXs outperform most local area networks is network record keeping. For several years, PBXs have featured station message detail reporting (SMDR) software to enable offices to track

Figure 3-16.
Data Can Travel from a
Mainframe to a PBX

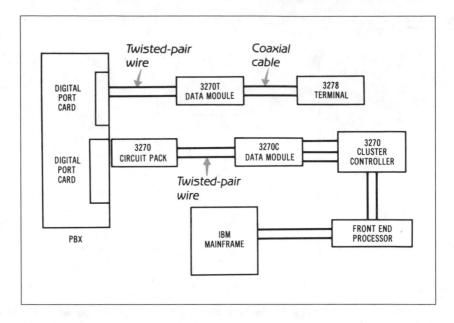

each person's phone calls. Law offices, for example, can use this software automatically to charge each call an attorney makes while working on a particular case to the client represented. This same SMDR function within a PBX can monitor all microcomputer use of resources and, if so desired, record charges to various workstations or departments for long-distance data line usage.

Another strong PBX resource management tool is automatic route selection (ARS). Since there are so many different kinds of long-distance lines now available, ARS can save companies substantial amounts of money.

Integrating Voice and Data

A digital PBX can integrate voice and data, and some can provide voice messages to accompany the text that flashes across a computer terminal.

Slowly the dream of many telecommunications pioneers is becoming a reality. Digital PBXs are able to integrate voice and data information, and some are even able to send this information simultaneously over the same line. Today a salesperson uses the company's PBX to add a voice message for a sales manager to a customer proposal drawn up on a Lotus 1-2-3 spreadsheet. The sales manager can call up the spreadsheet on a terminal and hear the accompanying message: "This proposal looks strange because of one complication. Let me explain. . . . "

In large companies, a middle manager is likely to receive as many internal calls from other departments as external calls from customers. One feature integrating voice and data that shows the utility of a PBX as a local area network is its ability to match an internal caller with a company directory. Imagine how much more efficient communication can be when a caller is greeted by name before introducing herself or himself! This is possible because the receiver's voice terminal flashes the caller's name as the terminal begins ringing.

ISDN AND THE FUTURE OFFICE

The Integrated Services Digital Network (ISDN) is a CCITT model that provides for the integration of voice and data as well as for a universal interface between different networks.

Study Group XVII of the CCITT worked from 1980 to 1984 to develop a set of standards for voice and data integration. The committee took a global view of future telecommunications in developing a plan for an architecture that would provide integrated access to circuit-switched and packet-switched networks and end-to-end digital transport of data. The Integrated Services Digital Network (ISDN) represents a network of the future that will include truly integrated voice, data, and even video traveling over the same pathways and moving smoothly from one type of network to another.

The ISDN concept of a universal interface means that each terminal will understand every other terminal. It will be possible to send information such as interactive videotex and facsimiles at the relatively high speed of 64 kbs. ISDN standards define a digital interface divided into two types of channels. B channels are used for customer information (voice, data, and video), and D channels are used to send signals and control information. These D channels use a packet-mode layered protocol based on the CCITT's X.25 standard.

The two major ISDN interfaces are the Basic-Rate Interface (BRI) designed for relatively small-capacity devices and the Primary-Rate Interface (PRI) designed for high-capacity devices such as PBXs.

There are two major interfaces defined by the CCITT committee that use these B and D channels. The Basic-Rate Interface (BRI) serves devices with relatively small capacity such as terminals. A second interface, Primary-Rate Interface (PRI), is used for large-capacity devices such as PBXs. Both interfaces use one D channel and several B channels transmitting at 64 kbps.

Since the PRI channel structure represents the form most PBXs will take in the future, let's take a closer look at this model. The CCITT model consists of twenty-four slots with twenty-three B channels and one D channel. Like the current T1, the maximum transfer rate on the PRI is 1.536 mbs. Perhaps this ISDN framework will become clearer if we view it within the context of the AT&T 510 Personal Terminal that combines both voice and data. As Figure 3-17 illustrates, the terminal is connected by a BRI (AT&T's Digital Communication Protocol) to the digital PBX (System 75). Then, through a PRI (AT&T's Digital Multiplexed Interface), the data is transmitted to a carrier network.

WHAT HAVE YOU LEARNED?

1. IBM's mainframe and minicomputers utilize Systems Network Architecture (SNA)
2. Network-addressable units (NAUs) consist of logical units (LUs), physical units (PUs), and system services control points (SSCPs).
3. LU 6.2 provides an application program interface (API) that will permit peer-to-peer communication.
4. An IBM PC or compatible with appropriate hardware and software can emulate an IBM 3270 terminal and communicate with a mainframe via a 3274 or 3276 cluster controller.
5. An IBM PC or compatible can serve as a local area network gateway. The PC is connected via coaxial cable with the cluster controller and provides terminal emulation for an entire local area network.

Figure 3-17.
AT&T's Integration of
Voice and Data

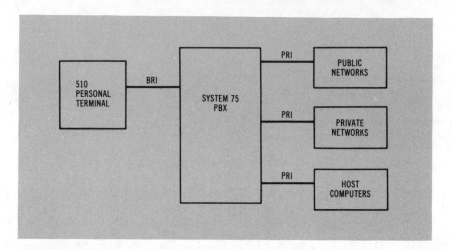

6. From a remote site, an IBM PC or compatible can emulate a cluster controller and serve as a gateway for a local area network.
7. An IBM PC or compatible can perform remote job entry (RJE) for a local area network.
8. A private branch network (PBX) telephone system can serve as a local area network linking together voice and data communications.

Quiz for Chapter 3

1. Under IBM's System Network Architecture (SNA), the protocol for data packets is
   a. HDLC
   b. SDLC
   c. SPCA
   d. IMOK

2. Network-addressable units (NAUs) consist of all of the following EXCEPT
   a. logical units (LU)
   b. synchronous units (SU)
   c. physical units (PU)
   d. system services control points (SSCP)

3. Under SNA, the path control network is concerned with
   a. traffic flow
   b. transmission priorities
   c. error recovery
   d. all of the above

4. An IBM PC or compatible can communicate with a mainframe computer via a cluster controller if the PC is equipped with
   a. a dot matrix printer
   b. a 30-megabyte hard disk
   c. 3270 terminal emulation hardware and software
   d. a communications front-end processor

5. Microcomputers that are part of a local area network can communicate with a mainframe located in the same building by using
   a. communications software
   b. an IBM PC or compatible LAN gateway connected via coaxial cable with a cluster controller
   c. laser technology
   d. fiber optics

6. A gateway PC that is used only for this function is known as a
   a. gateway server
   b. distributed server
   c. dedicated gateway
   d. remote job entry station

7. A mainframe database file is likely to consist of
   a. EBCDIC characters
   b. ASCII characters
   c. ANSI characters
   d. 8-bit words

8. An efficient method of uploading microcomputer information to a mainframe computer is to have the PC emulate a
   a. 3278 monochrome terminal
   b. 3279 color terminal
   c. 3770 remote job entry workstation
   d. 3705 front-end processor

9. To communicate with an IBM System 34/36/38, the PC should emulate a
   a. 3770 remote job entry workstation
   b. 3278 monochrome terminal
   c. 3279 color terminal
   d. 5250 terminal

10. A PBX stands for a
    a. public broadcasting exchange
    b. public branch exchange
    c. private branch exchange
    d. preferential broadband exchange

11. Converting analog signals to digital transmission and digital signals back to analog is performed by a(n)
    a. operator
    b. transformer
    c. coder-decoder
    d. switchboard

12. A digital PBX measures and samples signals 8000 times per second and translates these signals into 8-bit words using what process?
   a. Pulse Amplitude Modulation (PAM)
   b. Pulse Code Modulation (PCM)
   c. public data network (PDN)
   d. Pulse Amplitude Authorization (PAA)

13. A technique for transmitting a data stream through a coaxial cable bus by assigning time slots is known as
   a. Pulse Code Amplification (PCA)
   b. Time-Division Multiplexing (TDM)
   c. Frequency-Division Multiplexing (FDM)
   d. pulse code modulation (PCM)

14. A T1 high-speed link can transmit data at a maximum speed of
   a. 64 kbps
   b. 19.2 kbps
   c. 1.544 mbps
   d. 15 mbps

15. The standard used for transmitting packets of information to a public data network is
   a. 802.3
   b. X.25
   c. X.3
   d. 802.6

16. A network manager can monitor the data usage of each network user in a PBX-based local area network by using which PBX feature?
   a. ARS
   b. SMDR
   c. CCITT
   d. X.25

17. The Integrated Services Digital Network (ISDN) will provide
   a. integrated voice and data information
   b. an interface between different networks
   c. several channels of multiplexed information at 64 kbps
   d. all of the above

18. Under the ISDN model, small-capacity devices such as terminals will use the
   a. Basic-Rate Interface (BRI)
   b. Primary-Rate Interface (PRI)
   c. Universal-Rate Interface (URI)
   d. Terminal-Rate Interface (TRI)

19. The maximum transfer rate under PRI is
   a. 1.536 mbps
   b. 64 kbps
   c. 19.2 kbps
   d. 56 kbps

20. Under the ISDN model, a high-capacity device such as a PBX would use (a)
   a. Primary-Rate Interface (PRI)
   b. Basic-Rate Interface (BRI)
   c. T1 line
   d. all B channels

IBM's Local Area Networks

ABOUT THIS CHAPTER

Having discussed how local area networks work in theory, we will now examine how they work in practice. Since IBM is the acknowledged leader in this field, we will look at its DOS-based LANs, its OS/2-based LAN Server, and its major LAN architecture, the token ring.

PC NETWORK

PC Network is IBM's answer for companies needing a broadband network for carrying information such as video in addition to network data traffic. (A less sophisticated baseband version is also available for companies that need to link only a few workstations. This network uses coaxial cable and can accommodate IBM's Frequency 2 and Frequency 3 adapters, which provide additional frequencies for other information, such as data in the Manufacturing Automation Protocol (MAP) for the factory floor.

PC Network hardware consists of a Network Translator Unit (NTU) for frequency translation, an 8-way splitter to connect up to eight workstations, base expanders for expansion beyond eight nodes, and adapter cards for each workstation.

PC Network includes a Network Translator Unit (NTU) that translates broadband frequency from the return channel to the forward channel. A directional coupler connects the NTU to up to eight workstations through an 8-way splitter which is tied by cabling to the network adapter cards in the workstations' expansion slots. Figure 4-1 illustrates a basic PC Network configuration.

Each of these eight workstations can be a maximum of 200 feet from the 8-way splitter. As Figure 4-2 illustrates, you can connect an additional sixty-four workstations by using *base expanders* and IBM's short-distance (1 foot), medium-distance (400 feet), or long-distance cabling kits (800 feet).

The NTU has both a receive channel (50.75 MHz) and a send channel (219 MHz).

The NTU receives signals broadcast by network workstations (through the modems on their network adapter cards) at a 6-MHz channel centered at 50.75 MHz and then retransmits these signals across the network at a different 6-MHz channel centered at 219 MHz. The network workstations receive all these signals broadcast on the receive channel by the NTU and determine whether or not a particular message is directed to them. The NTU can also boost signals before retransmitting them in order to maintain a balanced network. Although the NTU does receive and transmit every network message, you must understand that it is not a network file server or central processor.

Figure 4-1.
Basic PC Network
Configuration

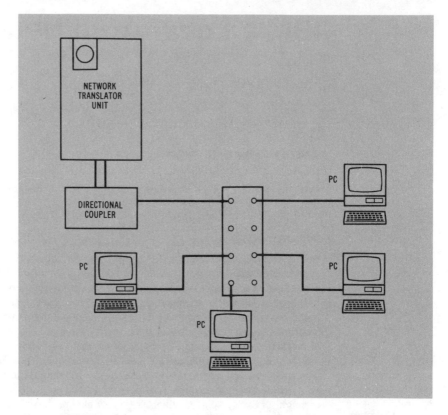

PC Network uses a bus topology without a master computer, a
simple architecture but one that requires significant planning before
installation. For example, you should use only half the ports in the network's
8-way splitters to ensure room for future growth.

All workstations on PC Network are potential file servers if they
have at least 320K of RAM. With proper access any network user can
retrieve files from any other user's hard disk. Dedicated file servers are not
necessary, but they do make the network run significantly faster.

Network Adapter Cards

Network adapter cards are
the real "brains" of PC
Network. They contain a
modem and use Frequency
Shift Keying (FSK) to
achieve a transmission
speed of 2 mbps.

The real heart of PC Network is the network adapter card required in each
workstation's expansion bus. This circuit card includes a modem that
translates the digital message from the PC into radio frequency (RF) signals,
which are then sent over the coaxial cable at the speed of 2 mbps to the
NTU. The modem achieves these transmission speeds by using a technique
known as *Frequency Shift Keying* (FSK), which modulates ones and zeros
during transmission by shifting between two closely spaced frequencies. Since
the modem is *frequency agile*, it cannot handle other channels.

The network adapter card uses a microprocessor with a
communications controller to identify and avoid data collisions by comparing
bits received with bits transmitted. The controller also converts incoming RF

Figure 4-2.
PC Network
Configuration with a
Base Expander

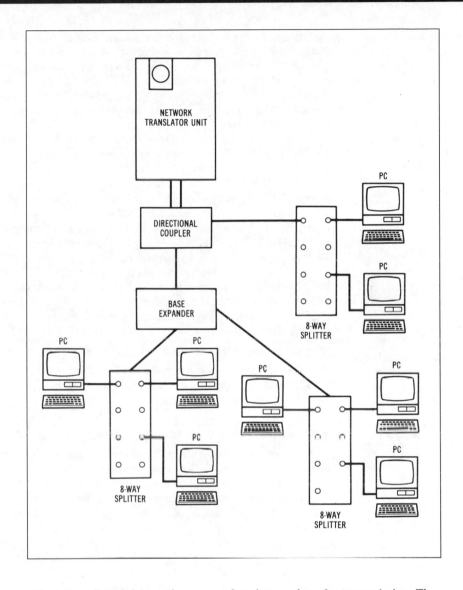

signals into digital data and arranges data into packets for transmission. The packets are framed with the same flag control characters as in the HDLC protocol: 01111110. This protocol, however, uses a variation of "bit stuffing" known as *zero insertion*, which inserts a zero after five straight ones. On receipt of the data packet, the zero is stripped away.

The ROM found on each network adapter card contains a unique 48-bit address. Whenever a data frame is transmitted, the first 48 bits of the frame after the initial flag will consist of the destination address. Each node's adapter card checks a data packet to see if its ROM address matches this destination address. If it does, the accompanying message has reached its destination. Nodes can also share the same group address. A data packet sent along the PC Network bus with a group address may find several users who are part of this group. Their addresses will share a least significant bit 1.

Finally, the network adapter card also provides end-to-end error detection and recovery by using a 32-bit cyclic redundancy check (CRC) sequence. This CRC frame is generated when a message is transmitted and then checked on receipt.

One of the major features of the network adapter card is the NETBIOS (Network Basic Input/Output System) interface between applications compatible with IBM PC-DOS and the network adapter controller. This ROM software manages all network traffic for that particular workstation and enables the network adapter card to perform the functions we have discussed so far, including collision and error detection, the transmission of data packets, and the reassembly of data on receipt of a packet. The NETBIOS also determines when a message has ended or when another station has failed to respond within a given period of time (timeout).

As we will discuss later in this chapter, the NETBIOS for the Token Ring Network is a superset of that for the PC Network. In other words, any application program that runs correctly on a PC Network should run correctly on the Token Ring Network. The converse is not necessarily true, however, although both networks do use the same IBM PC Network Program.

> The network adapter card contains the NETBIOS (Network Basic Input/Output System) in ROM, a microcode that provides the "brains" for the entire network.

The Baseband Version of PC Network

IBM also offers a baseband version of PC Network that allows up to eight workstations to be daisy-chained together in a bus configuration. You can also add an expander unit to connect up to ten daisy chains, so that a total of eighty workstations can be linked together in a star configuration.

THE IBM PC LOCAL AREA NETWORK PROGRAM

This powerful yet easy-to-use software package was originally called the PC Network Program, but IBM recently changed its name to the PC Local Area Network Program, perhaps to distinguish the program from the network hardware. Since so much literature refers to the program by its original name, however, we will also do so here, although you should be aware of this change in terminology.

The program permits the sharing of disk drives and printers as well as the sending and receiving of both messages and files. Beginning network users can rely on a series of menus within menus, whereas more experienced users can use network commands to send and receive information.

There are two different options for installation, Basic Services and Extended Services. Basic Services uses the command-line and menu-driven functions found in all earlier versions of this program. Since the majority of networks are installed with this option, our discussion will center on the Basic Services version of the program. Extended Services permits the resources of multiple servers to be defined, named, and accessed as a single set of resources. A master server, known as a domain controller, controls security for this set of resources. Figure 4-3 illustrates how Extended Services requires users to log in to a domain controller to gain access to the network.

**Figure 4-3.
The Logon in the
Extended Services
Version of PC LAN
Program** *(Courtesy of
IBM Corporation)*

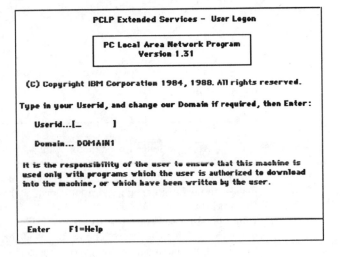

```
        PCLP Extended Services - User Logon

        ┌──────────────────────────────────┐
        │   PC Local Area Network Program   │
        │           Version 1.31            │
        └──────────────────────────────────┘

   (C) Copyright IBM Corporation 1984, 1988. All rights reserved.

   Type in your Userid, and change our Domain if required, then Enter:

       Userid...[_       ]

       Domain... DOMAIN1

   It is the responsibility of the user to ensure that this machine is
   used only with programs which the user is authorized to download
   into the machine, or which have been written by the user.


   Enter     F1=Help
```

PC Network Program Configurations

The PC Network Program
requires users to indicate
when entering the
network how they wish to
configure their
workstations, as a
Redirector, Receiver,
Messenger, or Server.

The PC Network Program has four different configurations:

Messenger (MSG),
Redirector (RDR),
Server (SRV), and
Receiver (RCV).

The Redirector configuration restricts the user to accepting and passing along either data or requests for applications directed to servers. The Receiver configuration, which includes the Redirector, also receives and logs in messages; it represents a minimum-user configuration. A full user would generally opt for the Messenger configuration, which provides full-screen message editing and message-forwarding capabilities in addition to all the functions of the Redirector and Receiver. Finally, the Server configuration controls disk drives, directories, and printers as well as incorporating the functions of the other three configurations.

Beginners will automatically go to the Main menu (Figure 4-4) and will not concern themselves with configuring their systems but will depend on the normal defaults built into the network. More experienced users, however, will use the Net Start command to configure their own network workstation.

Figure 4-4.
The PC Local Area
Network Main Menu
(Courtesy of IBM
Corporation)

```
                                        IBM PC Network

      Main Menu - Task Selection

      1. Message tasks

      2. Printer tasks

      3. Disk or directory tasks

      4. Print queue tasks

      5. Network status tasks

      6. Pause or cancel the network setup
      1 Choice
      Enter- Continue         F1- Help
      Esc- Exit
```

Experienced users will change their network configuration based on the amount of available memory needed to run specific application programs, the need to share additional resources, and the need for additional memory to hold long messages in a buffer.

An experienced user might want to reconfigure his or her network workstation for many reasons. The network default value for using network devices, for example, is five. If you needed to use more than five network devices to perform certain operations, or if you needed to share more than five workstation devices with the network, you would need to reconfigure your workstation. From time to time you might also need to change network default values for the size of the buffer used for printing (512 characters), the size of the buffer used for waiting messages (1600 characters), and the number of network computers that will be using devices (10).

The RAM installed on a network workstation can limit a workstation's ability to serve other network functions. To function as a file server, for example, a network workstation needs to have at least 320K of RAM for DOS and for the PC Network Program. A network user who wanted to run a program that requires 320K of RAM and use the workstation as a file server would need to install 640K of RAM to serve both purposes. As a file server, this workstation could then share its disk drives, directories, and printers, and as a workstation it could still share those resources found on other workstations. All configurations except the Redirector are able both to send and receive messages.

The Messenger configuration requires a minimum of 256K of RAM for the PC Network Program and DOS. With this configuration you can not only send and receive messages but also transfer messages to other computers and save messages directly to a file by logging them in. We will see very shortly how easy it is to send a message on this network.

When configured as a Receiver, a workstation requires 192K of RAM for the PC Network Program and DOS in order to send and receive messages, to save these messages by placing them into a log file (rather than by having to view them the moment they are received), and to share network disk drives, directories, and printers.

The Redirector configuration, on the other hand, requires only 128K of RAM and allows a workstation simply to send messages and to share network disk drives, directories, and printers.

The IBM PC Network Program User's Guide provides a handy
summary of these different configurations and their major functions:

**Table 4-1.
Configurations and
Functions** (Courtesy of
IBM Corporation)

Configuration	You can use the PC Network Program to:
SERVER (320K RAM required)	Send messages Use network disks, directories, and printers Receive messages Save (log) messages Use network request keys Receive messages for other names Transfer messages to other computers Share your disks, directories, and printers
MESSENGER (256K RAM required)	Send messages Use network disks, directories, and printers Receive messages Save (log) messages Use network request keys Receive messages for other names Transfer messages to other computers
RECEIVER (192K RAM required)	Send messages Use network disks, directories, and printers Receive messages Save (log) messages
REDIRECTOR (128K RAM required)	Send messages Use network disks, directories, and printers

In order to see why network users would choose one configuration
over another, it is useful to examine how these options are presented in a
menu format for new users by the PC Network Program. As indicated earlier,
Figure 4-4 illustrates the PC Network Program Main menu. Help is available
simply by pressing the <F1> key. We'll go through those network options
and examine the way the network actually works.

When PC Network sends and receives messages on the network it
keeps track of machines and not of people. Each network workstation must
have a name so that other network users can address it. This name can be up
to fifteen letters. Sometimes one name is not enough. The PC Network
Program permits a maximum of sixteen names for a particular workstation.
If several people in an accounting department share a workstation, for
example, the workstation could have the name "ACCOUNT" as well as
individual names of other departmental users.

Message Tasks Available under the PC Network Program

Figure 4-5 illustrates how messages are edited before being sent on the PC
Network Program. By using an asterisk (*) you can send the message to all
network workstations. A message can be up to 1600 characters in length (80
characters per line times 20 lines) except for *broadcast messages*, which are
sent to all computers on the network and are limited to 128 characters. This
message screen editor uses "word wrap" so that all lines contain complete
words. This feature might also make some messages look unprofessional,
however, by interspersing short lines with long lines. The <F3> key solves
this problem by adjusting paragraphs to make them look more even. Notice
that the lower right corner of the screen keeps track of the number of free
characters by subtracting the characters found in a message from 1600.

**Figure 4-5.
Screen for Editing
Messages** *(Courtesy of
IBM Corporation)*

```
                          Send Messages

    Send the message to: (* for all computers) Bill

    Type the message below:

    This is a test to see it work.

    Ctrl-Enter Send message          Esc- Previous menu or Exit
    Tab- cursor to next field        Ctrl-PgDn - Erase message
    Ctrl-Home - Return to Main Menu   F3 ADJUST PARAGRAPH F4 VIEW MESSAGES
    F1 - HELP   F2 - COMMAND LINE

    Message sent . . . and successfully received    Characters free 1571
```

The message function of the PC Network Program is a good
example of how the program uses the IBM PC's special keys and function
keys. The <F1> key requests additional information, the <TAB> key moves
the cursor from field to field, the <ESC> key exits a menu or moves
backward to view a previous menu screen, and the <CONTROL> and
<HOME> keys, when pressed simultaneously, bring a user back to the
program's Main menu. Once edited, a message can be sent simply by pressing
the <CONTROL> and <ENTER> keys simultaneously.

The PC Network Program also has a number of safety features
built-in to help network users avoid making serious mistakes. For example, if
a user inadvertently presses the <ESCAPE> key before sending a message,
the program asks the user to press the key again to confirm that he or she
was leaving this menu with the knowledge that the message would be erased
and not sent.

Notice that the PC Network Program asks for a specific name for
the addressee (the message's destination). Many network administrators will
publish a directory of network users and their network names to prevent
confusion when sending messages. For example, a large company would
likely have more than one Bob. Users in other departments may know a
certain Bob but not know his last name. This is why it is so practical for each
workstation's network adapter card to be able to handle sixteen different

names. Since Bob does payroll for the XYZ company, his workstation might have PAYROLL as one of its names.

The PC Network Program has a number of ways of handling incoming messages depending on how users have configured their network workstations. A user may have chosen to use the network request keys, for example, in which case receipt of a message will generate a message on the screen, as illustrated in Figure 4-6. If he or she chooses to press the <CONTROL> and <BREAK>keys to erase this message and continue working, the message will be put into a waiting area from which it can be retrieved through the Message Tasks menus. Because buffer room is limited, however, users should view their messages frequently and then erase them. If the user chooses to view the message, he or she presses the <CONTROL>-<ALTERNATE>-<BREAK> keys; the <ESCAPE> key returns the user to his or her work. Normally these three network request keys, when pressed simultaneously, interrupt work in progress and take the user directly to the network menus. After making whatever network menu selections desired, the user is returned to whatever he or she was doing prior to pressing these three keys.

**Figure 4-6.
PC LAN Program
Signals Incoming
Message** *(Courtesy of
IBM Corporation)*

```
MESSAGE FROM   | SALES|
_____

Press Ctrl-Break to Continue

Press Ctrl-Alt-Break to View Message
```

The third alternative when receiving messages is to configure a workstation so that it automatically saves incoming messages to a "log" file. Then, at your convenience, you can use the DOS command TYPE to view your saved messages. With this option your workstation will "beep" when a message arrives but not disrupt your current activities. With the Receiver configuration, messages are automatically logged to the workstation console and displayed unless you specify another location for them such as a log file. In this instance a log file can prevent the disruption of your current work and eliminate the need continually to erase the "garbage" caused by messages. You can also have messages sent to a logged printer rather than to a file, but the printer would need to be dedicated to this function and not shared with other network users.

Figure 4-7 illustrates how messages are viewed on the PC Network Program. Once again, the same function keys used on the Send Messages screen are used on this View Messages screen. Two additional options (Save Message and Print Message) can also be performed by using function keys. Notice that PC Network distinguishes between waiting messages (messages stored in memory) and saved messages (messages already saved and logged to a file).

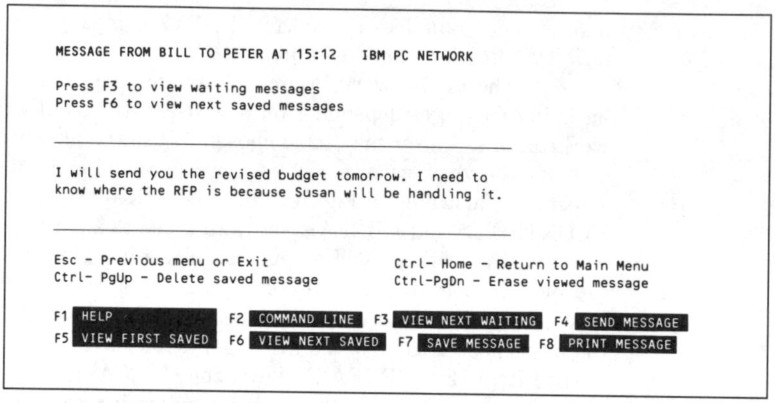

Figure 4-7.
Receiving Messages on
the PC LAN Program
(Courtesy of IBM
Corporation)

```
MESSAGE FROM BILL TO PETER AT 15:12    IBM PC NETWORK

Press F3 to view waiting messages
Press F6 to view next saved messages
_____

I will send you the revised budget tomorrow. I need to
know where the RFP is because Susan will be handling it.
_____

Esc - Previous menu or Exit             Ctrl- Home - Return to Main Menu
Ctrl- PgUp - Delete saved message       Ctrl-PgDn - Erase viewed message

F1  HELP                    F2  COMMAND LINE  F3  VIEW NEXT WAITING  F4  SEND MESSAGE
F5  VIEW FIRST SAVED        F6  VIEW NEXT SAVED  F7  SAVE MESSAGE   F8  PRINT MESSAGE
```

The network can save all incoming messages so that you will not be disturbed, receive messages for another name, and forward messages to another computer if users need to work at another network node.

A few additional message commands indicate the power of this PC Network feature. If you are faced with a deadline and do not want to be interrupted, you can tell the network to start saving messages. The network will continue to do this until told otherwise. Let's say that you expect an important message and need to see it the instant it arrives. You may give the command to stop saving messages. At this time the network will begin displaying your messages as they are received.

Another common need in an office is for someone to "cover" for another employee. Let's say that Bill and Susan are working on an important project. Susan must go to a meeting but asks Bill to "cover" for her so that they can act on the message as soon as it arrives. Bill can give the network the command to let him Start Receiving Messages for Another Name, and he then can indicate that Susan's messages should be sent to him. When Susan returns, Bill simply selects the message task entitled Stop Receiving Messages for Another Name.

Many large firms have call forwarding on their PBX telephone systems. PC Network has a similar feature in its message program. If Bill needs to spend the day working in the Accounting department, he can use the Forward Messages to Another Computer option and have all messages sent to that computer (ACCOUNT). Figure 4-8 illustrates the PC Network menu that would be used for this purpose. When Bill returns the following day, he selects Stop Forwarding Messages to Another Computer. Up to twelve names may be used on a network workstation at any given time.

Printer Tasks under the PC Network Program

It is possible to share up to three printers with the network. Printers can be designated as shared or local, and there are queues for each printer.

As Figure 4-4 illustrates, the second option available from the PC Network Main menu refers to Printer tasks and the fourth option to Print queue tasks, which provide a degree of control over network printers. Every printer attached to a workstation using PC Network has to be designated as either a local printer (limited to that particular workstation) or a network printer. Since the program's print management functions control all printing, a workstation user cannot simply use a PRINT command, even with a local printer, but must use the network NET PRINT command.

Figure 4-8.
Message Forwarding
with PC LAN Program
(Courtesy of IBM
Corporation)

```
                        Start or Stop Forwarding Messages



        1. Start forwarding messages

        2. Stop forwarding messages

        1 Choice

        Forward messages for (name on your computer)

         ┌──────┐
         │ Bill │
         └──────┘

        To (name on another computer)

         ┌─────────┐
         │ Account │
         └─────────┘

        Tab- cursor to next field          F1 - Help
        Enter - Continue                   Ctrl - Home - Return to Main Menu
        Esc - Previous menu
```

As Figure 4-9 illustrates, the Printer Tasks menu covers six printer options. Users may share up to three printers with the network. It is also possible to declare a printer a shared printer but not provide its name to other users. The result will be a printer that will perform like a local printer but use the network print management program.

Figure 4-9.
Printer Tasks Menu
(Courtesy of IBM
Corporation)

```
                            Printer Tasks



        1. Start or stop sharing your printer

        2. Start or stop using a network printer

        3. Print a file

        4. Change the print size on a network printer

        5. Display devices you are sharing

        6. Display network devices you are using

        1 Choice

        Enter  Continue                   F1 = Help
        Ctrl-Home - Return to Main Menu    Esc - Previous menu
```

Why would anyone ever decide not to share a printer with the network? If you have a major printing job that must be completed as quickly as possible, you obviously do not want to wait your turn. Secondly, there is a finite limit to the number of devices that can be shared with the network at any given time. You might want to share a different device such as a plotter or a modem, and thus you would need to remove one of your printers from the network.

Print servers do present some restrictions, however. Each server requires 256K of RAM and supports three printers. Up to one hundred files can be placed in a printer queue table where they will be printed in order in *background mode* while the computer's processor continues to perform other functions.

Network application programs are installed so that they automatically send print jobs to the printer queue. The new user is often unaware of this process since, with low levels of network printing, files may seem to print almost instantaneously.

The PC Network Program permits separate queues for each of the network printers. As Figure 4-10 illustrates, a user can check or change the print queue from a menu. Option 6 will cause the highlighted entry to "Print Now" rather than wait its turn. The program allows users to set up a *Separator Page* that will print out between files indicating who printed the file, the name of the file itself, and the current date and time. Files that are still "spooling" are being sent to the printer queue, and their status cannot be changed until they finish spooling.

**Figure 4-10.
Printer Server's Print
Queue** *(Courtesy of IBM
Corporation)*

```
       Check or Change the Print Queue IBM PC NETWORK


 1. Update queue      ID  User Name  Size   Device  Status
                      -Start of Queue-
 2. Hold              010 FRED      16422   LPT1    Printing

 3. Release           019 PAUL      12350   LPT1    Spooling

                      020 SUSAN       546   LPT2    Waiting
 4. Cancel
                      021 FRED      20195   LPT2    Waiting
 5. Print Next
                      -End of Queue-
 6. Print now

 1 Choice
                              PgUp and PgDn - Scroll List
 ⬆ and ⬇ - Select File        F1 - Help
 Enter - Change queue         Esc - Previous menu
 Ctrl-Home - Return to Main Menu
```

The IBM PC Network Program has a number of printer control commands. The NET PAUSE PRINT [=printdevice] pauses the network sharing of a specific printer, and the NET CONTINUE PRINT [=printdevice] resumes network printing. Companion server commands that also cause this result, but we will look at those when we examine the server functions found on the PC Network.

Sharing Disks and Directories with the Network

The third option under the PC Network Program's Main menu is "Disk or directory tasks," which consist of the following choices:

1. Start or stop sharing your disk or directory

2. Start or stop using a network disk or directory

3. Display devices you are sharing

4. Display devices you are using

The program permits users to share directories but not to designate particular files to be shared. As a result, you will need to place a file in its own directory if you wish to share only that particular file. A decision to share a directory is not automatically sent as a message to other network users. The PC Network Program assumes that you will make this directory available to those people who need to know about it or have legitimate reasons to use it.

In order to share application programs with other users, IBM suggests placing these programs in one subdirectory. The PC Network Program has an Installation Aid utility program that will create this subdirectory, install the application programs, and mark each program file as "read only." Because some application programs have files that require Read/Write/Create access, the PC Network Program creates several user subdirectories, each of which contains copies of these files. The Installation Aid utility will create these private subdirectories for each computer user that wants to run these application programs.

You can establish a password for a particular directory or subdirectory that you are sharing. Let's assume that we wished to share a very sensitive directory (TOPSEC) with a remote computer user named FRANK. You have decided to use the password ABCXYZ. You would enter the following:

NET SHARE FRANK=C:\TOPSEC ABCXYZ

This information could be placed in an AUTOEXEC.BAT file with an asterisk (*) replacing the secret password. When the batch file runs, the network will prompt you for the password.

Additional steps can be taken to increase the security found under PC Network. A file server's physical location offers some additional control. A company controller who has sensitive payroll records on an IBM PC AT being used as a file server can take the simple precaution of locking the machine with a key when one is provided. Some companies save valuable data onto diskettes, which are then stored under lock and key.

Virtually all network activities under the IBM PC Network Program can be accessed by direct commands or through the system of nested menus. This means that an experienced user who wished to share a directory with the network could use a command (NET SHARE) to accomplish this task. The network command structure uses the DOS hierarchial file-naming conventions. For example, if Bill wished to make the budget reports in his drive C directory \BUD\BUDRPT available to the entire network, he would use the following command:

NET SHARE \BUD\BUDRPT

The problem with this arrangement is that network users who want to access this file will have to provide its exact path. A user who wanted to treat Bill's directory as his own drive D, for example, would have to type the following:

NET USE D: \\BILL\BUD\BUDRPT

Bill could make everyone else's work much easier by using a network name for his directory. Let's assume that the network users already refer to Bill's famous budget reports as the "87 Budget Report." He could provide the network name BUDGET:

NET USE BUDGET=C:\BUD\BUDRPT

Now other network users who want to access this directory as their D directories, for example, could type the following:

NET USE D: \\BILL\BUDGET

Users who wish to share their entire disk rather than certain directories can do so by sharing their root directory (C:\). Everything in this drive C directory will then be available to other network users, including all subdirectories on drive C. Figure 4-11 illustrates how Bill could go about sharing a customer list in one of his subdirectories with the rest of the network.

**Figure 4-11.
Sharing a Directory with
the Network** *(Courtesy of
IBM Corporation)*

```
         Start Sharing Your Disk or Directory        IBM PC NETWORK


    DOS name for disk or directory
    c:\BILL\SALES\CUSLST
    _____

    Network name for your disk or directory
    CUSTMR

    Password for disk or directory (Optional)
    PROFIT

    Other users can
    1. Read only        4. Write/Create/Delete
    2. Read/Write       5. Read/Write/Create/Delete
    3. Write only

    4 Choice
        Tab - Cursor to next field        F1 - Help
        Enter - Continue                  Ctrl-Home - Return to Main Menu
        Esc - Previous menu
```

Figure 4-11 also shows that the IBM PC Network Program permits five different combinations of user access to directories that are shared with the network:

1. Read only
2. Read/Write
3. Write only
4. Write/Create/Delete
5. Read/Write/Create/Delete

The program's default value is Read/Write/Create/Delete. A user who wished to share a directory and who pressed the <Enter> key at this point would provide this level of access for all network users without realizing it. Users who need only to view information can be limited to "Read only" status, whereas other members of your particular project or department who need full access would require Read/Write/Create/Delete privileges. The PC Network Program does not provide the level of security of a more sophisticated program such as Novell's NetWare. Any user who knows the password (PROFIT) for Bill's device (in this case, his disk drive containing this subdirectory) will have the same level of access to this material as anyone else. Of course, Bill could decide not to share this particular directory, in which case network users would not be able to access the files in the directory even though they might have access to the disk drive.

One additional way to provide the same level of security for all network users is to offer this same subdirectory to the network several times with several different network names and device passwords. A company controller, for example, might want to set up a payroll subdirectory so that certain individuals could access it under one network name with read-only privileges. A payroll clerk who needs to change hours worked and hourly rate fields would use a different network name and have greater privileges, including the ability to change key fields.

Saving Time When Starting the PC Network Program

The PC Network Program permits you to save the configuration values established when you first entered the network in an AUTOEXEC.BAT file. If you wish to save your network setup, the program saves optional parameters including which resources you wish to share with the network and which resources you currently are using. If you are receiving messages for additional names, this will continue when you enter the network the next time.

You do need to ask yourself several questions before saving your network setup. Since memory is a valuable resource that affects the network's speed and ability to respond to users' requests, you need to decide precisely what you plan to be doing the next time you enter the network. If you are expecting an important, lengthy report, for example, you might have to change the buffer size for your messages from 512K bytes to 60,000 bytes. This decision, in turn, may affect your ability to run a large application program (such as Symphony) and still function as a network server.

The IBM PC Network Program does permit the user who is sharing resources to adjust the time and memory allocation of network functions versus local functions. The tasks the user performs on his or her own machine are known as *foreground tasks* whereas those performed by other network users are called *background tasks*. A network timer provides intervals composed of timer ticks of 18.175 milliseconds. The network's normal default value of 5/4 allocates approximately equal time to both foreground tasks (5 intervals) and background tasks (4 intervals). Five intervals are equivalent to 90.875 milliseconds (5×18.175 milliseconds). The *Time Slice Intervals* (TSI) parameter defines the way the file server will divide its time. The server carries out a foreground task until it reaches the time to perform a background task. It then checks to see if there is a background task, and, if so, it temporarily halts what it is doing and begins performing the background task.

Although the file server is incapable of multitasking and only performs one task at a time, it switches back and forth so many times within a second that the results may seem like multitasking. Still, there are some file-server tasks that can cripple the entire network's speed. One example is diskette formatting. During this relatively lengthy procedure the file server will not release DOS to enable the time-slicing procedure to work. Obviously, file servers should not be used to format diskettes. If larger numbers are allocated to foreground and background tasks, the network response will seem erratic. It may seem to take forever for certain tasks to be performed.

Other Ways to Boost Network Performance

A number of additional parameters can be adjusted in order to maximize PC Network performance, including the amount of memory used for disk sharing, print spooling, and background print performance. The Receive Request Buffer (/RQB), for example, can be adjusted to specify the maximum buffer available for transferring files between a file server and network workstations. The larger the number specified for /RQB, the more data the file server can send at any given time to the workstation. As a result, the file server does not need to perform as many send operations and thus can perform other network procedures more quickly.

The Request Buffers parameter (/REQ) determines how many user requests can be handled at any given time. This value can vary from 1 to 3, with 2 serving as the default figure. The larger this parameter, the more requests that can be processed and the faster the network performance. Whereas a "2" requires 16K of memory, a "3" requires 48K.

Network print buffer parameters also can enhance performance under the PC Network Program. The Print Buffer parameter (/PRB) specifies how much of a print file the print server can keep in its memory at any given time before it has to retrieve more of the file. The default value of 512K is sufficient unless printers are heavily used on the network. Similarly, the Print Priority (/PRP) parameter specifies how much of the foreground task interval is used for printing files while the server computer is performing other tasks. The default value for this parameter is 3, but a network user who wants greater responsiveness from his or her server computer should choose 1 or 2.

THE IBM TOKEN RING NETWORK: AN OVERVIEW

Although PC Network might be adequate for a small office environment, IBM does offer a more powerful, faster local area network that is capable of much greater expansion. The IBM Token Ring Network uses a star-wired ring topology and follows the protocols of the IEEE 802.5 standard for baseband signaling and token passing. The network uses unshielded twisted-pair telephone wire, designated by IBM as type 3 cabling, and IBM's type 1 and type 2 cabling as well as fiber optics. The Token Ring Network operates at 4 mbps and supports up to 260 devices using shielded twisted-pair cabling or 72 devices using twisted-pair telephone wire. A version operating at 16 mbps is also available, which we will discuss later in this chapter.

Although the Token Ring Network and PC Network run the same PC Network Program, there are major differences in the NETBIOS and the hardware of both systems. Whereas PC Network uses a NETBIOS found on ROM portions of the adapter cards required on each network workstation, the Token Ring Network uses a NETBIOS software program that is loaded into each machine. PC Network also uses a simple bus architecture, where there is always some danger of data collision, whereas in a token ring topology only one network workstation at a time has the token required to send messages.

HARDWARE REQUIRED FOR THE TOKEN RING NETWORK

The PC Adapter

The Token Ring Network requires an adapter card in an expansion slot of each node. Figure 4-12 illustrates the configuration of this circuit card. Data buffers and control blocks are exchanged between the network workstation's memory (RAM) and the adapter card. In fact, the card's RAM is actually mapped into the workstation's memory in a section IBM refers to as "*shared RAM.*" This technique reduces the overhead required for Input/Output (I/O) between adapter card and workstation.

Figure 4-12 also displays the two interfaces found on the adapter card. The Data Link–LLC Interface contains some microcode (ROM) that supports these logical link control functions as defined by the IEEE 802.2 standards. The Direct Interface allows a program to read logs on matters such as error-status information maintained by the adapter card.

The token ring adapter card contains microcode to provide error checking, token generation, address recognition, and data transmission.

Figure 4-12.
Token Ring Adapter
Card Structure (*Courtesy of IBM Corporation*)

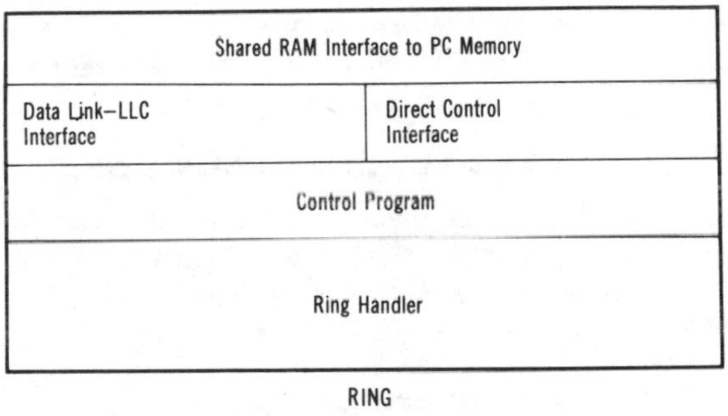

Shared RAM Interface to PC Memory	
Data Link–LLC Interface	Direct Control Interface
Control Program	
Ring Handler	

RING

The adapter card located in each network workstation handles token recognition and data transmission. Among the adapter's network responsibilities are frame recognition, token generation, address recognition, error checking and logging, time-out controls, and link-fault detection. One adapter on each network ring is designated as the *active token monitor*, whereas the other adapters function as passive monitors. This station becomes responsible for error-recovery procedures should the normal token activity become disrupted. Should something happen to the active token monitor, any one of the remaining adapter cards can assume an active role.

The adapter card comes with two different diagnostic programs. The Adapter Diagnostics Program is used *before* the adapter card is attached to the ring. It simply checks the adapter and the attaching cable and ensures that the card can perform self-diagnostics successfully. A second program checks the adapter card after it has been connected to the ring and ensures that it can perform the "open" functions required to connect it to the ring media. The adapter itself detects permanent errors such as the loss of a receiving signal and then generates a notification signal to initiate automatic network recovery. Recoverable errors, such as bit errors in the transmitted message, are detected by the adapter for subsequent reporting to a ring diagnostic program.

IBM actually markets two different token ring adapter cards. The Token Ring Network PC Adapter is the choice for workstations in a self-contained token ring network. PCs are attached directly to the token ring through this adapter, whereas System/36 computers are attached to the ring through an IBM PC AT equipped with the Token Ring Network PC Adapter II card. A link to IBM's AS/400 minicomputer is also available.

Multistation Access Unit (MSAU)

The Multistation Access Unit (MSAU) is a wiring concentrator that permits up to eight network workstations to be inserted or bypassed on the ring. This unit is mounted either on a rack located in a nearby wiring closet or in a housing on a wall or tabletop. The MSAU is actually a passive device with bypass circuitry that is designed to detect the presence or absence of a signal from a network workstation. Should the MSAU detect a defective device or damaged cable, it will bypass this particular workstation to avoid losing data or the token that circulates throughout the ring. Figure 4-13 illustrates how workstations are actually attached to the MSAU. Although this looks like a star architecture, it is really a ring topology within the MSAU. Each MSAU contains ten connector jacks, with eight ports to connect network workstations and two ports to connect other MSAUs.

TOKEN RING NETWORK CONNECTIVITY

One of the major strengths of the IBM Token Ring Network is that IBM provides the hardware and software required to connect this network with other networks, PBX systems, remote PCs, and mainframe computers. As we will see, it is easy to connect this network to the rest of the world.

Network Bridges

Two token ring networks can be joined together using a bridge. In fact, bridges can connect several token ring networks, each of which can contain up to 260 workstations. Bridges appear to be a normal node on a ring, but they route frames of information between rings by examining the destination addresses contained on the frames, addresses that identify a specific ring as well as a workstation within that ring. To perform this high-speed data transfer, a bridge normally is an IBM PC AT or one of several models of IBM industrial computers containing two Token Ring Network Adapter II cards and the IBM Bridge program. The RAM found in this bridge serves as a buffer to hold several frames awaiting their transfer to the network nodes corresponding to their destination addresses.

Several bridges can be connected together with a high-speed link known as a *backbone*. Figure 4-14 illustrates three token ring networks joined together with a backbone, which in this case is a token ring itself. The

The Multistation Access Unit (MSAU) is a wiring concentrator that permits up to eight network workstations to be inserted or deleted from the network.

A network node (usually an IBM PC AT) serves as a bridge to connect two or more token ring networks together.

Figure 4-13.
Three Multistation
Access Units

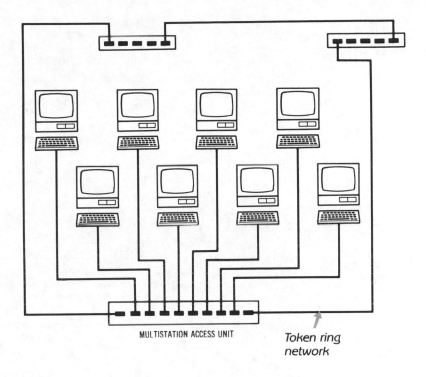

MULTISTATION ACCESS UNIT

Token ring
network

backbone need not be a higher speed token ring but may also consist of other kinds of high-speed channels, including an RF channel within a broadband cable TV system. In this situation each bridge would consist of a modem that would switch the data onto a broadband channel.

Connecting PC Network and the Token Ring Network

The Token Ring Network/ PC Network Interconnect Program can serve as a bridge when running on a dedicated PC workstation with adapter cards for both networks.

Many companies may find a need to connect a PC Network perhaps performing a departmental function with a larger token ring network that encompasses the entire company's activities. IBM offers the Token Ring Network/PC Network Interconnect Program to serve this purpose, which runs on a dedicated IBM PC along with the NETBIOS program. Since adapter cards from each network are installed in two of the PC's expansion slots, workstations in one network can share the resources of the other network through this "bridge" PC. This interconnect program can handle up to sixteen application names for each network, which means that one network can identify no more than sixteen attaching devices to the other network. Some applications also require the use of multiple names. Since the file-server function on the PC Network Program requires the use of three names, only a maximum of five file servers on one network can be identified to the other network. This limitation might make it necessary to run multiple interconnect programs in order to identify all the devices that workstations need to address. The interconnect program permits a maximum of thirty-two active sessions. When a name on one network connects with a name on the other

Figure 4-14.
Backbone Ring
Connecting Three
Token Ring Networks

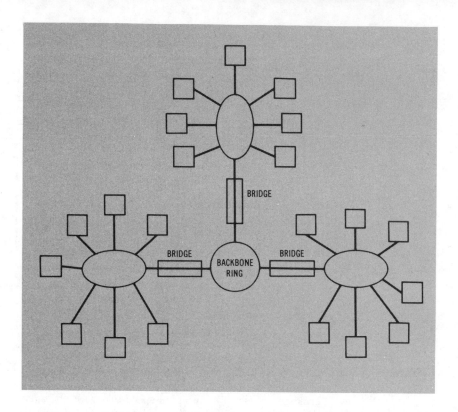

network, two sessions are created, one for each network. During its configuration phase the program identifies the devices on each network and stores them in a configuration file. The operational phase of the program concerns itself with receiving information from one network and then forwarding it to the other network.

While the interconnect program is running it monitors a number of on-line data, including the status of any adapter on either network. Since PC Network and the Token Ring Network require different kinds of status reports, there are different screens for each network's adapters. You can also examine interconnect status, which means that the program will display a list of network names that are currently connected. The network administrator can select a connected network pair and examine traffic statistics involving this particular session.

Connecting the Token Ring Network with System/370

Token Ring Network workstations can also be connected with IBM's System/370 world of SNA. A 3725 communication controller with token ring adapters can connect as many as eight token ring networks to an IBM mainframe computer. Workstations on these networks can then communicate with the mainframe computer using 3270 emulation mode. A gateway workstation on these networks can be connected to an IBM System/370 indirectly, through the network connection with the 3725, or directly, with an SDLC Adapter Card, the PC 3270 Emulation Program, and cabling. The gateway station can also function as a normal network workstation, depending on the amount of gateway activity, and as a network print server or file server.

The SNA Advanced Program-to-Program Communication (APPC)

The Advanced Program-to-Program Communications (APPC) program provides a program-to-program protocol (LU 6.2) that permits peer-to-peer conversations between applications running on an IBM PC, a System 36/38, System/370, Series 1, and another IBM PC. Although this program does not directly connect sessions on the Token Ring Network with sessions on the SDLC Link, it does provide an application programming interface so that a program can be written to communicate between these logical units.

Asynchronous Communications for the Token Ring Network and PC Network

IBM offers an asynchronous communications server program that enables workstations on the Token Ring Network or PC Network to access ASCII applications via switched communication lines. By using this program, network administrators can link workstations in their IBM network with a Rolm CBX II, a PBX, or public switched networks. Each asynchronous communications server gateway station provides up to two dial lines, and it is possible to have more than one of these nondedicated gateway stations on a network.

The asynchronous communications server program runs in background mode and establishes outbound calls to such valuable services as the IBM Information Network, The Source, and Dow Jones News/Retrieval Services. Because modems are shared resources on the network, this program provides cost-effective service for workstations that need this type of information. If all phone lines are being used, the program queues these requests. The program also accepts inbound calls for workstations on the network running communication programs, providing transparent ASCII data transfer between the caller and the network workstation. Although this program operates on both PC Network and the Token Ring Network, it will work on PC Network only if the PC running the PC Network Program is configured for Redirector functions.

An external ASCII device must perform a two-step procedure in order to establish communications, since remote asynchronous devices cannot have direct access to other resident-server functions such as file servers, print servers, or message servers. After establishing contact with the asynchronous communications server, the caller must provide the name of the network workstation. Some electronic mail programs that have their own private protocols will not work with this software, nor will host security applications that require the ability to disconnect and then immediately call back.

Connecting a Token Ring Network with a PBX

Just as AT&T has integrated its local area networks with its PBX telephone systems, so has IBM accomplished much the same thing between its Token Ring Network and Rolm's CBX II telephone equipment by using an asynchronous communications server and one of several digital interfaces, including Rolm's DataCom Module (DCM), Integrated Personal Computer Interface (IPCI), Integrated Personal Computer Interface AT (IPCI/AT), or Data Terminal Interface (DTI).

When attached to a Rolm PBX such as the CBX II, network workstations can share the CBX II's resources, including its modem pooling report capability. More importantly, the CBX II can switch among several different computer systems, including those with different protocols. With this PBX and protocol converters such as IBM's 3708, 3710, or 7171, an office consisting of several different types of office automation equipment can bridge the communication gap between the IBM world and the rest of the world that uses ASCII.

IBM sees this connection between the Token Ring Network and Rolm's CBX II as a way for PC workstations to access IBM Office Systems such as DisplayWrite/370, PROFS, and Personal Services/370. Because of its architecture, CBX II can operate attached ASCII terminals at much higher speeds than in the past. An IBM 3161/3163 and Rolm workstations such as the Cedar, Cypress, or Juniper can operate at up to 19.2 kbps through an IBM protocol converter. Figure 4-15 illustrates the many different devices, including Rolm's CBX II, that can be connected to the Token Ring Network.

Printing in the Token Ring Network

As we pointed out earlier, the PC Network Program offers printer-server functions including a printer queue. IBM does offer an additional program, the IBM Local Area Network Print Manager, to connect the Token Ring Network with its fast and powerful 3820 laser printer.

IBM's 16-mbps Token Ring

IBM offers a 16-mbps version of its Token Ring Network. Unlike the 4-mbs version, which can run on unshielded twisted-pair wire, this version requires IBM type 1, 2, or 9 shielded cabling and its own network adapter cards, which have 64K of onboard RAM compared to 8K in earlier versions. The new version supports frame sizes up to 18K, compared to the previous limit of 2K in the 4-mbs ring. These larger frame sizes are ideal for transmitting images in an engineering environment. These 16-mbs network interface cards may also be run at 4 mbs with more network efficiency because of their greater memory and additional circuitry.

The 16-mbps network uses a technique known as early token release. A workstation may transmit a token immediately after sending a frame of data instead of waiting for the original token to be returned. Using more than one token on the same ring at the same time increases network efficiency and speed.

Figure 4-15.
IBM's Token Ring
Connectivity *(Courtesy of*
IBM Corporation)

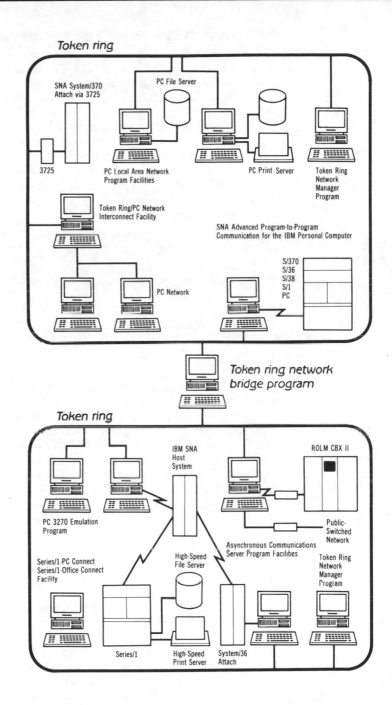

DATA TRANSMISSION ON THE TOKEN RING NETWORK

Unlike PC Network, which is a bus topology that uses Carrier Sense Multiple Access with Collision Detection (CSMA/CD) to avoid collisions, the Token Ring Network is a noncontention network. Only one network node can send information at any given time because of the nature of a token ring architecture.

Information to be sent across the network is formatted into frames. Figure 4-16 illustrates the fields found within these frames. Notice that the frame contains both the destination node address as well as the address of the source workstation. In very large networks with multiple rings tied together with bridges, an optional routing information subfield (RI) follows the address fields and indicates the sequence of bridges that must be transversed to reach the correct ring.

**Figure 4-16.
Token Ring Information
Frame**

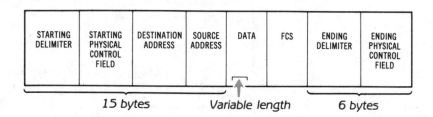

When a mailbox's flag is up, the postman knows that there is a letter to be picked up. In much the same fashion, the token that circulates around the ring has a bit sequence that tells the various nodes whether it is carrying a message or is free to be used. The first byte of the physical control field along with the starting delimiter field and ending delimiter field comprise a special token identifier. One of these bits is known as the "token bit," because, when set to zero, it is a token ready to be used. When a node has information to send, it captures this token and adds the source and destination addresses as well as the other fields seen in Figure 4-16. It then changes the zero to a one, meaning that this frame is now an information frame.

The information frame moves through the ring until it reaches the destination node. This workstation recognizes its own address in the destination address field, copies the information that has been sent, and then returns this token to the sender. The sender removes the header (the first 15 bytes) and issues a new token. This frame now is ready to circulate to the next node that needs to send a message. Each network node gets a chance to use the token because no one node is allowed to transmit continuously.

Errors can occur on a token ring network, so IBM has developed some safeguards to prevent network downtime. One such safeguard is the IBM Token Ring Manager Program, which is run by a node designated as the active token monitor. This program monitors the network for permanent errors and for *transient* errors, "soft," often intermittent errors that usually can be corrected by retransmission. Nodes detect these transient errors by monitoring all frames and verifying the validity of the frame check sequence that accompanies the message. Each node keeps track of these errors and reports them if they exceed a threshold amount. An operator can use a function called Soft Error Conditions to display the conditions of all stations reporting transient errors. The node discovering these errors sets the error detected flag in the physical trailer portion (6 bytes) of the frame.

In contrast to these "soft" errors, permanent errors represent a serious threat to the network's continued operation. When a node sends a message and receives the token back, it examines the token to see if the address-recognized flag has been set by the destination node. If the flag has not been set, the location of this defective node is identified. The wire concentrators are able to bypass such faults in the network and keep the network operating.

A complete disruption of the network signal can be caused when a receiver or transmitter of an active node fails or when a break occurs in the wiring. In the first case, the next node downstream from the defective node sends out a special network signal called a *beacon*, which contains the address of the node sending the message and the address of the node immediately upstream from it (presumably the defective node). In response, the wiring concentrator involved bypasses the defective node. Breaks in the wiring of the network may not be as easy to resolve. In fact, the entire ring may have to be reconfigured to bypass a particular break. If no obvious break is apparent in the network wiring each node should run its self-diagnostic tests to identify errors in its own wiring.

LAN SERVER

LAN Server runs under OS/2 Extended Edition. This file-server software provides what IBM terms requester/server relationships and what the rest of the industry refers to as server-client relationships. Regardless of the term used, the software running under a true multitasking operating system permits distributed data bases on a LAN to become a reality. Users need only request a particular record and the actual processing will take place elsewhere on the network. In addition to LAN Server, a network file server must also have the following software: OS/2 Communications Manager, Database Manager, and LAN Requester.

As in the case of the Extended Services version of PC Lan Program, LAN Server requires a minimum of one domain and a server acting as a domain controller.

Figure 4-17 illustrates a typical LAN Server screen. Unlike the DOS-based PC Lan Program, this program can use OS/2's greater power to track network activity and issue alerts. Its graphics-oriented user interface is consistent with IBM's Systems Application Architecture (SAA), the company's long-range plan for providing a uniform interface and transparent movement of information across its product line. LAN Server is clearly IBM's major file-server software for its largest customers, and, as such, it undoubtedly will garner increasing market share in the future.

Figure 4-17.
A Typical LAN Server
Screen *(Courtesy of IBM Corporation)*

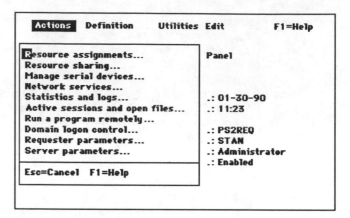

```
┌──────────────────────────────────────────────────────┐
│  Actions   Definition    Utilities  Edit      F1=Help │
│ ┌────────────────────────────────┐                    │
│ │Resource assignments...         │  Panel             │
│ │Resource sharing...             │                    │
│ │Manage serial devices...        │                    │
│ │Network services...             │                    │
│ │Statistics and logs...          │  .: 01-30-90       │
│ │Active sessions and open files..│  .: 11:23          │
│ │Run a program remotely...       │                    │
│ │Domain logon control...         │  .: PS2REQ         │
│ │Requester parameters...         │  .: STAN           │
│ │Server parameters...            │  .: Administrator  │
│ │                                │  .: Enabled        │
│ │Esc=Cancel  F1=Help             │                    │
│ └────────────────────────────────┘                    │
│                                                        │
└──────────────────────────────────────────────────────┘
```

WHAT HAVE YOU LEARNED?

1. PC Network is a broadband LAN using coaxial cable. A baseband version is also available.
2. The network adapter cards for PC Network contain modems as well as the NETBIOS, the "brains" of the network.
3. A PC Network workstation can be configured as a Redirector, Receiver, Messenger, or Server.
4. The Token Ring Network requires a NETBIOS software program.
5. The Token Ring Network and PC Network can be connected with the Token Ring Network/PC Network Interconnect Program by using a dedicated workstation with adapter cards from both networks.
6. The Token Ring Network can be connected with a PBX through an asynchronous communications server and a digital interface.
7. The Token Ring Network can be connected directly to IBM mainframes and minicomputers.
8. The Token Ring Manager Program monitors the network for both transient and permanent errors.

Quiz for Chapter 4

1. PC Network's broadband version uses which media?
  a. fiber optics
  b. coaxial cable
  c. twisted pair
  d. RS-232 serial cable

2. The actual broadband frequency translation on the PC Network is handled by the
  a. adapter cards
  b. network translation unit
  c. 8-way splitters
  d. base expanders

3. The broadband version of PC Network uses modems located
  a. in the Network Translator Units
  b. in the network adapter cards
  c. in the base expanders
  d. in the 8-way splitters

4. Modems can achieve a speed of 2 mbps on the network by
  a. Frequency Shift Keying
  b. modulating and demodulating signals
  c. bit stuffing
  d. accelerating bit packing

5. On PC Network the interface between PC-DOS applications and the network adapter controller is known as
  a. SNA
  b. BIOS
  c. UNIX
  d. HDLC

6. The PC Network configuration that can only accept requests for applications directed to servers and pass requests along to the servers is
  a. the Messenger
  b. the Redirector
  c. the Receiver
  d. the Server

7. Network Request Keys on PC Network consist of
  a. <CONTROL>-<ALT>-<BREAK>
  b. <CONTROL>-<ALT>-<DELETE>
  c. <CONTROL>-<ESCAPE>
  d. <CONTROL>-<PRTSCRN>

8. The PC Network command to share resources is
  a. LINK
  b. SHARE
  c. NET SHARE
  d. JOIN

9. Programs in PC Network normally are set up with the following default:
  a. Read/Write/Create/Delete
  b. Read Only
  c. Read/Write
  d. Write/Create/Delete

10. Tasks a user performs on his own machine are known as
  a. background tasks
  b. foreground tasks
  c. remote tasks
  d. server-initiated tasks

11. The Token Ring Network's topology follows IEEE standard
  a. 802.3
  b. 802.4
  c. 802.5
  d. 802.2

12. The Token Ring Network's wiring concentrators are found on its
   a. adapter cards
   b. network translation cards
   c. Multistation Access Units
   d. active network monitors

13. Two token ring networks can be joined together with a
   a. backbone
   b. bridge
   c. spinal tap
   d. T1 high-speed connection

14. Several bridges can be joined together with a
   a. backbone
   b. bridge
   c. spinal tap
   d. T1 high-speed connection

15. To establish peer-to-peer conversations between applications running on an IBM PC and a System/370 IBM provides
   a. modems
   b. an asynchronous communications server
   c. the Advanced Program-to-Program Communication Program
   d. synchronous connections

16. To establish cost-effective calls between network workstations and services such as The Source and Dow Jones News/Information Network, IBM provides
   a. SDLC protocol
   b. an asynchronous communications server
   c. HDLC protocol
   d. Dow Jones software

17. When a network workstation wishes to use a token, it must check to see
   a. if the token bit is set to zero
   b. if the token bit is set to one
   c. if the token bit has been removed
   d. if the token beacon signal is on

18. Transient network errors are
   a. vagrant bits looking for a free transmission
   b. errors caused by user error
   c. errors normally corrected by retransmission
   d. errors that extend across a bridge to a second network

Novell's NetWare

ABOUT THIS CHAPTER

In this chapter we'll survey the LAN software that dominates today's market, Novell's NetWare. In particular, we will examine NetWare's file-server software, its sophisticated options for network security and accounting, and some of its powerful utility programs. We will also look at Novell's blueprint for the future and its newest product, NetWare 386, a product designed for a new generation of local area networks based on Intel's 80386 and 80486 microprocessors.

NOVELL'S PHILOSOPHY

Novell's approach to serving the local area network user is unique. Although the company still offers a few network interface cards, it has chosen to concentrate its efforts on producing software that will run on other vendors' network hardware. NetWare runs on virtually any IBM or compatible, and versions support all the major LAN hardware discussed in this book, including the Apple Macintosh and 3Com products. Novell's philosophy is to make itself a de facto standard for the industry by dominating the marketplace. If a major corporation insists on purchasing IBM's Token Ring Network, Novell is happy to supply compatible NetWare to enhance the token ring's performance.

TOPOLOGY

NetWare supports a variety of network architectures including a star, a bus, a token ring, and a cluster of stars.

Novell offers several different starter kits that can be configured, depending on the hardware selected, as a star, a string of stars, a token ring, and even a bus. Running NetWare on 3Com's Ethernet hardware results in a bus topology. On Arcnet hardware NetWare functions in an efficient token bus environment. Northern Telecom and other PBX manufacturers offer their customers NetWare that uses the star topology of a PBX. And Proteon runs NetWare on hardware configured as a string of stars.

NETWARE AND THE CONCEPT OF A FILE SERVER

NetWare is designed for true network file-server support. To understand this approach, it is helpful to study how a file server functions under Novell's software. Under the OSI model, Novell's file-server software resides in the application layer and DOS resides in the presentation layer. In effect, the file-server software forms a shell around DOS in order to intercept application program commands before they can reach DOS—a procedure that is transparent to the workstation user, who simply asks for a data file or a program without worrying about where either is located.

To understand this interaction between the file server and the individual workstations, let's look at what happens when a workstation issues a request for a particular file. As Figure 5-1 illustrates, the network interface to the network file server (the "interface shell") resides in each workstation, where it intercepts DOS commands from an application program. When an application program requests a specific file, the shell must first determine whether the request is for a local file (residing on the workstation's own disk drives) or for information located on a network file server. If the information is located on the workstation's own drives, the request is passed back to DOS and handled as a normal I/O operation. The user would then notice that the red light on the disk drive goes on as a file is located and loaded into the workstation's CPU for processing.

Figure 5-1.
Network Interface Shell
(Copyright 1986, Novell,
Inc., all rights reserved)

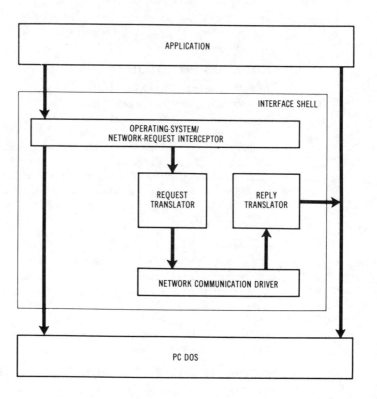

If the requested file is located on a file server, however, the request translator issues a "read" request to the file server, which locates the file and transmits it to the workstation in the form of a reply packet. The packet is received by a reply translator, which converts this information into a form that DOS can handle. DOS then provides the application program with this data. This procedure is so fast that the local and the network response will appear indistinguishable.

Techniques for Speeding up the File Server

Directory hashing is a method of mapping and indexing directories and their files in order to minimize the number of entries a file server must examine when searching for a specific file.

Disk caching is a technique for keeping often-requested files in RAM for rapid response to workstation requests.

Novell's NetWare uses a number of techniques to speed up the response time of its file servers. One technique is *directory hashing*, which can be likened to an efficient indexing system. The software maps all the directory files and keeps all of this information in RAM. When a workstation requests a file, the file server need only examine a few directory entries to locate the particular file. Since this information is in RAM and not on disk, the procedure is very fast.

A second technique for rapid file-server response, *disk caching*, illustrates just how intelligent a Novell file server can be. In effect, the file server anticipates future workstation file requests and keeps an image of frequently requested portions of its drive in RAM. When a workstation requests additional material from this area of the server's hard disk drive, the information is already located in RAM and does not require access to the hard disk. Since disk access is in milliseconds and RAM access is in microseconds, a "smart" file server can use disk caching to realize significant time savings for network users. Second and third requests for information that has been cached can be processed one hundred times faster. Another advantage of disk caching is that the file server can perform all disk writes as a "background" operation, which means that it can perform other procedures while sending this information to requesting workstations.

Elevator seeking is a technique enabling the file server to determine the order for executing file requests based on the current location of the disk heads.

Another technique used to speed up Novell's file-server response time is *elevator seeking*. Imagine a file clerk who is given a series of files to locate. The first three files are Johnson, Anderson, and Jackson. Since two of the files are located in the same drawer, the clerk would pull these simultaneously rather than in the order listed. Similarly, in elevator seeking the file server executes requests in the most effective manner possible in relation to the current position of the disk heads. The result is an increase of throughput of up to 50 percent and a decrease in the wear and tear on the disk drives.

FILE MANAGEMENT UNDER NETWARE

NetWare allows the system administrator to define not only access to specific files but also the nature of the files themselves. Some programs might be single-user MS-DOS or PC-DOS applications that certain users want to run in a multiuser environment. The system administrator can designate a program or file as shareable (capable of being shared) or nonshareable (restricted to one user at a time). NetWare also contains a default file-locking function, which means that different users can access these single-user programs one at a time.

If a file is nonshareable, different users can view the file in read-only mode, but they cannot write to it while it is being used in read/write mode by a specific user. Shareable programs and files with record-locking capability operate in true multiuser fashion: several users can read and write to them simultaneously as long as only one user is writing to a specific record at a time. One feature of NetWare is that an application program can specify all the records it needs before telling the file server to lock these records. This technique ensures that two application programs needing overlapping records cannot create a deadlock in which both wait for records that simply are not available.

Setting up Directories under NetWare

NetWare uses a hierarchical file structure, a diagram of which would resemble a mature tree, with main branches having smaller branches that, in turn, have even smaller branches of their own. As an example, imagine that the Widget Corporation has just installed a NetWare network with several distributed file servers. Now it is time to set up some directories on the first file server.

Let's assume that the Sales and Personnel departments will be using this file server. Beth and Barbara are the two sales administrators, and Phil, Paul, and Peter handle personnel functions. As Figure 5-2 illustrates, Widget has named its first file server FS1. Under the Sales directory are two subdirectories, Beth and Barbara. Each sales administrator has created further subdirectories under her own directory. Beth has established the subdirectories EASTERN.RGN, CUSTOMER.LST, and WESTERN.RGN and two additional subdirectories under WESTERN.RGN: SALES.RPTS and PROSPECTS. Barbara has not yet created as many subdirectories, but she certainly has that option in the future.

Likewise, the Personnel department has created directories for each of its administrators. Since Phil, Paul, and Peter all have distinct functions, each has created two subdirectories to handle his specialized reports.

The system administrator loads appropriate files within the directories and subdirectories of both departments. Beth's CUSTOMER.LST subdirectory for example, contains the files CURRCUST.E, CURRCUST.W, OLDCUST.E, and OLDCUST.W. To announce a new program designed to entice former Widget customers living in the Western region to buy widgets again, Beth writes a form letter and performs a mail merge with the OLDCUST.W and OLDCUST.E files.

When designating subdirectories, Novell follows the convention of using a slash ("/") or a backslash ("\") to separate a directory from its subdirectory. The names of all succeeding subdirectories must also be separated in the same manner. To indicate the pathway for OLDCUST.W, for example, Beth would type:

FS1/SYS:SALES/BETH/WESTERN.RGN/CUSTOMER.LST/
OLDCUST.W

Since we have written a pathway for OLDCUST.W, the last directory named is the directory we wished to specify.

Mapping Network Drives: A NetWare Shortcut

Network drives are logical and not physical drives.

NetWare requires that directories be assigned to a specific network drive. Network drives point to network directories and not to physical disk drives. Each workstation may assign twenty-six logical drive letters (A through Z).

**Figure 5-2.
NetWare's File
Structure**

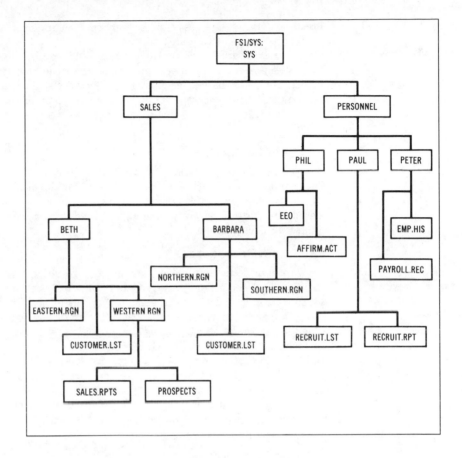

Let's assume that you want to assign the WESTERN.RGN directory to
network drive F. You would type the following:

MAP F:=FS1/SYS:SALES/BETH/WESTERN.RGN

Typing the colon following the drive letter assigns this directory to the drive.
Now you can type F: from a DOS prompt to go directly to this directory. By
assigning frequently used directories to different network drives, you can
jump back and forth among files without having to remember pathways and
correctly type in the long names.

Search Drives Save Time

Search drives permit users
to locate files even though
they might not know in
which directory the files
reside.

One of the most common network error messages indicates that a file cannot
be found. This usually means that the file does not exist in the directory in
which you are working. Often you cannot remember exactly where it resides.
To avoid this situation, NetWare permits you to define up to sixteen search
drives (Search1:, Search2:, etc.), which enable DOS to locate program files in
directories other than your default directory. A major advantage of this
approach is that, rather than having to copy a program into several individual

directories, users can access a single copy from their current directories since the copy is mapped to a search drive.

Search drives also can be mapped to directories on different file servers. The result is that a system administrator can make file access painless for novice users, since they need only specify a particular file or program that has been mapped to a search drive. Even if the file is located on a distant file server, it will appear on the user's screen as if it resided on his or her local disk drive.

SYSTEM SECURITY

Although vendors who market only network security systems may offer more elaborate systems, Novell's NetWare offers by far the most extensive security system available as part of a network package. NetWare provides file-server security in four different ways: the login procedure, trustee rights, directory rights, and file attributes.

The Login Procedure

NetWare requires a valid username, file-server name, and password when logging in.

NetWare provides security when logging in by requiring a valid username (user identity) and a valid password. As a matter of convenience, the network administrator normally allows the user to use his or her first name as the username. Fred's username, then, is simply FRED. The user must also know which file server he or she is using. Fred's login to file server FS1, for example, might look like this: LOGIN FS1/FRED. (NetWare doesn't care if users use uppercase, lowercase, or a combination.) NetWare now waits for a password to be typed. At this stage the software doesn't announce whether the login is correct or incorrect but waits for all three variables. For security, in the event of an unacceptable login NetWare will not indicate whether the username, file server, or password is incorrectly typed. Let's observe Fred's login procedure. Fred begins by typing the command:

LOGIN <ENTER>
Enter your login name:
FS1/FRED <ENTER>
Enter your password:

To maintain security, Fred's password will not appear on the screen when he types it. You should note that the password is associated with the user and not with the machine. With his or her username and password, a user can work on any available workstation.

Trustee Rights

Each user has up to eight usage rights assigned by the network supervisor.

The network administrator, referred to by Novell as the "network supervisor," is responsible for the network's security as well as its operation. The supervisor makes each user a "trustee" and provides each with specific rights in certain directories. These rights normally extend through all subsequent subdirectories unless the supervisor specifically limits a user's access. These rights also may be extended to the user either as an individual or as part of a user group. The range of eight possible trustee rights is listed here:

Read from open files
Write to open files
Open existing files
Create (and simultaneously open) new files
Delete existing files
Parental (create, rename, and erase subdirectories of the directory)
Set trustee and directory rights in the directory
Set trustee and directory rights in its subdirectories
Search the directory
Modify file attributes

Users can be given any combination of these rights. A user with Open, Read, and Write rights, for example, can open a file, read its contents, and write to the file. Without Search rights, however, the user would have to know the precise name of the file in order to access it. Similarly, without the Delete right, a user would be powerless to delete any existing files.

NetWare trustee security has many different levels and potential combinations. To delete an entire subdirectory, for instance, a user needs Parental rights as well as Delete rights. The network supervisor also establishes directory security. Normally, when a directory is created, all trustees enjoy all directory rights, but, if needed, the supervisor can limit these trustee rights within the directory. For example, within a specific directory, all or certain users might be limited to reading and not changing information. A "maximum-rights mask" for a directory means that users enjoy all eight trustee rights within that directory. Since this is a mask, only those user rights that are also directory rights will represent a user's rights within the directory.

Through network equivalences a supervisor can make the trustee rights of a particular user equivalent to the rights of a user group or a number of different individuals.

The network supervisor assigns each user to a user group and then may assign trustee rights directly to the entire group. These rights may also be assigned to user groups indirectly through equivalences. A user or user group can have up to thirty-two security equivalences. A supervisor may establish that one user group has all the rights already found within another user group, in which case the two groups become equivalent. The supervisor may set up a group called "Everyone" and make the rights of all user groups equivalent to those of this group. Obviously, this is more efficient than setting rights for each user. All members of the word-processing pool, for example, are part of the same user group and share the same trustee rights. A supervisor can also temporarily make an assistant's rights equivalent to his or her own, thereby enabling the assistant to function as the supervisor. A user's total rights comprise those as an individual user, those as part of a user group, and all the trustee rights of any other users or user groups for which this user has a security equivalence.

File Attributes Security

A user who establishes a file can set its attributes by using the FLAG command. File attributes prevail over individual trustee rights.

NetWare security permits a user to determine whether an individual file may be modified. Let's assume that Frieda has been having trouble with other network users changing the contents of a particular file (CSTCONFG). Her rights include Modify privileges for this file's directory. Using the FLAG command, she restricts the file's use to read-only. Frieda is in her default directory where the file resides, so to effect the change she types:

FLAG CSTCONFG SHAREABLE READ-ONLY <ENTER>

Now the CSTCONFG file can be shared by other users who can read it but not change its contents. Frieda could have changed all the files in her default directory to the same shareable read-only status by typing:

FLAG *.* SHAREABLE READ-ONLY <ENTER>

With the FLAG command you can select four different combinations of attributes for a file or group of files:

Shareable, Read-only
Shareable, Read-write
Non-Shareable, Read-only
Non-Shareable, Read-write

By typing FLAG and pressing <ENTER> within a directory, you can see a list of the flags on files within that directory.

File attributes take precedence over trustee rights because NetWare uses a logical AND function to determine final rights. Let's assume that Stan has Read and Write rights as a user, and that the CUST file has been flagged as Shareable, Read-only. NetWare examines Stan's user rights and the file attributes using an AND function that accepts only those terms that appear in both lists. Since the Read function appears in both lists, Stan can read only the CUST file.

NETWORK UTILITIES

The four levels of network security we have been discussing are all handled by NetWare's powerful series of utility programs. At this point we'll examine the two utility programs that are used in conjunction with network security: SYSCON and FILER.

The SYSCON Utility

SYSCON enables users to view information about the file servers they are logged into, their login procedure, the user groups that they belong to, their trustee rights, and their network security equivalences.

The SYSCON utility is used for system configuration and handles many of the security functions we have been discussing, such as establishing passwords, user groups, access to file servers, trustee rights, and equivalences. Because some of its functions can be performed by nonsupervisors, SYSCON is loaded into the SYS:PUBLIC directory. SYSCON is a menu-driven program. From DOS, typing SYSCON and pressing <ENTER> gives the Available Topics menu shown in Figure 5-3. Even though you might not be a network supervisor you can still view information regarding your own status on the network. As illustrated in Figure 5-4, the

Available Topics for users include Change Current Server, File-Server Information, Group Information, System Login Script, and User Information.

Figure 5-3.
SYSCON's Main Menu

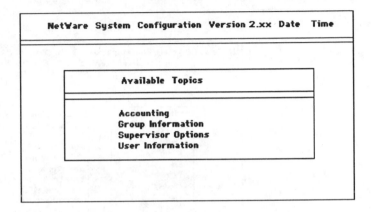

Figure 5-4.
Viewing Users on a File Server

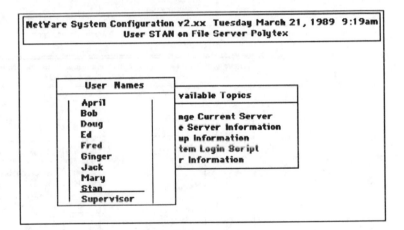

Figure 5-5 displays the groups to which a particular user belongs. A personnel department, for example, might want to make all staff members part of the PERSONNEL group, which would entitle them to read-only privileges. Any member of this group would be able to look up a personnel file for basic information, but only certain members of the department would have individual trustee assignments enabling them to change a file.

Novell's NetWare allows users to examine their own security equivalences and trustee assignments. In Figure 5-6 Stan has chosen to examine his security equivalences and discovered that he has security equivalences with Bill as well as with the groups EVERYONE and WRITER. As we saw earlier, this system makes it easy to add new users and duplicate trustee rights without having to list each of several dozen files that a user should be able to retrieve. A new clerk in the Personnel department who will cover Frieda's assignments during her summer vacation can be given a security equivalence to Frieda, automatically giving him or her all the group and individual rights Frieda now enjoys. When Frieda returns from vacation, the clerk's security equivalence can be reduced to that of another department clerk.

**Figure 5-5.
Identifying a User's
Groups**

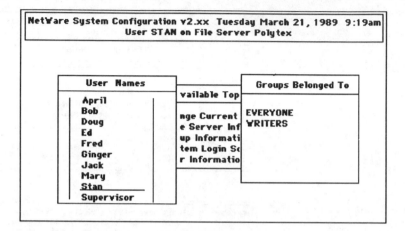

**Figure 5-6.
Displaying Security
Equivalences**

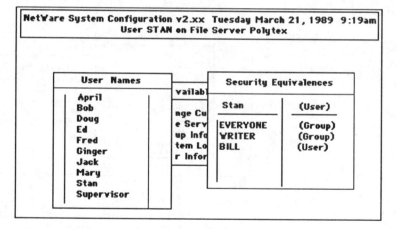

Enhancing Security with SYSCON's Accounting Restrictions

SYSCON contains a number of accounting functions that enable a supervisor to control the degree of network access granted users and the costs of operating the network. As Figure 5-7 reveals, a supervisor can designate the hours an employee can use the network. In this example, Carol has been restricted to using the network between 7:00 am and 7:00 pm on weekdays. Other accounting restrictions illustrated in Figure 5-8 enable a supervisor to establish an account expiration date for a temporary employee. Supervisors can also require users to change passwords at certain intervals and to use passwords of certain lengths. Finally, additional options (not pictured here) permit a supervisor to charge users for their disk storage and processing time. Users can even be charged higher rates during peak computing time to discourage unnecessary file transfers and report printing.

Figure 5-7.
Carol May Log in
between 7:00 am and
7:00 pm

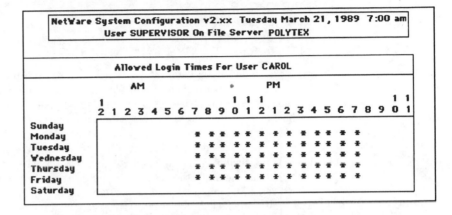

Figure 5-8.
Setting Intruder
Detection/Lockout

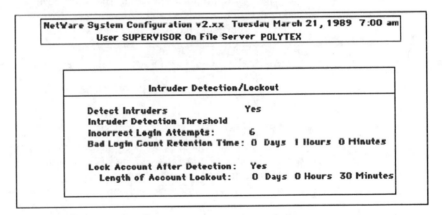

NetWare's Login Scripts

Login scripts automatically map network search drives, display key information upon logging in, and load the proper DOS software into network workstations.

At any given time, a user can use the NetWare utilities menu to examine his or her login script and make any necessary changes. The login script is a shortcut, a way to tell NetWare how to go through a preassigned set of steps to customize the network's environment and to display certain information when you log in to the network. Although each user can design an individual login script, one of the major advantages of this procedure is that the network supervisor can set up a login script for a new user that will shield the novice from the intricacies of a network environment. The SETLOGIN command defines a login script.

Although NetWare permits the mapping of different network search drives, this information is erased each time the user logs off the system. One of the major uses of a login script is to provide NetWare with this information automatically when the login script is executed. A login script for Peter might include the following:

```
MAP *1=SYS:PAUL
MAP *2=SYS:SUPER
MAP *3=SYS:PUBLIC
MAP *4=SYS:SYSTEM
MAP *5=SYS:FS1/SYS:SALES/CUST.LST
```

With this login script, Peter is able to access files in different directories without even knowing where these files exist. By typing CUST.LST, for example, Peter will retrieve this information without knowing the full pathname. As a new user, Peter need not even know what a pathname is as long as his network supervisor has set up this login script for him.

NetWare allows a number of different variables to be placed in a login script, including the time, day of the week, month, and year. The login script can also identify the specific file server the user is addressing. Scripts uses a command language that is clearly explained in Novell's documentation. The commands include an IF . . . THEN combination that permits you to individualize scripts for each day of the week. Frieda, for example, might want to remind herself of a staff meeting that is always held Mondays at 10:00 am. She could have the following login script:

```
IF DAY OF WEEK="Monday" THEN
WRITE "Another week. Don't forget the staff meeting at 10:00 am."
```

When Frieda logs in on a Monday morning, her computer screen will display the following:

Another week. Don't forget the staff meeting at 10:00 am.

You can individualize each day's script not only with the date and time and standing appointments but also with the actual set of procedures normally performed that day. For example, a payroll clerk may go through the routine of printing checks only on the first and fifteenth of a month. The script could specify that on these dates the network should log the clerk into a different file server where the check-printing program resides, load the program, and make sure that the appropriate printer is on-line. The clerk would need only to use the correct login name and password to begin the check-writing procedure.

Another useful login script command is INCLUDE. This command enables you to establish a series of text files that can serve as subscripts for your login. As many as ten levels of INCLUDE commands can access different subscripts, which have a number of very practical uses. Let's say that several people are working on a project with a tight deadline. Although some of these individuals are scattered throughout a large four-story building and others are at remote locations, it is essential that they all know the progress of the project on a daily basis. A project manager could establish an announcements file under the PROJECT directory. Each night before leaving work (or even late at night from home with the proper remote equipment), the project manager could use the word-processing program to write a text

The INCLUDE command enables you to link a number of text files and place them in a login script.

...all members of the team. Each member's login script ...n INCLUDE command to access this file. As a team login script might include the following:

:K="Monday" THEN BEGIN
~ week. Don't forget the staff meeting at 10:00 am."
PROJECT/ANNCMENT

4 2077.01.01.10 08/13/91 12.13 3558
SOFTWARE, ETC.   APPLETON, WI
6041019   19.95
        SUBTOTAL   19.95
        SALES TAX   1.00
        TOTAL   20.95
        CHECK   20.95

ALL RETURNS MUST BE ACCOMPANIED BY A
RECEIPT WITHIN 30 DAYS -- THANK YOU

...and its login script procedure address a critical problem ...r companies, that of a proliferation of types of computers ...ems. On a NetWare file server, differing operating systems ...ause of the interpretive shell. CP/M 86 files can coexist ...and MS-DOS 3.3 files. A company can establish an ...ommand within users' login scripts to ensure that a user ...PC-DOS 2.1, for example, loads the proper 2.1 versions of ...not 3.3 versions. Novell suggests the following LOGIN ...ch directories for differing machines and operating systems:

PUBLIC\%MACHINE\%OS VERSION

The FILER Utility

FILER permits users to display and change key information about directories and files that they control.

The FILER menu utility program controls volume, directory, file, and subdirectory information. Earlier we discussed a situation in which Frieda wanted to ensure that other users did not change a file within a directory she had established. To do so, Frieda could change the directory's maximum-rights mask or change the file's attributes. Let's assume that Frieda wished to make the change at the directory level. She could examine the maximum-rights mask for that current directory using the FILER utility. The maximum rights consist of the following:

        Create New Files
        Delete Files
        Modify File Names/Flags
        Open Existing Files
        Parental Rights
        Read From Files
        Search For Files
        Write To Files

Frieda places the selection bar (displayed on the screen) on the right she wishes to delete and then presses the <Delete> key. NetWare will ask if she wishes to revoke this particular right (Yes or No). When she presses her <Select> key, the right is revoked and removed from the maximum-rights mask.

The FILER utility also permits adding and deleting trustee rights for a directory, viewing and deleting trustee rights for a directory, and viewing and deleting file attributes. A security feature available under FILER is the capacity to specify a directory exclusion pattern. A network supervisor, for example, could establish a network directory exclusion pattern for all directories whose names begin with PROJ. This would mean that secretive information in the Jove, Jupiter, and Saturn projects (PROJJOV, PROJJUP, and PROJSAT) would not be displayed with a directory listing. It is also possible to specify a file exclusion pattern within directories. Let's say that the directories of each of the secret projects contains a budget file (PROJBUD) that only the project manager needs to see or use. A file exclusion pattern for the .BUD pattern ensures that even those users with sufficient security to enter the project directories won't be able to see the budget files when they request a listing of all the files in that particular directory.

PRINTING UTILITIES

PRINTDEF

The PRINTDEF utility defines print devices, modes of printing, and types of forms.

PRINTDEF is a printer definition utility program that enables the network supervisor to define the types of network print devices (printers, plotters, etc.), the modes of network printing (draft-quality or final printout), and even types of forms (wide, $8\frac{1}{2}'' \times 11''$, and so forth). By typing PRINTDEF and pressing <ENTER>, you will see the PrintDef Options screen; selecting "Print Devices" at this point reveals a list of whatever print devices have been defined. A network supervisor can define the control codes associated with the network's various printers once and then use other NetWare printing utilities to create customized printing jobs.

Using PRINTDEF, a supervisor can define several print modes required for a specific print job. A desktop publishing program's print definition might include emphasized printing and proportional spacing. Budget analysts, on the other hand, might want a print job defined for wide spreadsheets in compressed mode.

CAPTURE/ENDCAP

CAPTURE is particularly valuable for a network supervisor who must install software that insists on sending all print data to LPT1.

The CAPTURE/ENDCAP utility is designed to allow you to redirect a workstation's LPT ports to network printer devices, queues, and files. CAPTURE can redirect up to three LPT ports. Since these ports are logical, a PC need not have three physical ports. In fact, CAPTURE does not work with serial ports COM1 and COM2.

CAPTURE is particularly valuable for a network supervisor who must install software that insists on sending all print data to LPT1. We can redirect the print data to the network print queue 2 as follows:

CAPTURE LOCAL=1 QUEUE=PRINTQ_2

Note that these CAPTURE commands are temporary and are effective only until another CAPTURE command is executed, until an ENDCAP command is used, or until you log out of the file server.

PRINTCON

The PRINTCON utility sets up print-job configurations using the options available under the NPRINT and PCONSOLE utilities.

The PRINTCON utility sets up print-job configurations using the options available under the NPRINT and PCONSOLE utilities. A supervisor may define standard configurations for specific users and their documents since this data is stored in each user's mail directory on the server they normally log into. Figure 5-9 illustrates a typical print job for a routine text file using a laser printer. Once these configurations are defined, a user simply selects a configuration without having to specify print options. For example, we can specify Carol's LOTUS standard printer configuration as well as her WORDPERF configuration once, and as a result she will never again have to grapple with answering printer definition questions.

**Figure 5-9.
A Typical Print-Job
Configuration**

```
┌──────────────────────────────────────────────────────────────┐
│  ┌──────────────────────────────────────────────────────────┐ │
│  │  Configure Print Jobs  Vx.xx   Date      Time            │ │
│  │        User SUPERVISOR on File Server POLYTEX            │ │
│  └──────────────────────────────────────────────────────────┘ │
│                                                                │
│  ┌──────────────────────────────────────────────────────────┐ │
│  │       Edit Print Job Configuration "Stan's_report"       │ │
│  │                                                          │ │
│  │   Number of copies:   1          Form name:   CONTINUOUS │ │
│  │   Suppress form feed: No         Print banner:  No       │ │
│  │   File contents:      Text       Banner name:            │ │
│  │   Tab size:           6          Banner file:            │ │
│  │                                                          │ │
│  │   Local printer:      1          Enable timeout: No      │ │
│  │   Auto endcap:        Yes        Timeout count:          │ │
│  │   File server:        POLYTEX                            │ │
│  │   Print queue:        PRINTQ_1                           │ │
│  │   Device:             HP LASERJET                        │ │
│  │   Mode:               (Re-initialize)                    │ │
│  └──────────────────────────────────────────────────────────┘ │
└──────────────────────────────────────────────────────────────┘
```

NPRINT

NPRINT is a fast way to print a document on a network using print configurations already established.

Once a job configuration has been set up under PRINTCON, it can be used with the NPRINT command. Since PRINTCON contains a detailed description of your form, your printer, the number of copies, and so forth, all you need specify with the NPRINT command is the file you wish to print:

NPRINT file job –BUDMONTH <ENTER>

The specific parameters you defined in the BUDMONTH configuration will be used for printing the document. As another example, assume you wanted to print three copies of the file WESTERN without a banner. We would issue the following command:

NPRINT SYS:MARKETNG\SALES\REGIONS\WESTERN C=3 NB <ENTER>

PCONSOLE

The PCONSOLE utility controls network printing. This program enables you to access and print files on other file servers, examine jobs waiting in a print queue for printing, change the way a job is printed, physically change the contents of a print queue, and view information about both print servers and print queues. In Figure 5-10, Hilda is both a user and a designated print-queue operator (designated by her network supervisor) viewing a particular print job in a print queue.

**Figure 5-10.
A Print-Queue Entry
Window**

```
NetWare Print Console Vx.xx              Date  Time
         User HILDA on File Server POLYTEX Connection 12


              Print Queue Entry Information


Print job:          5        File size:      17435
Client:             SERV[3]
Description:        LPT1Catch
Status:             Read to Be Serviced, Waiting for Print Server
User Hold:          No                Job Entry Date: May 4, 1989
Operator Hold:      No                Job Entry Time: 8:33:12 am
Service Sequence:   1
Number of Copies:   1                 Form:           1
File contents:      Text              Print banner:   Yes
Tab size:           8                 Banner name:    STAND
Suppress form feed: No                Banner file:    BNNR
Defer printing:     No                Target date:
Target server:      {Any Server}      Target time:
```

NETWARE BRIDGES AND GATEWAYS TO OTHER NETWORKS

Bridge Software

Novell's bridge software permits the linking of two networks. A bridge PC must contain the network interface cards for both networks as well as the bridge software.

NetWare makes it possible for networks to communicate with other networks as well as with mainframe computers. A bridge connects networks using different hardware. One network, for example, might use Arcnet's interface cards and cabling whereas another might use IBM's token ring interface cards and cabling. NetWare provides bridge software, which permits these two networks to share information. The software resides on a bridge workstation, usually dedicated to this purpose. The computer must have at least one floppy disk drive and two available expansion slots to hold the two networks' corresponding interface cards. The cards are cabled to their respective networks, but the bridge is designed to remain invisible to both sets of network users.

SNA Gateway for Micro-Mainframe Communications

Novell's SNA gateway hardware and software provides micro-mainframe communications through a gateway PC and IBM 3270 terminal emulation for the entire network.

Novell's SNA gateway software provides five different hardware options: token ring, coax, CoaxMux, remote synchronous, and remote high-speed synchronous. In a token ring network, a NetWare gateway can accommodate up to 128 host terminal or printer sessions to as many as ninety-seven workstations. NetWare gateway software permits multiple gateways on the same network, the sending of mainframe print jobs to LAN printers, the ability to view the current status of the gateway, and the ability to pool LU sessions.

Since IBM mainframes use synchronous communications, Novell recommends its Synchronous/V.35 Adapter Board, which contains an RS-232 to V.35 interface. When used with an Intel 80386-based workstation serving as a gateway, transmission speeds of up to 64 kbps are possible. Figure 5-11 illustrates how the gateway workstation connects the network with an IBM mainframe via modems.

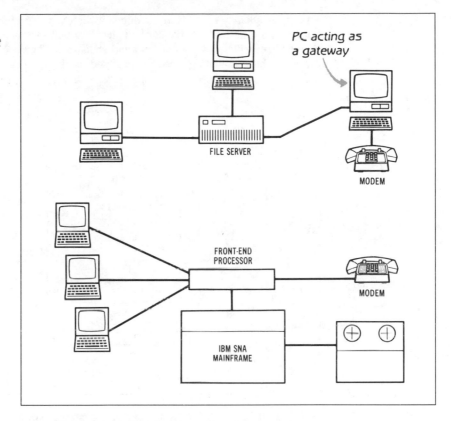

Asynchronous Communications Server

Novell also offers asynchronous communications server (ASC) software that
can be used with a Wide Area Network Interface Module (WNIM) so that a
workstation acting as a server may support simultaneous asynchronous
connections for up to four different workstations. Up to four WNIM boards
may be installed on a network, which means that up to sixteen concurrent
asynchronous ports are possible under NetWare.

SYSTEM FAULT TOLERANT NETWARE

Novell offers three levels
of System Fault Tolerant
NetWare, whose features
include the duplication of
file allocation tables, disk
drives, and even the file
server.

Any company that relies completely on computers for information processing
is fearful of a system failure. Novell has developed System Fault Tolerant
NetWare to overcome this potential disaster. This special version of NetWare
comes in three different levels, each with progressively more protection. What
makes this approach so unusual is that Novell not only provides the software
tools for hardware duplication (to prevent downtime) but also allows users to
purchase off-the-shelf hardware in order to realize a significant cost savings.

The Level I NetWare protects against partial destruction of the file
server by providing redundant directory structures. The file server maintains
extra copies of file allocation tables and directory entries on different disk
cylinders for each shared network volume. If a directory sector fails, the file

server immediately shifts to the redundant directory. Through a feature known as a "hot fix" the file server places the bad sector in a bad block sector table and stores the data in another location. The user is not even aware of this automatic procedure, depicted in Figure 5-12.

**Figure 5-12.
The Hot Fix Feature of
SFT NetWare**

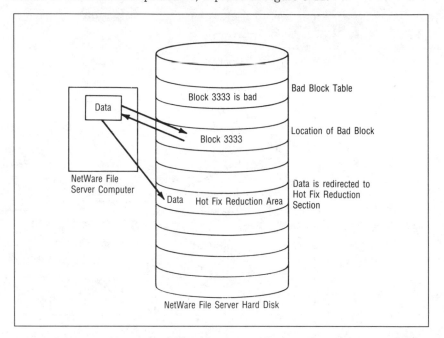

When a Level I system is powered up, it performs a complete self-consistency check on each redundant directory and file allocation table. After each network disk writes the system performs a read-after-write verification to ensure that data written to the file server is rereadable. Level I software also includes a VOLFIX utility program that scans the surface of a disk looking for potential surface faults and ensures that the file server will bypass potential trouble spots and place data on safe areas.

Level II software includes the protection found in Level I plus a number of additional features. At this level, Novell offers two options to protect the LAN against the total failure of the file server. The first option is mirrored drives, which involves supporting two duplicate hard disk drives with a single hard disk controller, as illustrated in Figure 5-13. Every time the file server performs a disk-write function, it mirrors this image on the duplicate file server and verifies both hard disk drives to ensure complete accuracy. In case of a system failure, the system switches to the mirrored file server and resumes operations.

**Figure 5-13.
Disk Mirroring with SFT
NetWare**

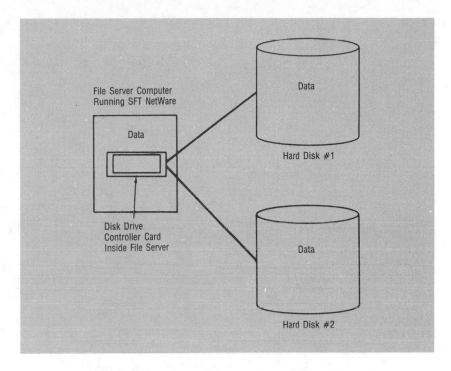

File Server Computer
Running SFT NetWare

Data

Data

Hard Disk #1

Disk Drive
Controller Card
Inside File Server

Data

Hard Disk #2

With duplexed drives the disk controller, the disk drive, and even the cables and interfaces are duplicated. Because both drives perform disk reads, file server performance is virtually doubled.

The Transaction Tracking System (TSS) ensures that the data integrity of a database is maintained if the network is disrupted in the middle of a database transaction.

The second option under Level II is for duplexed drives. As illustrated in Figure 5-14, they duplicate virtually all the network hardware, including the disk controller, interface, and power supply. If a disk controller or disk drive fails, the system automatically switches to the duplexed alternative and records this fact in a log. The performance of a duplexed system is far superior to that of a single system because of split seeks. If a certain file is requested, the system checks to see which disk system can respond more quickly, and if two requests occur simultaneously each drive handles one of the disk reads. In effect, this technique doubles the performance of a file server.

Level II also includes a Novell feature known as the Transaction Tracking System (TTS), which is designed to ensure the data integrity of multiuser databases. The system views each change in a database as a transaction that is either complete or incomplete. If a user is in the middle of a database transaction when the system fails, the TTS rolls the database back to the point just before the transaction began. This action is known as "automatic rollback." A second procedure performed by the TTS is "rollforward recovery," which means that the system keeps a complete log of all transactions to ensure that everything can be recovered in the event of a complete system failure.

Level III software incorporates all features from Level II and adds a duplicate file server connected by a high-speed bus. If a file server fails, the second file server immediately assumes control over network operations.

Figure 5-14.
Disk Duplexing with
SFT NetWare

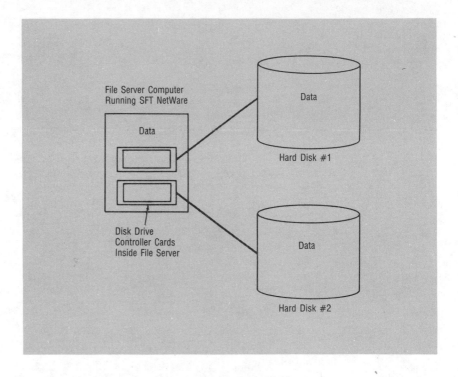

NOVELL, NETWARE, AND THE FUTURE

In this section we'll examine Novell's future plans for NetWare. We'll look at Novell's vision of a universal architecture that accommodates a number of different protocols concurrently. We'll also see how NetWare 386 comes very close to achieving Novell's vision of a seamless network platform.

Over the past several years Novell has developed a plan, an architecture that it believes is consistent with a future characterized by increased connectivity, seamless flow of information between large and small computers, and multivendor compatibility.

Novell believes that the computer industry is now in a second stage of LAN connectivity, one in which LANs are connected to mainframe computers by gateways. In addition to increasing the number of available terminal emulation sessions, gateways now provide file-transfer capabilities for a network user.

This second stage of LAN connectivity is still not user-friendly. A network user wishing to connect with an IBM mainframe must know a lot about that system, including how to access the gateway, how to log on to a mainframe, and how to use a 3270 terminal.

Ease-of-use, peer-to-peer connectivity, and end user transparency will characterize a third stage of LAN connectivity.

The major emphasis today is still on the mainframe or host computer. The LAN user is concerned with accessing mainframe applications and not with direct peer-to-peer communications between a microcomputer program and a mainframe program. This concept of peer-to-peer communications and the concepts of ease-of-use and user transparency are what will characterize the next stage of LAN connectivity.

Novell sees this third stage of LAN connectivity as a time in which a single record of a database can be updated with information from various programs running on different-sized computers that use different protocols and operating systems. All these differences will be resolved by NetWare in a manner transparent to the end user.

Novell demonstrates its seriousness about its universal network architecture (UNA) by including MHS in every package of NetWare. Licensed from Action Technology, MHS provides the key CCITT X.400 electronic mail standards that will enable electronic mail programs running on different computers to provide a universal "envelope" that can be properly opened and decoded by the electronic mail program of the destination local area network.

NetWare v2.1 and above reflects Novell's philosophy in yet another way. IBM has been modifying its Systems Network Architecture to incorporate peer-to-peer communications so that programs can communicate directly with other programs without having to go through a mainframe computer. NetWare v2.1 and above permits Advanced Program-to-Program Communications (APPC) through the addition of Value-Added Processes (VAPs). We'll return to VAPs later in this chapter.

NetWare and the Use of Heterogeneous File Servers

Novell is committed to having a variety of different types of computers serving as file servers.

Novell has been developing file-server software that enables a variety of different types of computers to serve as file servers under NetWare. With NetWare VMS, for example, a DEC VAX computer now can function as a NetWare file server. The VAX's file server capabilities are transparent to the end user, who still sees DOS files in their familiar format.

NetWare for the Macintosh now permits an IBM DOS-based machine to serve as a file server for an AppleTalk network. Once again, NetWare translated the native AppleTalk commands from Macintosh workstations into its own Network Core Protocol, processed the commands, and then translated its own commands back into the AppleTalk protocol the Apple workstations could understand. This entire process was transparent to Apple users as well as to PC users.

In December 1988 Novell announced that its NetWare server strategy would support the Network File Systems (NFS) protocol, IBM's Server Message Block (SMB) protocol, and, for LAN Manager clients, the NetBeui/DLC protocol. Novell's long-range NetWare server strategy, though, is to provide a broad platform that can support several different kinds of file servers, including those running under UNIX, VMS, and OS/2. Novell also committed itself to developing a powerful version of NetWare that can use platforms based on the Intel 80386 and 80486 microprocessors. Support of OS/2 will include support for Microsoft's Named Pipes and IBM's APPC. Figure 5-15 represents what Novell calls its "Novell Vision" of a heterogeneous file-server environment.

Native-mode file servers perform with much greater efficiency than host-mode file servers.

Novell differentiates between "native-mode" file servers and "host" file servers. Native-mode file servers such as a dedicated NetWare Intel 80386-based file server are inherently more efficient since they are designed

Figure 5-15.
The Novell Vision
(Courtesy of Novell,

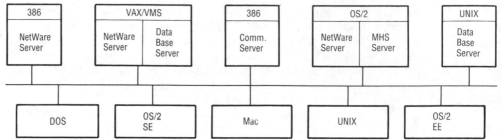

for a specific hardware platform. Host-mode servers, on the other hand, run on top of an operating system such as UNIX or OS/2 that also supports such services as file and print functions.

A movement is underway within the computer industry toward server-based database applications using such host-based server platforms as OS/2 and UNIX. Novell has indicated that it will support both its own native-mode server and host servers supporting database applications. Novell's commitment in this area is evidenced by its signing of Fox Software as the original equipment manufacturer (OEM) of its NetWare structured query language (SQL). The two companies have agreed jointly to develop a database server based on NetWare SQL using features found in Fox Software's FoxPro database program.

FoxPro uses a language similar to dBASE, and the FoxServer processes requests to see if they are in SQL format or dBASE format. This approach will enable developers to create applications in either dBASE or SQL to work on the SQL server. Eventually the software will support DOS, OS/2, and Macintosh operating systems that use NetWare.

PORTABLE NETWARE

Portable NetWare, written in the C language, provides a scaled-down version of 80386-based NetWare.

Novell has developed a version of NetWare that will run on platforms from mainframe and minicomputer vendors. Portable NetWare represents a scaled-down version of its Intel 80386-based software that will be licensed to computer companies for recompilation on their own systems. Portable NetWare runs as a host operating system application so that minicomputers can serve both as hosts and as NetWare servers. Among the computer vendors who have agreed to port NetWare to their machines so that their computers can serve as file servers are Prime, Data General, Hewlett Packard, NCR, and Unisys.

As we just indicated, network users will be able to communicate with these larger machines both as terminals and as network workstations. As terminals they will be able to run minicomputer and mainframe software in much the same way that NetWare VMS users can have their workstations emulate a DEC terminal and run DEC programs. Network users will also be able to run PC-based SQL database programs and then save their files on the larger machines in NetWare file format.

Novell has written its portable NetWare in the C programming language to make it easier to port it from machine to machine. The software is compliant with the U.S. government's Posix standard for operating system interoperability.

NETWARE'S MOVEMENT TOWARD PROTOCOL TRANSPARENCY

Novell has been moving toward its vision of a virtually universal NetWare platform that would provide support for multiple protocols. This platform would enable a user to have transparent access to a number of computing resources that might include multiple server and client protocols and various subnetwork protocols.

A key to understanding this concept is to realize that Novell views the future as a time when the microcomputer will be at the center of computing and not a mere appendage to mainframe computers. Apple Computer's John Sculley has expressed much the same viewpoint. To make this dream come true, however, the artificial barriers separating computing resources must be eliminated.

Novell envisions a time when its software will break down the barriers to communication caused by various protocol differences among UNIX-based minicomputers, DEC computers running VMS, SNA-based IBM mainframe computers, and other computing resources such as Sun workstations running NFS protocol.

NOVELL'S OPEN LINK INTERFACE

Open Link Interface (OLI) software provides an interface between up to sixteen different LAN adapter cards and up to thirty-two different protocol stacks

Open Link Interface (OLI) software provides an interface between LAN adapter cards and protocol stacks that, in many ways, is a Novell response to LAN Manager's Network Device Interface and Protocol Manager features. This interface can handle as many as thirty-two transport protocols and sixteen different adapters simultaneously. A single network can therefore support multiple protocols and different types of adapter cards. Instead of a network manager having to grapple with the issue of multiple protocols, OLI will make the entire matter transparent to users. In effect, OLI acts as a standard network interface so that vendors need only develop network software with one generic driver. OLI will provide the necessary translations required as well as the appropriate network drivers.

OLI is composed of a link support layer that contains two programming interfaces, Multiple Link Interface (MLI) for LAN adapter device drivers and Multiple Protocol Interface (MPI) for LAN protocols. The link support layer coordinates the sending and receiving of packets by sorting the packets it receives into the correct protocol stack, which could consist of as many as thirty-two queues for such disparate protocols as IPX/SPX, TCP/IP, OSI, and AppleTalk.

Among the many vendors who welcomed Novell's OLI announcement in early 1989 were Apple, Compaq, and Western Digital Corporation. Sytek Corporation also indicated that it will support OLI by incorporating it into its Multiple Protocol Architecture and LocalNet Integrated Network Connectivity products. Sytek will develop drivers for baseband and broadband network adapter cards using Novell's Multiple Link Interface. Novell indicated that it would provide OLI-compliant drivers for its own LAN adapters as well as for those offered by IBM and 3Com

Corporation. OLI is consistent with Novell's philosophy of offering a universal platform for different network operating systems.

VALUE-ADDED PROCESSES (VAPS)

Value-Added Processes (VAPs) are software interfaces that permit third-party developers to write programs to these interfaces so that their applications will run a NetWare server through the VAP interface.

A Value-Added Process (VAP) is a special program running on a dedicated server that permits the server to host additional applications that users can access without requiring additional servers. A VAP is actually a software interface that permits third-party developers to write programs to these interfaces so that their applications will run on the NetWare server through the VAP interface. To the NetWare operating system, a VAP appears to be a logical workstation that can make all kinds of requests for operating system functions. A VAP can request that a particular process be scheduled and run, order that a report be generated, or request that a printer queue be emptied. In effect, the VAP is the process that permits the application program to run and perform its functions.

The computer industry's movement toward SQL database servers illustrates the usefulness of NetWare's concept of a VAP. A database management system can run as a VAP on a server without requiring a second, dedicated server for database management.

Dozens of VAPS can communicate with each other using Internetwork Packet Exchange (IPX) protocol, thus facilitating the application programs they support while keeping the user aware only of the application program currently running. NetWare for the Macintosh is actually a VAP application known as DTALK when it communicates with Apple's LocalTalk hardware and ETALK when it communicates with Ethernet hardware. Additional VAPS are required to manage Macintosh printing functions and to manage the NetWare printing queue.

NETWARE 386

In May 1989 Novell announced NetWare 386 v3.0 and v3.1, the products it intends to use as its "server platform for the 1990s." NetWare 386 supports up to 250 nodes per server and up to 32 gigabyte volumes with 32 physical drivers per volume for a total of 1,024 physical drives per server. It allows 100,000 concurrent open files and 25,000 concurrent transactions. It also can handle more than two million directory entries per volume with a maximum file size of 4 gigabytes and a maximum volume size of 32 terabytes. A level-three system fault tolerance feature not yet available eventually will permit redundant file servers and third-party applications.

Novell's NetWare 386 approach is modular. Users are able to add functions to their server platform using server-based applications called NetWare Loadable Modules (NLMs). Among the features available as NLMs are printing functions, LAN drivers, and various NetWare utilities. In the near future Novell expects database, electronic mail, and office automation servers to be written as NLMs so they can be loaded or unloaded while the server is running. Figure 5-16 illustrates this feature of NetWare 386 architecture. The only drawback to NLMs is that existing VAPs that work on NetWare 286 servers will have to be completely rewritten to work in this

NLM environment. Also, all current 286 drives have to be reformatted for the 386 version.

**Figure 5-16.
Netware 386
Architecture** *(Courtesy of Novell, Inc.)*

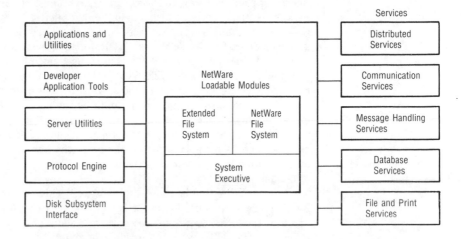

NetWare 386 will support XNS, TCP/IP, OSI, and SNA.

As illustrated in Figure 5-17, NetWare 386 will concurrently support multiple transport protocols, including Xerox Networking System (XNS), Transport Control Protocol/Internet Protocol (TCP/IP), Open Systems Interconnection (OSI), and Systems Network Architecture (SNA). Novell has indicated that by the end of 1990 NetWare 386 will also support Microsoft's Named Pipes and Server Message Block, IBM's NETBIOS Extended User Interface, Advanced Program-to-Program Communications (APPC), Apple's AppleTalk and Apple Filing Protocol (AFP), and Sun Microsystems's Network Filing System (NFS).

**Figure 5-17.
NetWare 386 Supports
Multiple Protocols**

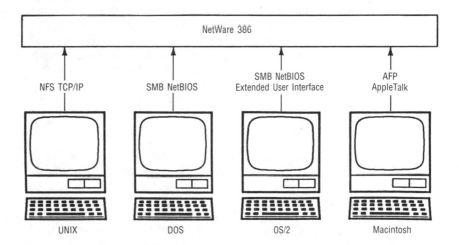

NetWare 386 adds a number of significant network management features, including better network statistical reporting, better print services (including print servers), and password encryption. Version 3.1 will provide network status reports and even monitors and alerts, as well as access to management functions from remote consoles and extended (installable) file system support for CD ROMs and WORM drives. NetWare 386 can configure its server memory automatically, which reduces installation time substantially. An Extended File Salvage facility enables NetWare 386 to retain all user-deleted files until the server runs out of disk space (unless those files have been flagged for purging by the user). When there is no longer any disk space available, the files are purged in order of deletion.

NetWare 386 incorporates other evidence of artificial intelligence. It can fine tune its own operation by observing the number of users accessing an application and by adjusting the amount of memory needed at each stage of optimum caching.

NetWare 386 is also 80486 "aware." This means that if an Intel 80486 processor is installed in the server, the operating system is aware of it and uses the extra 80486 instructions available to perform with greater efficiency. The 80386 version provides approximately three times the performance of Novell's 80286-based products.

Communications are obviously a primary concern for network supervisors considering NetWare 386. Novell has announced that version 3.1 (due in 1990) will support a global naming directory, an important feature for companies with several networks at different locations. NetWare 386 also will support Ethernet, token ring, LocalTalk, Arcnet, Synchronous Data Link Control, and T-1 and asynchronous media.

Version 3.1 will add global directory services and additional network management functions. Novell intends to base its network reporting system on the categories and packet formats of the OSI Common Management Information Protocol (CMIP), which will enable NetWare networks to report information to other CMIP-based systems and to IBM's NetView mainframe network management system.

Novell is offering a NetWare Programmers' Workbench that provides developers with everything necessary to write distributed applications in the NetWare 386 environment, including two C programming language compilers supplied to Novell by Watcom Systems (a C Network Compiler and a C Network Compiler/386), NetWare 386, and NetWare RPC for the 386. Novell also has announced development kits for NetWare 386 Open Link Interface and driver development kits for DOS and OS/2.

WHAT HAVE WE LEARNED?

1. System Fault Tolerant NetWare is designed to provide redundancy of key hardware and software elements to prevent network failure.
2. Three techniques Netware uses to speed up its file-server response time are directory hashing, disk caching, and elevator seeking.
3. By mapping network drives and using search drives, a user can retrieve a file without knowing where it is located.

4. NetWare's many levels of network security include the login procedure, trustee rights, directory rights, and file attributes.
5. New network users can immediately enjoy all the rights of another network user if they have the same network equivalences.
6. NetWare users can learn information about their login scripts by using the SYSCON utility.
7. Using the FILER utility, network users can establish directory and file exclusion patterns.
8. Novell's NetWare bridge software and hardware permit two networks to be linked.
9. Novell's SNA gateway software permits up to 128 concurrent SNA sessions with an IBM mainframe.
10. NetWare can search for potential bad disk sectors and then avoid them using the VOLFIX utility program feature of System Fault Tolerant NetWare.
11. The integrity of a database is maintained even in the event of network failure by the Transaction Tracking System (TTS).

Quiz for Chapter 5

1. Arcnet uses a series of active and passive hubs tied together with
  a. fiber optics
  b. twisted-pair wire
  c. coaxial cable
  d. lasers

2. NetWare file servers keep often requested files in RAM for rapid response to requests. This is known as
  a. directory hashing
  b. disk caching
  c. elevator seeking
  d. rapid-response retrieval

3. NetWare minimizes wear and tear on disk drives by retrieving files that are closest to the present location of the heads instead of simply processing retrieval requests in the order in which they are received. This technique is known as
  a. directory hashing
  b. disk caching
  c. rapid file retrieval
  d. elevator seeking

4. NetWare workstations need not contain floppy disk drives as long as they have
  a. a remote system reset prom
  b. NetWare v2.11 and above
  c. EGA graphics
  d. at least 256K of RAM

5. Workstations using different versions of DOS can coexist on a NetWare network because
  a. each workstation does not use the file server
  b. NetWare provides an interpretive shell
  c. the differences in DOS versions are not significant
  d. different machines need different versions of DOS

6. The PCONSOLE menu utility is designed to handle
  a. printing requests
  b. photocopying requests
  c. filing requests
  d. micro-mainframe communications

7. Novell's System Fault Tolerant NetWare automatically places bad sectors in a bad block table using
  a. a hot fix feature
  b. elevator seeking
  c. mirrored disk drives
  d. the Transaction Tracking System

8. The automatic rollback feature of the Transaction Tracking System ensures the integrity of a database by
  a. duplicating each data entry
  b. rolling back to before the data entry if the entry was disrupted before it was complete
  c. keeping a log of all data entries
  d. completing an entry if it is disrupted

9. The concept of mirrored drives means that:
   a. all drives are the mirror opposites of each other
   b. a second drive keeps an exact copy of the file server's information
   c. all hardware and software are duplicated, including disk controllers and interfaces
   d. if one disk drive becomes cracked, the other drive also is cracked

10. Duplexed drives increase the speed of a file server by about
    a. three times
    b. four times
    c. two times
    d. six times

11. System Fault Tolerant NetWare is able to locate potential bad blocks and then avoid them by using the following utility program:
    a. VOLFIX
    b. PCONSOLE
    c. FILER
    d. NOGOOD

12. Portable NetWare is written in
    a. Cobol
    b. Fortran
    c. C
    d. 4GL

13. NetWare enables the file server to locate a file quickly without searching through every directory by using
    a. disk caching
    b. directory hashing
    c. elevator seeking
    d. remote system reset proms

14. Network disk drives are really
    a. hard disk drives
    b. floppy disk drives
    c. network file servers
    d. logical disk drives

15. Different networks can be linked using
    a. a remote PC
    b. a bridge PC
    c. a disk server
    d. spooled disk files

16. NetWare local area networks can communicate with IBM mainframe computers using
    a. a bridge PC
    b. an SNA gateway PC
    c. an asynchronous communications server
    d. both b and c

17. A program running on a server that permits the server to host additional applications is known as a
    a. vaperware product
    b. vampire link
    c. VAMP
    d. VAP

18. Users can shorten the login procedure by
    a. using the NetWare manuals
    b. using electronic mail
    c. using elevator seeking
    d. using login scripts

3Com's Local Area Networks

ABOUT THIS CHAPTER

A company named 3Com is one of the major local area network manufacturers, offering file servers and customized workstations as well as advanced network software. 3Com provides upward compatibility for companies that wish to install its DOS-based 3+Share software and later upgrade to the more sophisticated OS/2-based 3+ Open series. In this chapter we will look closely at the company's file servers and at its wide range of network software that provides electronic mail, printer management, bridges to other networks, and communications with mainframe computers.

NETWORK DATA COLLISION DETECTION AND AVOIDANCE

3Com's local area networks use the standard Ethernet data packet that contains information on source and destination addresses, the type of protocol used, and error checking.

Under Ethernet the physical layer generates a 64-bit preamble so that all network workstations can synchronize the data stream. The preamble consists of a unique pattern of 1s and 0s that indicate the start of a new data packet. As Figure 6-1 illustrates, the Ethernet packet contains destination and source address fields, a type field (to indicate the higher level protocols that might be used), a data field, and a cyclic redundancy check (CRC).

**Figure 6-1.
Ethernet Packet Format**

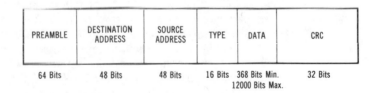

PREAMBLE	DESTINATION ADDRESS	SOURCE ADDRESS	TYPE	DATA	CRC
64 Bits	48 Bits	48 Bits	16 Bits	368 Bits Min. 12000 Bits Max.	32 Bits

3Com's network software uses a CSMA/CD approach to avoid data collisions, which are most likely to occur during the time interval when a workstation sends a transmit signal until the signal returns, indicating that the workstation may claim the channel.

In compliance with the IEEE 802.3 standards, 3Com's Ethernet network software delivers the data packets to network workstations using CSMA/CD (Carrier Sense Multiple Access with Collision Detection) to avoid data collisions along the bus. Since this is a *contention* (competition) scheme in which workstations compete for the right to send a message, a station that is about to send a message through the network listens to see if another station has sent a transmitting signal. If it does not hear this signal, the workstation promptly sends its own signal alerting the network that it has acquired the channel and is about to send a message. Thus, this node does not really acquire the channel until its transmitting signal completes a round trip through the network.

In the event of a data collision, a jam signal is generated, and workstations wait different random intervals before trying again to gain a channel.

With this CSMA/CD approach it is possible to build a very large Ethernet network by combining thick and thin cabling and using repeaters. On very large networks, however, there is a significant time lapse between the time when a workstation acquires a channel and transmits its signal and the time when such a message is received further down the bus.

If a data collision occurs, the transmitting station detects this event and its physical layer turns on a collision-detect signal. The transmit link management elements of the data link layer respond by generating a *jam* signal that notifies the network of this collision and initiates a temporary hiatus during which no signals are transmitted. The transmitting station then waits an additional interval before beginning to retransmit its message. In the event of another collision, the workstations wait additional random intervals before trying to retransmit.

NETWORK HARDWARE

File Servers

3Com's 3Server/400 and 3Server/500 series of file servers are built around the Intel 80386 microprocessor and contain several features designed to optimize network file-server performance.

3Com offers a 3Server/400 series based on an Intel 80386 platform that supports up to 14 megabytes of memory. For MIS managers looking for minicomputer speed and security, 3Com offers its 3Server/500, a 20-MHz 80386-based file server with base RAM of 2 or 8 megabytes (expandable to 16 megabytes). For enhanced security, the 3Server/500 has no keyboard, floppy disk drive, or monitor. A 33-MHz version of this unit should also be available by the time you read this chapter.

3Server/500 uses triported RAM, an architecture that separately controls the I/O bus of the Small-Computer System Interface (SCSI) for disk drives, tape backup units, printer ports, four AT-compatible slots, and two 32-bit memory cards.

What also distinguishes this file server is its massive capacity for secondary storage. SCSI disk storage can be 150, 320, or 630 megabytes; this capacity can be extended with up to five external drives to 6 gigabytes. A 250-megabyte or 2.3-gigabyte tape drive is available as a backup unit.

3Com currently bundles its file server with its 3Station diskless network workstations and 3+ Open LAN Manager system software (including electronic mail and internetworking software) into a "3+ Client-Server System."

3Com file servers are dedicated units that are designed for optimized network performance. They are limited to this specific function, however, and cannot be used to fill the role of an AT workstation.

Tape Backup

The 3Backup tape backup unit can backup all file servers on a network. 3+Backup software permits selective backup of those files that have changed.

3Com file servers also come with two SCSI ports to connect optional tape backup units or additional disk drives. Since 3Com offers the option of both thick and thin Ethernet cabling, the 3Server comes with BNC (thin Ethernet) and DIX (thick Ethernet) connectors. One major advantage of using a 3Server 60-megabyte streaming tape backup unit with the file server is that a separate SCSI channel avoids degrading disk performance during backup. With 3+Backup software, the 3+Backup unit becomes even more valuable. This unit can back up all network file servers on a single unit. It can provide complete backup of an entire server's files as well as incremental backup of any files changed since the last backup, and it can schedule full or incremental backup for automatic operation and initiate these processes unattended. With this combination of hardware and software a user can also initiate multiple backups on the same tape, restrict backups to a new tape, and restore files either on a file-by-file basis for all files below a specified directory or through a complete restoration of all files.

A network administrator can use 3+Backup to restore files from system-level backup tapes in four different ways. It is possible to restore all files on a server, restore all files on a specific 3Server disk, restore all files within a directory and its subdirectories, and restore one or more specific files. The 3+Backup unit prevents anyone accessing it from carrying out backup, restore, erase, or directory commands while you are performing one of these operations. In this way it provides some protection against catastrophe.

Network Architecture and Media

3Com offers a baseband bus network operating at 10 mbps that adheres to the IEEE 802.3 standard and a bus with a logical token ring network that adheres to the IEEE 802.5 standard of 4 mbps.

Historically 3Com's major focus has been on very fast (10-mbps) baseband bus networks. The company's newest direction has been to add a connection to the IEEE 802.5 token ring standard, specifically to IBM's Token Ring Network, as well as to offer its own token ring architecture.

The baseband transmission speed of 10 mbps over a bus is achieved using a 3Com network adapter card. 3Com's EtherLink card is designed to fit into the half-slot of an IBM PC or compatible. This circuit card contains a single coaxial cable connector and many jumpers, which are used to change the card's address (which must be unique), its interrupts, or its Direct Memory Access (DMA) channel.

For the PC AT bus 3Com also markets an EtherLink Plus card, a full-sized card with its own Intel 80186 microprocessor and RAM. Though more expensive, this adapter provides higher performance since it can respond to the faster interrupts generated by the Intel 80286-based PC AT. Whereas EtherLink card provides an 8-kilobyte buffer, the EtherLink Plus card provides a buffer of 64 kilobytes. A workstation that rarely needs to access the network can probably get by with a small buffer, but a network file server that supplies information for all network users should have a large buffer. In general, however, a larger buffer does provide higher network performance.

3Com networks may use standard (thick) Ethernet cable, thin cable, or a combination of both.

3Com's network adapter cards can each transmit 3280 feet (1000 meters) using standard (thick) Ethernet cable. This thick cabling (.4 inch in diameter) uses an external transceiver box for each workstation. Network workstations must be a minimum of 7.5 feet apart.

Although the standard cabling permits a larger network, it costs more and is more difficult to install than thin cabling. With thin Ethernet cabling (.2 inch in diameter), the total length of a network segment cannot surpass 1000 feet (300 meters) and network workstations must be a minimum of 3 feet apart. The Etherlink adapter card for a thin-cabled network contains its own on-board transceiver. Figure 6-2 illustrates how a BNC connector links a network's workstations and thin coaxial cabling together. One attractive feature of the 3Com local area networks is that it is possible to customize a network to meet a particular company's needs by combining thin and thick cabling and several file servers.

**Figure 6-2.
3Com Bus Network with
Thin Coaxial Cabling**

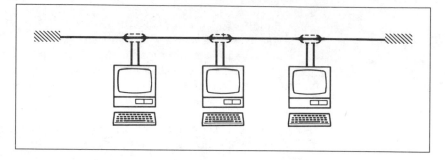

Although the type of cabling used determines the length of a particular *segment* of an Ethernet LAN, Multiple segments can be linked together by using *repeaters*. These units rebroadcast the signal and prevent data degradation. Figure 6-3 illustrates how an office with various departments can have different cabling segments linked together with repeaters.

**Figure 6-3.
Ethernet Network with
Multiple Segments and
Repeaters**

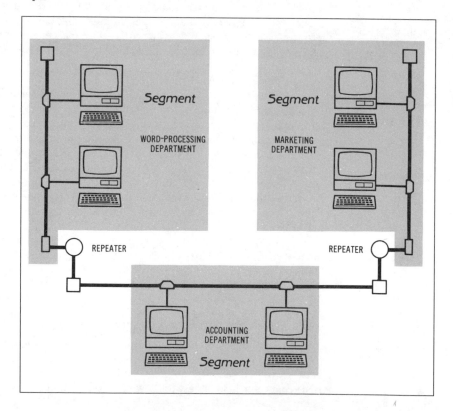

3Com's Token Ring Network Alternatives

Realizing the dominant position that IBM's Token Ring Network has achieved in the LAN marketplace, 3Com has developed hardware and software to enable its networks to connect with token ring networks. TokenConnection for a 3Server consists of two circuit boards, a Ring Interface board, and the Processor Interface board. In effect, these components replace the back panel of 3Server. TokenConnection has a token ring port and two synchronous serial ports. In order to assure IBM compatibility, 3Com has chosen to use the Texas Instruments TMS380 Token Ring Chip Set. Since this chip set was developed jointly by Texas Instruments and IBM, it guarantees IBM compatibility. 3Com also markets RingTap and the TokenPlus cabling system, which are totally compatible with IBM's Token Ring Network PC Adapter cables.

As Figure 6-4 illustrates, 3Com offers an internal ring topology with an external bus topology, in which the RingTaps are connected to the token ring adapters found in each network workstation. 3Com also produces its own TokenLink Plus adapter cards for IBM PCs, XTs, ATs, and compatibles, as shown in Figure 6-5. These adapter cards offer IEEE 802.5 and IEEE 802.2 logical link control interfaces on a baseband token ring network of 4 mbps. Each card contains 256K of RAM, which can be used for downloading protocol software with the IBM-compatible NETBIOS interface, and 16K of ROM, which provides boot and diagnostic firmware.

**Figure 6-4.
An Internal Ring
Topology with an
External Bus Topology**

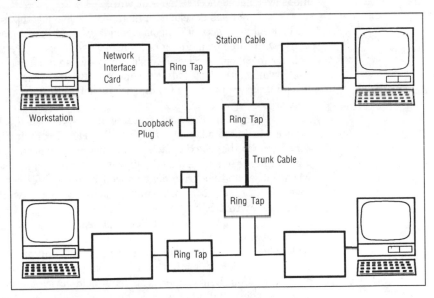

The RingTaps consist of small boxes that connect to the token ring adapter cards with thumb screws. The TokenPlus cabling system links several of these RingTaps together with trunk cables. A Y-MAU cable is used to

Figure 6-5.
3Com TokenLink Plus
Adapter Card *(Reprinted*
with the permission of
3Com Corporation)

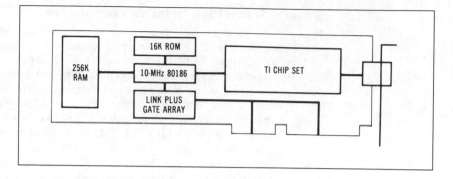

connect the TokenPlus cabling system with IBM's Multistation Access Unit. The 3Com cable design for its token ring network uses doubled, shielded twisted-pair wire.

3Com's Twisted-Pair Approach

3Com uses a single twisted-pair and the PairTamer adapter to transmit at 10 mbps over twisted-pair wire.

Until recently the LAN industry standard for twisted-pair wire has been a transmission speed of 1 mbps. Recently an IEEE task force in charge of standardizing Ethernet over unshielded twisted-pair wire has developed a new standard known as 10baseT, which describes a transmission speed of 10 mbps over baseband twisted-pair wire.

3Com has developed a method of achieving this transmission speed on its local area networks using a single twisted-pair. Since most offices are wired with three or more pairs of unshielded copper wire and use only one pair for telephone service, 3Com's ability to use a single pair almost ensures cable availability. An additional benefit to 3Com's twisted-pair solution is that it permits users to mix twisted-pair, coaxial, and fiber-optic cable on a single network.

The 3Com approach features an adapter called a PairTamer that connects to 3Com adapter cards. The PairTamer contains both a coaxial connector for thin coaxial cable and a modular connector for twisted-pair wire. In general, since twisted-pair wiring runs from a desktop to a central wiring closet and not from desktop to desktop, PairTamers are used to link together Ethernet nodes of as many as twenty-five network workstations connected by thin coaxial cable.

3Com's MultiConnect Repeater resides in a wiring closet and ties the entire network together. It accepts transceiver modules for several different types of cabling. Figure 6-6 illustrates how this approach works.

In order to ensure that the cabling is working properly, 3Com also offers the 3Com LanScanner. This hand-held device measures the resistance, electrical noise, and other electrical characteristics on a twisted-pair or thin coaxial cable. It is an excellent tool for discovering any shorts in the cabling.

Figure 6-6.
3Com's PairTamer

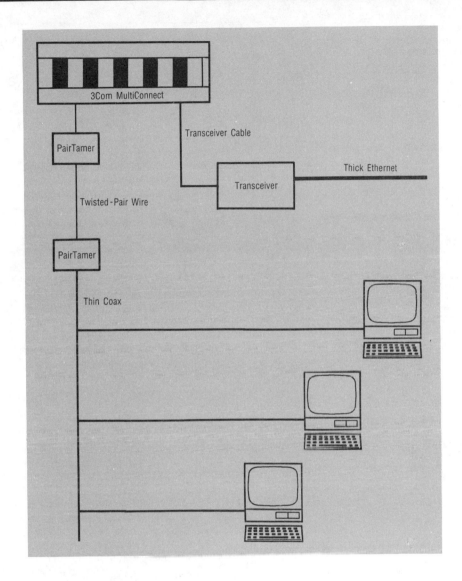

NETWORK SOFTWARE

3+Share

3+Share is the heart of the 3+ DOS-based LAN. It provides internetworking, mail, file, name, and print services.

3+Share forms the basis for all the advanced features of the 3+ series, including internetworking (connecting networks together via 3+Route), mainframe-minicomputer gateways (3+3270), configurable menus (3+Menus), remote dial-in access to the network (3+Remote), backup capabilities (3+Backup), and electronic mail (3+Mail). The command structure is remarkably simple, as you can see from Table 6-1, which summarizes 3+Share user commands.

6

**Table 6-1.
3+Share User
Commands**

Command	Function
LOGIN	Login to the network
LOGOUT	Logout from the network
3F User Commands	
3F	Start program file
3F DIR	List names of shared directories
3F HELP	Get help with the File Service
3F LINK	Link to a shared directory
3F LOGIN	Login to the network
3F LOGOUT	Logout from the network
3F MODIFY	Modify a shared directory
3F SHARE	Share a directory
3F STAT	Show 3Share server information
3F UNLINK	Unlink from a shared directory
3F UNSHARE	Delete a shared directory
3N User Commands	
3N	Start program name
3N ASSIGN	Assign a sharename for 3Share
3N DIR	List 3N names
3N HELP	Display helpful information
3N LOGIN	Login to the network
3N LOGOUT	Logout from the network
3N MODIFY	Modify 3N information
3N SET	Set 3N defaults
3N STAT	Display 3N information
3P User Commands	
3P	Start program print
3P DELETE	Delete a file from the print queue
3P DIR	List names of shared printers
3P HELP	Display helpful information
3P LINK	Link to a shared printer
3P LOGIN	Login to the network
3P LOGOUT	Logout from the network
3P SET	Set printer options
3P STAT	Show 3Share printer information
3P QSTAT	List a printer queue
3P UNLINK	Unlink from a shared printer

Because 3+Share uses the Microsoft Redirector and emulates
NETBIOS functions supporting the Redirector, most software compatible with

the IBM PC LAN and the Token Ring Network will run on these networks without change.

The Name Service

The Name Service is a database that requires a user's name, domain, and organization. This information then becomes available to all the other 3+ programs.

One of the most basic functions found under 3+Share is the Name Service, a database of users and servers. All the 3+ software accesses this information. 3N is the user program that interfaces with the Name Service and pulls information from the database to provide user login verification, lists of users, and so on. To login, a user must provide three different types of information using this format:

name:domain:organization

The person's name is followed by his or her geographical location (domain) and company (organization). A typical entry might look like this:

Fred Goodman:Accounting:DeVry

The Name Service does have a default domain and organization. Under most circumstances Fred would not have to type these default values. In addition to his or her name, a user may have one or more aliases that usually take the short form of a user's name. Fred Goodman's alias, for example, is FredG. Let's assume that for security reasons DeVry wants all employees to log on to the network with a password in addition to their alias. Fred, who selected his childhood nickname "Scrappy" as his password, would type the following each time he logs on to the network:

FredG /PASS=Scrappy

The network responds by recognizing the password and returning Fred's three-part network name :

Fred Goodman:Accounting:DeVry

The first time Fred used the network, the network administrator added him to the Name Service and assigned him a file server. The 3+Share program assigned Fred a home directory (Fredhome) in which to keep his files. Using the standard MS-DOS hierarchial directory structure, Fred was able to create a number of subdirectories under his home directory. One of these subdirectories (Account) contains an accounts receivable file with valuable customer histories (Cust.his) that Fred frequently accesses.

The *pathway* to this particular file through MS-DOS's tree-like structure can be written as follows:

C: \Fredhome\Account\Cust.his

Shared Directories

The major reason for using a local area network is to share information. To share files a user needs to tell 3+Share that a particular directory is available to be shared using 3Com's 3F user interface for 3+Share's file service. Let's assume that salespeople want to check on some of Fred's customer histories. Fred decides to share this file with other users by giving it the sharename "customer" and limiting access to read-only:

3F SHARE cust.his=E:\customer /R

If Fred were concerned about security, he could have required a password such as "victory":

3F SHARE cust.his=E:\customer /PASS=victory /R

You may assign a number of different access rights to your sharename directory, including the following:

/R	Read
/RW	Read/Write
/RWC	Read/Write/Create
/WC	Write/Create
/W	Write
/SHAR	Read/Write/Create/Share
/PRIV	Private
/PUB	Public

It is important to remember that the network's default value is "Private." If you have different network users who require different levels of access for a particular directory, you can give that file several different sharenames with different passwords for each sharename. All the subdirectories under a particular directory share the same access rights for that directory.

3+Share's Print Service

3Com provides the 3P user interface program for 3+Share's Print Service. The program is started by typing 3P. Through this program it is possible to list or link shared printers and directories, set special printing options for a printer, and examine printing queues. By typing 3P HELP a user can see a complete list of print commands with a brief description of each command.

One of the most powerful yet easy-to-use print commands is 3P SET, which enables you to establish special printing options for a printer. The 3Com format for this command is illustrative of its flexibility:

3P SET[prnid:][/HOLD[=OFF]][/COPIES=#][/PRI=#]
[/DEFER[=OFF]][/RELEASE][/FORM=#][/SPOOL=#]

The printer identifier can be LPT1, LPT2, or LPT3. The HOLD parameter holds all printing jobs until you use HOLD=OFF or a UNLINK command. This latter command is used when you wish to ensure that all files are printed together in batch form.

The COPIES parameter permits you to make multiple copies of the same document, up to 99 copies at a time. The normal default value here is 1. The PRI parameter permits you to assign your files a priority in the print queue from 1 (the lowest priority) to 99 (the highest priority). The default value is 50.

The DEFER parameter allows you to defer the printing of a file no matter what its place is in the print queue. If you defer a file until its place in the queue has already passed, the software automatically moves it to the top of the print queue. The RELEASE command releases deferred files for printing.

The final two print option parameters are FORM and SPOOL. FORM specifies which particular form you want your file to print. The printer will then wait until that form is loaded before it begins printing. The default value here is form number 1. The SPOOL parameter indicates the spool identifier of the file that is assigned by the 3P program. If you specify a spool identifier, only that particular file will be affected by your print specifications. If you do not specify a number, all the options you have set will apply to all files you send to the printer.

Since there are default values for all these options, you list only the parameters you wish to set when using the 3P program. To print all your files in the printer's queue on a specific form, for example, you would type:

SET LPT1: /FORM=10

Remote Access

3+Remote software permits remote workstations to dial into a network and set all network services, including file server, print server, and electronic mail.

Using the 3+Remote software package a remote workstation can dial into a 3+ local area network. Remote users can thus enjoy all 3+ series services, including 3+Share electronic mail as well as access to all the file and print functions of the network. The software provides full error checking of transmitted data; if an error is detected, the software will automatically retransmit lost data packets. To make it easier and faster for remote users to access a network, the software supports up to nine prioritized telephone numbers that can be up to thirty digits long. The 3Com program supports automatic hang-up for inactivity time-out; this feature is configurable. It also supports automatic, prioritized alternate phone numbers with a user profile to maintain predefined dialing, modem, and port information. The program is fully integrated with 3+Mail. Figure 6-7 shows the 3+Remote software linking three remote users with a 3Com network.

Linking a 3+Share LAN to an IBM Mainframe Computer

Network workstations can emulate an IBM 3278 or 3279 terminal and communicate with an IBM mainframe computer by using 3+3270 software and an IBM SDLC card.

A 3Com 3+Share LAN can be linked to an IBM mainframe by using 3Com software that causes network workstations to emulate an IBM 3278 or 3279 terminal. A very fast 80386-based workstation is an ideal choice for a dedicated communications server, which must also have an IBM SDLC card.

As Figure 6-8 reveals, it is possible to have two or more dedicated communications servers on a 3Com network. Since servers support only single host sessions, it is not possible to switch between host and PC sessions. The software does support up to thirty-two LUs, which are pooled among fifty users on a first-come-first-served basis. Though this may sound like quite a few sessions, you must remember that each terminal and printer in use counts as a session.

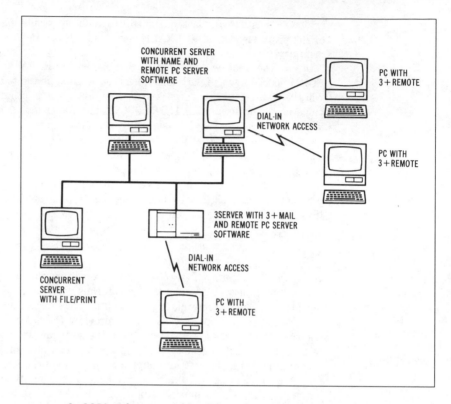

3+3270 software enables PC workstations to transfer files on the network. (The required host software, however, must be purchased directly from Forte Communications.) The ASCII-to-EBCDIC conversion process is handled at the workstation. 3Com uses the Microcom MNP protocol, a standard used by Telenet, GEISCO, and The Source. This terminal emulation software also allows you to spool output to any network printer, disk drive, or user workstation. Before you can print to a local printer, however, you must first spool files to a local or network storage device.

Internetworking with 3+NetConnect and 3+Route

3+NetConnect enables companies to interconnect different types of networks, including Ethernet and token ring. 3+Route software provides internetworking capabilities such as the ability of a workstation to access files and resources on other networks without knowing their pathways.

Companies often need to connect networks in the same building that might have different hardware and packet configurations. 3+NetConnect provides a bridge between two Ethernet LANs and between an Ethernet and a token ring network. 3+Route is a program based on Xerox's XNS internet protocol, which enables several different local area networks to be linked together. Because of the Name Service, all users can access resources by name without having to define a path from their workstation to the resource. 3+Route provides (with 3+Mail) full electronic mail service to the interconnected network users.

The 3+Route software permits a network supervisor to establish authorized calling times to reduce telephone costs. He or she can set up as many as eight access windows with time schedules on each for dialing out.

Figure 6-8.
3+3270 Connecting a
LAN to an IBM
Mainframe *(Reprinted*
with the permission of
3Com Corporation)

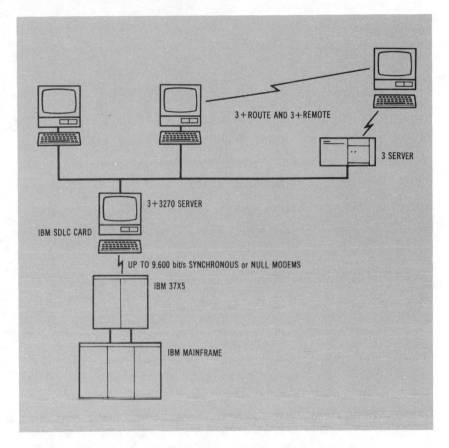

For busy internetwork traffic the program will support up to five ports on a 3Server with the Port Expansion Board, which automatically looks up telephone numbers for dialing other networks. If a primary number is busy, you can specify up to fifty alternate telephone numbers. 3+Route supports up to 2400 baud dial-in or 9600 baud direct while being run concurrently with 3+Share or 3+Mail. If greater speed is required, 3+Route's XNS protocol also supports Bridge Communication's high-performance communication servers. Figure 6-9 shows a local area network using 3+Route.

ELECTRONIC MAIL ON 3COM NETWORKS

Major 3+Mail Features

3+Mail has store-and-forward capability, which means that users can edit, save, and print messages as well as add attachments and require notification of receipt.

The 3Com Mail Service has store-and-forward capability, which means that messages can be transmitted with instructions to deliver them at a later date. This software enables users to compose a message, save it in a file for later editing, and add attachments to it before transmitting it. These attachments can be spreadsheets as well as word-processing documents.

Some other major features of the Mail Service include the ability to print, save, or delete messages received and the ability to rearrange messages

Figure 6-9.
3+Route Providing
Internetwork
Connections *(Reprinted*
with the permission of
3Com Corporation)

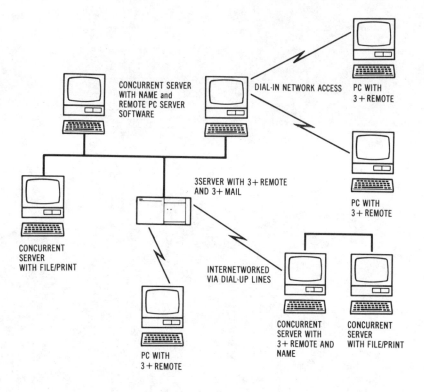

just as you might rearrange the incoming mail on your desk according to
sender or date. The Mail Service also provides the option of return receipts,
so that a user can request automatic notification of when a recipient reads a
message. This eliminates the common corporate excuse that "I missed the
meeting because I never saw your memo." A Mail Minder Service alerts users
that they have mail waiting to be read in much the same way that the Post
Office will leave a note on your door indicating that you have mail waiting to
be picked up. The Mail Service also allows you to search for specific
messages based on criteria you select, such as all letters from John Jones.
Under 3+ Open the Mail Service has the following parameters:

Maximum message length: 20 kilobytes (about 10 pages)
Maximum number of individually named recipients: 1,000
Maximum number of attachment files: 25

In this chapter, we'll discuss these major Mail Service features by
observing how a typical network user relies on electronic mail to help with
many routine tasks. 3+Mail is essentially the same whether it is run on a
DOS-based file server under 3+Share or on an OS/2-based server using LAN
Manager. Since Mary Worth, the personnel director for Polytex General, will
serve as our example, we'll spend some time looking over her shoulder as she
endures a typical Monday morning.

Mary Logs On to the Network and the Mail Service

When Mary sits down at her desk, she turns on her computer to become part of the Polytex General 3Com 3+ Open local area network. She first must log on to the network with a name that the Name Service will recognize:

login2 maryw:Pers:Polytex <ENTER>

Mary's applications directory, which contains the Mail Service, is located on drive E, whereas her home directory is on drive H. She first must link to this applications directory found on the LAN Manager server named ADMIN:

net use e: \\admin\os2apps

Under an MS-DOS 3Com network, Mary would have typed "dosapps" rather than "os2apps." She now links to her home directory (mworth) on drive H:

net use h: \\mworth <ENTER>

Finally, now that Mary has linked to her home directory, she can access her inbox found on drive E by starting the Mail Service:

h: <ENTER>
mail2 e: \inbox <ENTER>

Under an MS-DOS LAN, Mary would have typed "mail" rather than "mail2."

Mary Examines Her Inbox

When Mary examines her inbox, which is illustrated in Figure 6-10, she finds several messages. The messages with asterisks are those that Mary has not yet read. The RE and FYI designations indicate that a message is a reply to a previous message or a forwarded message. ATC reveals that the document is an attachment. The subject portion of this inbox display of mail is also important because Mary may later choose to sort her mail according to a specific subject or to group all mail on similar subjects in file folders.

**Figure 6-10.
Examining an Inbox**

```
DOS  Locate  Arrange By   Folder  Mark  Send  /for menu

  10    09-12-90   Frank Wilson       FYI: New Training Schedule
  12    09-13-90   Sue Willoby        RE: New Hire Pay Procedures
 *14    09-14-90   Frank Zaslow       RE: Budget Request
 *15    09-14-90   Neil Jackson       RE: EEO
 *15A   09-14-90   Neil Jackson       ATC: EEO Statistics
 *16    09-14-90   Mary LaBorde       RE: New Employee Welcome
 *17    09-14-90   Sharon Leider      RE: Training Proposal
 *18    09-14-90   Gil Gilbert        RE: Computer Training




F1=Help F2=Show F3=Del F4=Print F5=File F6=Repl F7=Forw F8=Get F9= New F10=Done
```

The 3+ Open Mail program is menu-driven, and these menus serve a wide variety of functions. The OS (operating system) menu permits you to return to the operating system by exiting the Mail Service. The Locate menu is used to locate a specific message or messages based on criteria you specify.

The Arrange By menu is used to sort mail in a variety of ways, such as by subject, date, or sender. The Folders menu is used to manipulate folders, including creating, opening, and copying them. The Mark menu is used to mark or unmark messages in an inbox or open folder. Finally, the Send menu is used to designate whether a message requires a return receipt or whether all messages are being sent in a batch.

Notice that the bottom of Mary's screen contains some function key options. She can find additional help on any Mail Service topic by using her <F1> key. Mary uses her <F8> key to retrieve her mail, which is transferred from the network mail server to her workstation. She can use her cursor keys to move down her screen and highlight the specific message she wants to read. If Mary has received dozens of messages, she can use her <PgDn> and <PgUp> keys to move through the list. She also can use her <End> and <Home> keys to move to the end of the list or back to the beginning of the list.

Once Mary has highlighted the message she wants to read first, she presses her <F2> key to retrieve it. Table 6-1 lists the major inbox function keys available to her with 3Com's Mail Service.

Mary Reads Her Mail

Mary highlighted a message from Frank Zaslow before pressing her <F2> key to retrieve it. Figure 6-11 reveals how the message is displayed on her screen. If the message is short, Mary can retrieve additional messages using her <F2> key and display them on the same screen. Once Mary has selected and retrieved Frank's message, the asterisk indicating it is an unread message will no longer be present. It is possible to replace the asterisk with a letter or symbol of your own choice to represent a particular type of correspondence you wish to identify for later sorting. If Mary found that she had received several letters referring to affirmative action, even though this was not the subject listed, she could place an "A" in front of each message on her list so that she could later locate these items and group them in a folder. Alternately, her symbol could represent an action that she wanted to take at a later time. She might place a "P" next to messages she wanted to print and an "F" next to messages requiring filing.

**Figure 6-11.
Frank Zaslow's
Message Displayed on
the Screen**

```
    Date: 09-14-90
    From: Frank Zaslow:ADMIN:Poly
      To: Mary Worth
      cc: Bill Sadler
    Subj: Budget
    ------------------------------------------------------
    Mary, do you see any problem in getting your new
    budget to me by tomorrow? I have to consolidate
    all department budgets and make my presentation
    Friday. Let me know whether you can meet this
    deadline.
```

Once Mary reads Frank's message, she has several options available through both the function keys and the pull-down menus. She can choose to delete the message by using the <F3> key, print it by pressing <F4>, file it using <F5>, or forward it using <F7>.

Printing a Message

To print a hard copy of Frank's message while it is still displayed on her screen, Mary presses <F4>. Since Frank's message is listed as message #3, the Mail Service will display the following:

Printing e:\inbox\3\msg

If Mary wished to print a message that was not displayed on her screen, she would use her cursor keys to move through the inbox until the line containing the specific message was highlighted, and then she would press <F4>.

Replying to a Message

Let's assume that Mary wants to reply to Frank's message. When she presses <F6> to reply, the message header and text body of Frank's message are displayed with space above in which to type her message. Frank will be able to see immediately which message Carol is responding to. Notice that the From and To fields are filled in by the program. If Mary wants a copy of this reply, she will press <F6>, which adds her to the cc list. By pressing <F5> she can add all the people in Frank's original cc list to her cc list for this reply. Figure 6-12 displays Mary's reply. When she is finished, she presses <F10> to leave the message editor portion of 3+ Open Mail and then <F6> to send her message.

**Figure 6-12.
Mary Replies to a
Message**

```
Date: 09-14-90
From: Mary Worth
  To: Frank Zaslow:ADMIN:Poly
  cc: Bill Sadler
Subj: Budget
----------------------------------------------------------------

I will work on the budget today and have it on your desk by
noon tomorrow.  I have decided to include the new training
program we discussed.
```

Marking and Deleting Messages

Before writing any more messages, Mary decides that she wants to straighten out her electronic desk. She uses her cursor keys to move down through the list of messages in her inbox. When the cursor highlights a message she wants to delete, Mary presses the <Space Bar>. This action causes a greater than sign > to appear to the left of the listed message:

> 14   09-14-90   Frank Zaslow   Budget

For this example, let's assume that Mary finds seven messages to be deleted. After marking all messages she wants to delete, Mary presses the slash key

</> and then <M> to open the Mark menu. Figure 6-13 illustrates that at this point Mary can choose between selecting all or none of the messages she has marked. She selects "All" and presses <F3> to delete these messages.

Figure 6-13.
Selecting Messages to
be Deleted

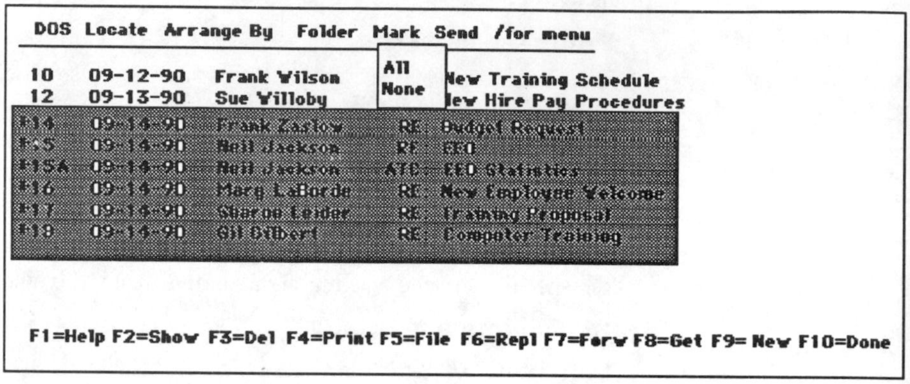

```
  DOS Locate  Arrange By   Folder  Mark  Send  /for menu

  10    09-12-90   Frank Wilson    All    New Training Schedule
  12    09-13-90   Sue Willoby     None   New Hire Pay Procedures
 #14    09-14-90   Frank Zaslow    RE: Budget Request
 #15    09-14-90   Neil Jackson    RE: EEO
 #15A   09-14-90   Neil Jackson    ATC: EEO Statistics
 #16    09-14-90   Mary LaBorde    RE: New Employee Welcome
 #17    09-14-90   Sharon Leider   RE: Training Proposal
 #18    09-14-90   Gil Dilbert     RE: Computer Training


 F1=Help F2=Show F3=Del F4=Print F5=File F6=Repl F7=Forw F8=Get F9= New F10=Done
```

There is a safeguard built into the deletion process. At this point the Mail Service will display the following question:

deleting 7 message (s) - are you sure? (y/n) ?

Mary presses <Y> and then <Return> and then presses <F3> to confirm her request for deletion.

Sending Mail with Attachments

Now that her inbox is straightened out, Mary decides she needs to send a message that will include some attachments. She presses <F9> to begin her message. The Mail Service will display a message header with "From" and "To" fields, with the "From" field already filled in with Mary's name. Mary will send this message to Bill Davis, so she types in his name and presses <Return>.

Mary can send the same message to several people by adding their names after Bill's and separating each name with a comma. As we shall see later in this chapter, the Mail Service also permits messages to be sent to groups. If Mary adds the name of a particular group such as the Budget Committee, the Mail Service will search its own records and send the message to everyone listed as a member of this group.

The cc field permits Mary to list anyone who should receive a courtesy copy of this message. It is simply an optional field and need not be filled in. Mary presses <Return> to bypass it and comes to the "Subj" field. This field may be up to thirty characters in length. For very short messages, some experienced Mail-service users will jot down a brief phrase in this field and bypass the text field entirely.

The next field, "Attachment," is where Mary lists the attachments she wants included with her message. As Figure 6-14 illustrates, Mary has indicated that she wants two Lotus 1-2-3 files, E:\EEO1.WKS and E:\EEO2.WKS, attached to her message. Notice that she must include the exact pathway so that the Mail Service can locate these files and include them when it transmits the message.

**Figure 6-14.
Attaching Worksheet
Files to a Message**

```
    Date: 09-14-90
    From: Mary Verth
      To: Bill Davis
    Subj: EEO Analysis
  Attach: E:\EEO1.WKS
          E:\EEO2.WKS

---------------------------------------------
Bill, the attached analysis shows that our affirmative
action efforts are starting to have an effect; I'm
particularly proud of the improvement in management
level recruitment (EEO2).
```

In an inbox each attachment is listed with a capital letter next to the message number. The letters ATC: precede the subject line of the attached message:

16   9-14-90   Bill Smith Affirmative Action Report
16A   9-14-90   Bill Smith ATC: EEO Guidelines
16B   9-14-90   Bill Smith ATC: EEO Report

As indicated earlier, the Mail Service permits a maximum of twenty-five attachments to a message. If an attachment is an application program data file such as the Lotus 1-2-3 spreadsheet Mary attached to her message, the recipient will need to save it first and then open it from the appropriate application program. In this case, for example, Bill highlights the appropriate attachment line in his inbox and then saves Mary's Lotus 1-2-3 spreadsheet file by pressing <F5>. The Mail Service then asks him for a path name. If he wants to save the file to a data disk on drive B, he might type the following:

B: \EEO1.WKS   <Return>

Adding a File to a Message

Let's assume that, while she is typing her message to Bill, Mary realizes that she needs to discuss some new EEO (equal-employment-opportunity) guidelines. She would like to include these guidelines on the same page as her message because she wants to discuss them and make it easy for Bill to understand the key points she will make. Since the guidelines are in a text file without any special word-processing control codes, Mary will be able to place them in her Mail Service message.

Mary places her cursor at the point where she wants the EEO guidelines file included and presses <Escape>, </>, and then <M> to display the Messages menu. Figure 6-15 displays her options at this point. Mary uses her cursor keys to highlight the "Include" option and then presses <Return>. She then types the name of the file and its pathway if it is located in any directory other than the current directory:

f: \eeo\guidelne <Return>

Besides limiting you to including text files, the Mail Service also does not allow files to exceed 20 kilobytes in size (approximately seven pages).

**Figure 6-15.
Displaying Message
Options**

Editing a Message

As Mary writes her message to Bill she can use the Mail Text Editor (MED), which provides some basic word-processing features such as the ability to delete words, entire lines, and blank spaces. It also permits some basic block functions such as marking a block of text and then copying it, moving it, or deleting it. Table 6-2 displays the MED function key definitions available to a Mail Service user. While composing a document Mary may also use various keyboard combinations to move rapidly through her document. Table 6-3 illustrates the MED keyboard definitions.

**Table 6-2.
MED Functions**
*(Reprinted with the
permission of 3Com
Corporation)*

Function Key	Description/Action
\<F1\> (Help)	Displays help information.
\<F2\> (Fill)	Removes excess space within paragraph created by additions and deletions.
\<F3\> (DelW)	Deletes the word where the cursor is located.
\<F4\> (Del2)	Deletes text from the cursor position to the end of the line.
\<F5\> (DelL)	Deletes the line where the cursor is located.
\<F6\> (Mark)	Marks text to be moved, copied, or deleted. Move the cursor to the beginning of the text you want to mark, then press \<F6\>; move the cursor to the end of the text you want to mark, then press \<F6\> again.
\<F10\> (Done)	Press \<F10\> to exit MED.

Leaving a Message Unfinished and Then Returning to It

While Mary is composing her message to Bill, her secretary interrupts to inform her that a department head would like her to meet and briefly chat with an applicant in his office. Mary saves her unfinished message, referred to by the Mail Service as an in-progress message (IP), by pressing \<F10\>. She presses \<F10\> again to indicate that she is done for the moment with the message but does not want to sent it. The Mail Service then asks her if she wishes to save the message to a current folder. Mary presses \<Y\> and \<Return\>, and the message is saved in Mary's inbox. If she had a folder open, it would have been saved in the folder.

After returning from the courtesy interview, Mary moves her cursor

Table 6-3.
MED Keyboard
definitions *(Reprinted*
with the permission of
3Com Corporation)

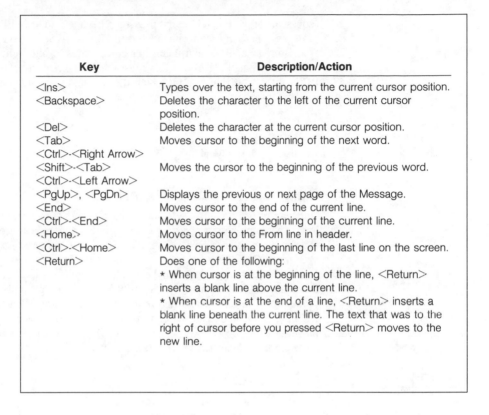

Key	Description/Action
<Ins>	Types over the text, starting from the current cursor position.
<Backspace>	Deletes the character to the left of the current cursor position.
<Del>	Deletes the character at the current cursor position.
<Tab> <Ctrl>-<Right Arrow>	Moves cursor to the beginning of the next word.
<Shift>-<Tab> <Ctrl>-<Left Arrow>	Moves the cursor to the beginning of the previous word.
<PgUp>, <PgDn>	Displays the previous or next page of the Message.
<End>	Moves cursor to the end of the current line.
<Ctrl>-<End>	Moves cursor to the beginning of the current line.
<Home>	Moves cursor to the From line in header.
<Ctrl>-<Home>	Moves cursor to the beginning of the last line on the screen.
<Return>	Does one of the following: * When cursor is at the beginning of the line, <Return> inserts a blank line above the current line. * When cursor is at the end of a line, <Return> inserts a blank line beneath the current line. The text that was to the right of cursor before you pressed <Return> moves to the new line.

keys to highlight the message she was writing to Bill and then presses <F2> to open it followed by <F7> to edit it. After completing the message, Mary presses <F10> to exit the Mail Text Editor and <F6> to send the message.

At this point Mary has sent the message displayed on her screen, but she has not saved this version. The version listed in her inbox is the previous incomplete version she saved before exiting the Mail Service to conduct her interview. Mary may decide that she wants to save this final version, or she may choose to delete the incomplete version listed in her inbox. We'll assume that she decides not to save the message and to delete the earlier version in her inbox using the procedure already discussed in this chapter.

Requesting a Return Receipt

Let's assume that, when it comes time for Mary to send her message to Bill, she decides that she wants a receipt indicating that the message arrived safely and was read, since Bill has a habit of turning off his Mail Service beep option and not checking his mail regularly. If the message is not acknowledged, she plans to call him or, if he doesn't answer his phone, to resort to the desperate and primitive option of leaving a message taped to his chair.

With 3+ Open Mail or version 1.3 or later of 3+Mail it is possible to request a return receipt. Mary presses <Escape> followed by </> and <S> to display the Send menu illustrated in Figure 6-16. She selects the "Registered Send" option using her cursor keys to highlight it and presses <Return>. When Bill reads this message, Mary receives a message marked RCPT indicating the date on which the message was opened and the name of the person opening it.

**Figure 6-16.
The Send Menu**

Using Folders to Organize Messages

One way of organizing electronic mail messages is to place them in folders in much the same way a person would organize paper messages. If Mary wants to keep all messages on EEO in one folder, she can create a folder by pressing </> followed by <F> to access the Folders menu displayed in Figure 6-17. Using her cursor keys, Mary highlights the "New Folder" option and then presses <Return>. The Mail Service then prompts her to provide a name (up to thirty-six characters long) for this folder. The eight-character DOS pathway restriction will shorten a name that exceeds this parameter, however. Mary types EEO and presses <Return>, thereby saving the message to a folder rather than saving it as a file to disk.

**Figure 6-17.
The Folders Menu**

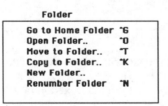

Messages can also be moved from the inbox or from one folder to another folder. Let's assume that Mary wants to move a message related to EEO that is currently in her inbox to her new EEO folder. She can use her cursor keys to highlight the specific message in her inbox, use the Mark menu option to mark the file, and press her </> and <F> keys to access the Folder menu. She can then use her cursor keys to highlight the "Move to Folder" or "Copy to Folder" option, depending on whether or not she wants to leave a copy of the message in her inbox. Finally, she completes the task by pressing <Enter>. Remember to copy or move messages associated with their attachments and not simply the attachments.

Searching for Mail Messages

Let's assume that Mary accumulates a good deal of electronic mail, which she dutifully tries to organize into meaningfully arranged folders. Occasionally, though, she needs to find information that may be scattered in a number of different places. Let's say that a particular employee, Fred Friendly, is now being accused of discrimination. Mary wants to locate every message she has received from Friendly, written with Friendly as the subject, or received that mentioned Friendly by name.

Although this task will take several steps, it is far easier and far more efficient than a manual search. Mary accesses the Locate menu by pressing </> followed by <L>, and here she finds several different options. She may choose to search through all messages from Friendly, look for all messages that mention Friendly in the Subj field, or search through the text in all messages. She may search through selected folders that she marks or may ask that all folders be selected.

Mary would probably choose initially to search through all folders for messages with Friendly as the subject. She might then search a second time through the text of the messages in her folders for "Friendly." If Mary had been coding all messages relating to Friendly by placing an F in the left margin of her inbox entry, she might also ask for a search based on the Note F.

Letting the Mail Minder Check for Mail

Having read her messages and sent some messages, Mary now is ready to exit the Mail Service program, so she presses <F10>. She also could accomplish this task by pressing <Ctrl> and <Q>. Although Mary has exited the Mail Service program in order to use her spreadsheet software, she does want to be notified if any important mail arrives. 3Com includes the 3+Mail Minder program with its Mail Service. This program is loaded into memory whenever Mary starts her workstation and remains there until she turns it off because the network supervisor edited her AUTOEXEC.BAT file on her 3+ workstation start-up diskette to include the command:

MMINDER

This program checks for incoming mail and then beeps and displays the window seen in Figure 6-18 when mail is received. The program will not interrupt another program running in graphics mode to display its window, but it will beep, assuming that the Beep parameter has been turned on. If Mary chooses not to be interrupted with a beep and sets Beep = OFF, she may still check to see if any mail has arrived even though she is working in another program. All she needs to do is to press the following key combination.

<Alt> + <Left Shift> + <M>

The Mail Minder will display either the message "You have Mail" or the message "No Mail."

Other Mail Minder parameters besides the beep include which key you wish to use to display the Mail Minder status window, how often you wish the window to check for new mail (1 to 32767 minutes, with a default value of 15 minutes), and the row and column locations where you want the status window to be displayed. All this information can be placed into an AUTOEXEC.BAT file so that you do not have to retype these parameters every time you run 3+Mail.

**Figure 6-18.
Message Minder
Indicates There's Mail**

```
┌─ 3+Mail Minder 1.2.1 ──────────┐
│                                │
│ You have Mail                  │
│                                │
│ ESC:  Close this window        │
│   C:  Check again              │
│   B:  Change beeping: /BEEP=OFF │
│   A:  Change Popup:   /AUTO=ON  │
│                                │
└────────────────────────────────┘
```

THE 3+ OPEN LOCAL AREA NETWORK

3Com has developed its 3+ Open LAN based on Microsoft's OS/2 operating system. In this section, we'll examine how this new 3Com product uses the many features that OS/2 offers.

OS/2 and LAN Manager

LAN Manager is Microsoft's network operating system that uses OS/2's rich collection of commands to perform its varied duties. It is comprised of two major components, a Redirector and a Server. Since OS/2 permits file servers to be nondedicated, the two components can in some cases reside on the same machine. In most cases, though, the Redirector portion of LAN Manager resides in each workstation where it intercepts and redirects calls from the I/O operating system to the network, where they can then be managed. The Redirector also starts and stops network operations and configures a workstation's use of network resources.

A file-server portion of LAN Manager assumes responsibility for file management, printer service, scheduling, and security. It also maintains statistics, monitors the network, and issues alerts if something goes wrong. 3Com licenses LAN Manager from Microsoft and uses it as the foundation of its OS/2-based 3+ Open network operating system.

In effect, LAN Manager is a platform that can be used by a LAN manufacturer such as 3Com to mount its own network operating system. LAN Manager supports a number of standard protocols such as NETBIOS.

What about communications between a 3+ Open LAN workstation and networks that do not use NETBIOS? 3Com has developed a brand-new approach to this problem, Demand Protocol Architecture (DPA), which includes a resident protocol manager that can deliver a host of protocols (including TCP/IP and some OSI protocols) to a workstation when it demands one. A workstation can request whatever protocol it needs to communicate with a particular type of computer system without having to maintain all protocols in its RAM.

3Com Network Driver Interface Specifications under OS/2

Microsoft and 3Com have jointly developed the Network Driver Interface Specifications (NDIS) found in OS/2. This set of specifications provides an interface falling within the data link layer of the OSI model that links together MAC hardware functions and MAC software.

The major significance of this new set of interface specifications is that it frees higher level protocols running under OS/2, such as those found in the transport layer, from any hardware specificity. Any network adapter card will work under NDIS, assuming it contains NDIS-compliant drivers. This interface ensures that 3Com LAN software running under OS/2 can run on token ring networks as well as on Ethernet networks.

3+ Open Features

3+ Open includes a menu-driven user interface that employs a mouse and pull-down menus that can be customized. Experienced users might prefer to use the available command structure. Security is greatly enhanced over the 3+Share version and includes the ability to assign access rights to user groups.

3+ Open supports Microsoft's Named Pipes, Mail Slots, and messaging applications programming interfaces. 3Com has reduced the size of workstation shell software from that in 3+ Open's first release by using the Demand Protocol Architecture discussed earlier in this chapter. This approach frees up enough RAM so that a DOS-based workstation on a 3+ Open LAN can load and unload multiple transport protocols on the fly. The reduced memory requirement also means that there is enough RAM under DOS to run programs such as Microsoft Windows and the Ashton-Tate/ Microsoft/Sybase SQL Server via the Named Pipes interface.

3+ Open NetConnect and 3+ Open Route provide internetworking for a 3+ Open network. Data-transfer speeds ranging from 300 to 19,200 bps are possible under 3+ Open Route. 3Com's Name Service makes internetworking connections transparent to users. 3Com also offers the Maxess SNA Gateway as a 3270 IBM SNA gateway for 3+ Open LANs. This hardware-software package supports up to thirty-two concurrent sessions, with each workstation able to run multiple sessions simultaneously. Users can use a hot key to shift back and forth between the 3270 and DOS environments. The package also supports multiple gateways on a single network.

SYSTEM FAULT TOLERANCE ON 3COM LANS

3+Fault Tolerant\DM software permits disk mirroring. The mirrored disk takes over in the event that the original hard disk fails, and up to 128 megabytes of data can be mirrored per server.

3+Fault Tolerant\SM software provides server mirroring. This approach is similar to disk mirroring but involves the entire server. If data has not yet been saved from a server to the failed original disk drive, it will be saved automatically to the mirrored server. Up to 256 megabytes of data per server can be mirrored.

WHAT HAVE YOU LEARNED?

1. 3Com offers a high-speed (10-mbps) LAN that uses a bus topology following the IEEE 802.3 standards.
2. Both 3+Share and 3+ Open are contention networks using a CSMA/CD approach.
3. 3Com offers a token ring network (TokenConnection) that follows the IEEE 802.5 standards of 4 mbps.

4. The 3+Share LAN is capable of remote access, internetwork connections, and multiuser software record locking under MS-DOS.
5. 3+ Open runs under the OS/2 operating system.
6. Micro-mainframe communication is possible on a 3Com network with 3+3270 software under 3+Share and Maxess SNA Gateway under 3+ Open.
7. 3+Mail permits electronic mail between different networks as long as 3+Route is also used.
8. 3+Mail contains a powerful editor (MED) that can be used independently of the electronic mail program to edit programs and text files.

Quiz for Chapter 6

1. 3+Share runs under
   a. DOS
   b. ProDOS
   c. UNIX
   d. OS/2

2. Ethernet illustrates a
   a. noncontention network
   b. token bus network
   c. contention network
   d. token ring network

3. A domain and an alias are associated with the
   a. Print Service
   b. File Service
   c. Name Service
   d. Mail Service

4. The 3Backup unit interfaces with 3Server through a
   a. parallel interface
   b. serial interface
   c. SCSI interface
   d. synchronous interface

5. 3Backup is capable of
   a. incremental backups of data
   b. automatic unattended backups of data
   c. backups of all file servers on the network
   d. all of the above

6. Thick (standard) Ethernet cabling can support network segments of up to
   a. 1000 feet
   b. 2550 feet
   c. 3280 feet
   d. 5280 feet

7. It is possible to connect multiple network segments with
   a. coaxial cable
   b. t-connectors
   c. transmitters
   d. repeaters

8. An Ethernet packet begins with a 64 bit
   a. introduction field
   b. data field
   c. error-checking field
   d. preamble field

9. A PC workstation located at another site can communicate with a 3+ series network by using
   a. 3+Remote
   b. 3+Route
   c. 3+3270
   d. 3+Path

10. A company that wishes to upgrade from the early EtherSeries to the 3+ LANs would use
   a. 3+Route
   b. 3+Path
   c. 3+Remote
   d. 3+Upgrade

11. The adapter card that must be installed in an expansion slot of each 3+ series workstation is called a(n)
   a. asynchronous communications card
   b. EtherLink Plus
   c. SerialLink
   d. 3+3270 card

12. The database that is used by all 3+ series programs is called
   a. the Name Service
   b. 3+Name
   c. Name+
   d. FileManager+

13. The three types of information needed when creating a user on a 3Com network are
   a. name, domain, organization
   b. name, position, title
   c. name, name of network, machine name
   d. user name, alias, nickname

14. People who wish to use a short
form of their user profile can use
a name known as their
   a. nickname
   b. alias
   c. user name
   d. company name

15. 3+Route offers
   a. automatic hangup
   b. alternate phone number list
   c. full error checking
   d. all of the above

16. The IEEE standard for
transmission at 10 mbps using
twisted-pair wire is called
   a. 10baseT
   b. TWP10
   c. BaseT10
   d. 10TBase

17. 3+Route is based on
   a. TCP/IP
   b. XNS
   c. NFS
   d. AFP

18. The 3+ Print Service permits the
customization of a particular print
job using
   a. 3+Set
   b. 3+Print
   c. 3+Custom
   d. 3+Option

19. 3+Mail provides security with
   a. login passwords
   b. passwords for inbox
directories
   c. encrypted messages
   d. all of the above

20. 3+Mail contains a powerful
message editor known as
   a. MESED
   b. MED
   c. ED
   d. WRITE

Macintosh Local Area Networks

ABOUT THIS CHAPTER

In this chapter, we'll examine some of the major Macintosh local area
networks. In addition to profiling Apple's LocalTalk hardware and
AppleShare software, which comprises an AppleTalk network, we will also
look at Novell's NetWare, 3Com's 3+Share, and Sun Systems' TOPS for the
Macintosh.

APPLE'S MACINTOSH HARDWARE AND SOFTWARE

LocalTalk

LocalTalk is the hardware
in an AppleTalk network.

LocalTalk is Apple's built-in network interface in its Macintosh computers
and LaserWriters. It handles the physical requirements of network
transmission as well as media access and can transmit data at 230.4 kbps
using a CSMA/CD method of controlling media access. The LocalTalk cabling
system consists of shielded twisted-pair wiring that is configured, according
to Apple, into a "multidrop bus." A drop cable connects a Macintosh to a
connection box, which in turn is connected to the network.

AppleTalk, on the other hand, is Apple's family of network software
protocols that controls everything from routing to file access. Before
examining specific network products we'll spend some time looking at these
important protocols.

APPLETALK PROTOCOLS AND THE OSI MODEL

Background

Apple has long desired to become a major provider of Fortune 500 local area
networks based on its Macintosh, but only recently has the company
developed a strategy that seems to be working. By developing a set of
protocols that are consistent with the OSI model discussed in Chapter 2,
Apple has provided major corporations with some assurance that its
Macintosh-based networks will be able to communicate with any IBM PC-
based LANs, since IBM has also moved toward OSI-model compatibility. If
both computer giants provide OSI-compliant networks that use the same
international standards, then it is reasonable to assume that these networks
will be compatible.

Apple designed its AppleTalk network to be consistent with the OSI
model. AppleTalk Filing Protocol (AFP) follows the layered approach
developed by the ISO to facilitate communications among heterogeneous
networks. Since AFP is critical to Apple's desire to make Macintosh-based

LANs an integral part of corporate America, it is worth taking some time to examine this protocol.

The Physical Layer

Figure 7-1 illustrates the structure of the protocols found in an AppleTalk network within the context of the OSI model. At the physical layer, Apple provides an interface for its own LocalTalk hardware. The LocalTalk circuitry is included with every Macintosh so that only a LocalTalk cable is needed to connect Macintosh computers together. As mentioned earlier, the problem with LocalTalk for larger networks is its limited transmission speed of approximately 230 kbps.

**Figure 7-1.
The AppleTalk Suite of Protocols**

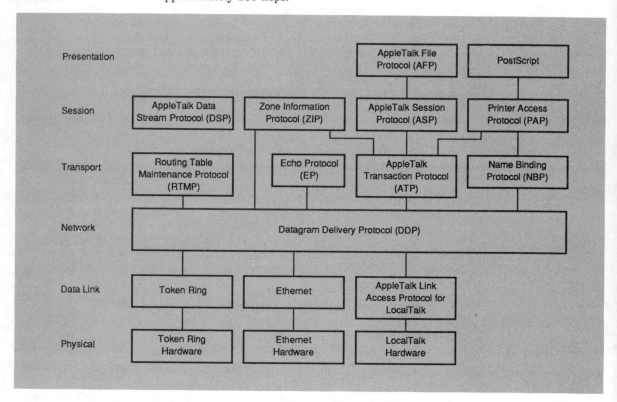

Apple File Protocol also supports Ethernet and the Token Ring Network for users requiring greater speed than LocalTalk hardware's 230 kbps.

Companies requiring faster network transmission can also implement Ethernet (10 mbps) and IBM's Token Ring Network (4 mbps) on an AppleTalk network. Both of these approaches would require the addition of network interface cards in each network workstation as well as appropriate network software. Apple as well as several other vendors offer this equipment.

The Data Link Layer

At the data link layer, an AppleTalk network provides a link-access protocol for Apple's own AppleTalk and for Ethernet and IBM's token ring hardware. In the not-too-distant future, there will also be a protocol for the popular Standard Microsystems' Arcnet. These link-access protocols provide the data link layer with directions for formatting a packet into frames with specifically defined fields as well as with a header and a trailer that include important control information. These protocols also provide specific directions for handling data collisions. As indicated earlier, Apple uses a traditional CSMA/CD approach for both detecting and avoiding data collisions.

The Network Layer

The network layer can access routing tables to establish a network path and use the Name Binding protocol to translate the network server's name into an acceptable internet address.

The network layer deals with the physical details of ensuring that a packet will be routed correctly from one network to another. Apple includes a Datagram Delivery Protocol (DDP) that provides a means of addressing specific logical ports or sockets on different networks. This protocol establishes the route a datagram (a self-contained packet of data) will take from its source workstation address to its destination workstation address.

The DDP is essential for Apple's interconnectivity with other networks because it can access vital information from routing tables to establish a network path for the datagram. The DDP can also use the Name Binding protocol found in the transport layer above it to translate the network server's name into an acceptable internet address.

The Transport Layer

The Routing Table Maintenance (RTM) protocol can provide alternative routes if a particular bridge is disabled.

An AppleTalk network's transport layer consists of four distinct protocols, all designed to facilitate the arrangements necessary to route a datagram from one network to another. Whereas the network layer handles the nitty-gritty details of the routing, the transport layer decides exactly what types of transport services are required, including acknowledgment of delivery, error checking, and so forth. The Routing Table Maintenance (RTM) protocol provides the information necessary for bridges to connect similar networks and for routers to connect different networks. For example, RTM gives detailed information on which bridges must be addressed (and how many "hops" it will take) to transmit a datagram from network 1 to network 4, and it can provide not only the preferred route for transport but also alternative routes if a particular bridge is disabled.

We have already mentioned a second transport-layer protocol, the Name Binding Protocol (NBP), in conjunction with the activities of the network layer. This protocol is responsible for matching workstation and server names with internet addresses. We might think of NBP as a service similar to one provided by many post offices. Although post offices like to process mail with complete addresses, often a letter addressed simply to "The Gas Company" will be properly routed to the city's lone gas company. The actual addressing, then, is transparent to the network user.

Transaction Protocol (TP)

The Transaction Protocol (TP) provides a guaranteed class of service for transporting datagrams, making it possible to receive an acknowledgment that a datagram was delivered error-free. This protocol is a critical component of OSI-compatible transport layers since a specific class of service may be required by certain network application programs.

The Echo Protocol (EP) is the final standard found in an AppleTalk network's transport layer. It provides an "echo" function by enabling the destination workstation to echo the contents of a datagram to the source network workstation. This echoing technique lets the network know that a workstation is responding and active and measures any round-trip delays encountered.

The Session Layer

The session layer on OSI-compatible networks establishes a communications session. In an AppleTalk network, this layer contains four protocols: the Data-Stream Protocol (DSP), Zone Information Protocol (ZIP), Session Protocol (SP), and Printer-Access Protocol (PAP).

The Data-Stream Protocol (DSP)

The Data-Stream Protocol (DSP) establishes communications sessions between nodes, which is the major task of the session layer. DSP can establish full-duplex communications, detect and eliminate duplicate datagrams, and request retransmission to ensure error-free service.

The Zone Information Protocol (ZIP)

The Zone Information Protocol (ZIP) maps networks into a series of zone names, which are instrumental in helping the NBP determine which networks are found in which specific zones. This information is also critical for establishing a delivery path for both routers and bridges.

Session Protocol (SP)

The Session Protocol (SP) found at the session layer in an Appletalk network places datagrams in correct sequence when they arrive out of order. SP also packages data into correctly sized datagrams and establishes break points during conversation sessions to ensure an efficient communication session.

Printer-Access Protocol (PAP)

The Printer-Access Protocol (PAP) in an AppleTalk network primarily provides streamlike service for printers and streaming tape systems when a network wishes to communicate with such devices.

The Presentation Layer

The presentation layer in an OSI-compatible network handles the way data is presented and the type of syntax used. In an AppleTalk network, two major protocols are found in the presentation layer, the AppleTalk Filing Protocol (AFP) and Postscript protocol.

The AppleTalk Filing Protocol (AFP)

The AppleTalk Filing Protocol (AFP) provides a critical interface for Apple's AppleShare file-server software and for Novell's NetWare file-server software. AFP also provides a Macintosh-like interface for other computers that now can serve as file servers on a Macintosh AppleTalk network.

AFP is concerned primarily with file structure. It provides the foundation for a network's hierarchical structure of volumes, directories, and files as well as appropriate login techniques. It also enables AppleTalk workstations to access a local or even a remote file server. A special translator program within AFP ensures that native AppleTalk file-system calls are translated into whatever equivalent required by the file server being accessed.

PostScript Protocol (PP)

The PostScript Protocol (PP) found at the presentation layer of an AppleTalk network provides the appropriate interface to ensure effective communications between network workstations and PostScript devices such as Apple's own LaserWriter.

APPLESHARE

AppleShare is Apple's file-server software for an AppleTalk network. Hard disks attached to the file server are known as *volumes*. Within each volume files are stored in folders, which correspond to directories under MS-DOS. Interestingly enough, security and access is at the folder level and not the file level. AppleShare's administrative software is called Admin, and it is used for such supervisory chores as setting up network users and work groups and creating reports for network users. These reports can provide such valuable information as the size and accessibility of individual folders on a volume.

Security features are built into the login procedure and the folder-access procedure and even allow a user to make files in a folder invisible to anyone but the person placing the files there. Figure 7-2 illustrates how a user can create this level of security.

**Figure 7-2.
Determining Access to
a Folder under
AppleShare**

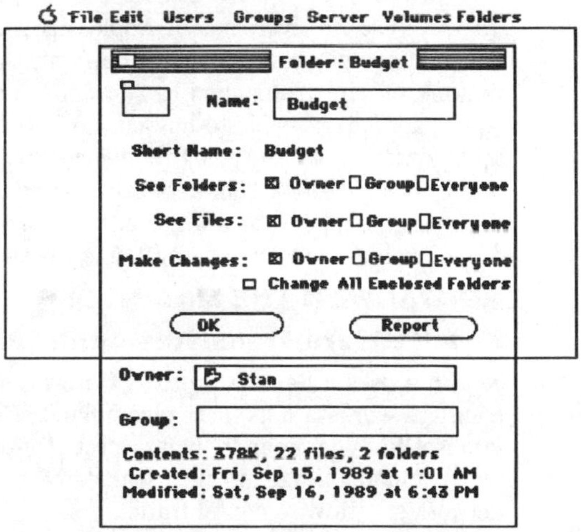

AppleShare makes full use of the Macintosh graphics interface. Figure 7-3 illustrates how an administrator can create a new user. Apple IIe and Apple IIGS computers can function as AppleShare workstations and can share their files with other network users of an AppleShare file server. Apple IIe computers require an Apple II Workstation Card whereas the Apple IIGS has LocalTalk hardware built-in. PC users can also connect to an AppleTalk network by installing a LocalTalk PC card, which enables them to access AppleShare files and printers. AppleShare PC software includes the MS-DOS Redirector, which converts all DOS file-system requests to server message blocks (SMBs). A special program then converts SMBs to AFP calls that can be understood on an AppleTalk network. The PC user will still see a conventional MS-DOS screen since Apple's software follows all MS-DOS conventions.

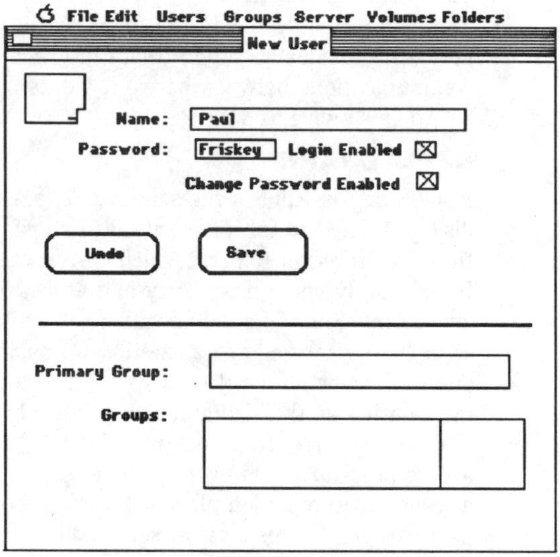

**Figure 7-3.
Creating a New User
under AppleShare**

The first versions of AppleTalk software limited users to 32 workstations per zone, a workgroup unit that is arbitrarily assigned by a network administrator, and to 254 nodes per network. Under Phase 2 AppleTalk it is possible to have up to 256 zones per network with support for up to sixteen million AppleTalk devices and routing support for up to 1024 interconnected AppleTalk networks. Although these numbers are theoretical, the routing support for a large number of workstations does make it easier for companies that have several small networks needing interconnectivity.

NETWARE ON THE MACINTOSH

How NetWare Translates AppleTalk Network Commands

NetWare uses a Service
Protocol Gateway (SPG)
VAP to translate the
Apple system calls of
Macintosh workstations
into NetWare commands.

NetWare uses a Service Protocol Gateway (SPG) illustrated in Figure 7-4 to translate workstations' native commands (in this case AppleTalk system calls) into NetWare commands. It interprets these commands and then responds with commands that are then translated back into a form acceptable to the network's hardware configuration.

**Figure 7-4.
The Service Protocol
Gateway Translates
Protocols**

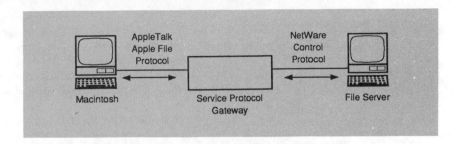

NetWare's Service Protocol Gateway is a Value-Added Process (VAP) that translates AppleTalk commands into its own Network Core Protocol (NCP). SPG in effect is an application that runs on top of a network operating system and allows NetWare and third-party processes to be linked into a network operating system running on a file server or bridge. For a NetWare file server to provide file services to Macintosh workstations, the SPG VAP and a special LAN driver VAP must be installed as well as additional VAPs for print services.

Bridging the Gap between the Macintosh and IBM PC

Since NetWare is a distinct network operating system that is hardware-independent, it provides an effective bridge between the IBM and Apple worlds. A Macintosh workstation using NetWare v2.15 (and above) can see and access both the Macintosh and the PC files displayed on its NetWare file server. DOS files are stored in standard HFS format, and files produced by application programs available for both machines (Microsoft Word, PageMaker, and WordPerfect, for example) do not need to be converted.

Under NetWare, a Macintosh network can use an IBM Intel 80286-based or 80386-based computer as a file server.

One major advantage of Novell's approach is that a Macintosh network can use Intel 80286-based and 80386-based computers as file servers. These units provide high performance at lower prices than comparable Macintosh units. Also, since NetWare can handle up to 2 gigabytes of disk storage on a single file server, large-capacity hard disks are still less expensive for IBM machines than their Macintosh counterparts.

DOS-based workstations on a Macintosh network under NetWare can use Apple printers.

Equally important, NetWare supports Macintosh print spooling, which is compatible with the AppleTalk Printer-Access Protocol (PAP). IBM PC workstations under DOS or OS/2 can access ImageWriters and LaserWriters that are part of an AppleTalk network. These printers can be configured on IBM software respectively as C Itoh Prowriters and Diablo 630 printers. The network also has Postscript printer drivers built into its AppleTalk protocol suite.

Because NetWare is able to distinguish its own IPX packet format from Apple's format for its own file server, AppleShare file servers can also be accessed on a NetWare network. Similarly, Macintosh computers using EtherPort network interface cards and running NetWare can access IBM PC workstations with standard Ethernet network interface cards that are also running NetWare.

NetWare for the Macintosh contains a utility program that converts Apple filenames to DOS filenames, since the two operating systems have different rules for naming files. DOS limits filenames to eight characters without spaces in between the letters whereas Apple files can contain up to thirty-one characters. DOS interprets a period in a filename as the separator between filename and extension and lists the first three letters after a period as the extension. The Apple filename MY PROPOSAL would translate into the DOS filename MY, and the Apple file MR.AND MRS. SMITH would become MR.AND.

One problem with this automatic conversion process is that, since the program truncates Apple names, two files could appear to have the same DOS name. The solution is that the Apple filenames are converted with the last character in the second filename of the DOS display appearing as a number, so that the Macintosh files MY.FILE 1 and MY.FILE would appear on a DOS workstation's screen as MY.FIL and M1.FIL. DOS files are displayed in Apple folders with the word DOS appearing in the document icon (picture) and all letters appearing in upper case. Figure 7-5 indicates what a Macintosh user would see.

**Figure 7-5.
DOS and Apple Files
Displayed**

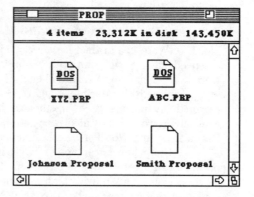

How NetWare Volumes are Depicted on the Macintosh

NetWare will display a list of available volumes in a volume dialogue box. You may select as many volumes as you wish to work with. One very nice feature of this login process is that you can specify that your name and password be saved along with the list of volumes you have selected. From that point on, whenever you log in to the network, you'll be logged into these volumes automatically.

NetWare volumes on the Macintosh are depicted using the Macintosh icons. The SYS volume, for example, can be selected and clicked to reveal several file folders including LOGIN, MAIL, PUBLIC, and SYSTEM.

You may drop files into dropbox folders but not see what is inside.

As Figure 7-6 reveals, a volume can contain several different types of folders: gray, dropbox, plain, black-tab gray, and black-tab plain. A gray folder is unavailable for use, which means that you cannot open it, copy files into it, or make any modifications. The arrow above dropbox folders symbolizes that you can drop files into these folders, but you cannot see what's inside.

Figure 7-6.
Different Types of
Folders Available

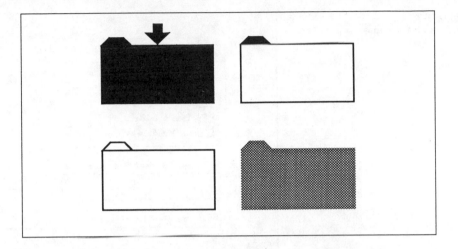

Plain folders, on the other hand, permit you to open them and see the files contained therein. Your rights, a subject we will discuss shortly, determine what else you can do with these files.

Finally, black-tab folders enable you to modify the folder's security. You can change your own rights inside the folder, which may result in a change of the folder's color from gray to plain.

To create a new folder, you simply select the New Folders command from the File menu. When an unlabeled new file folder appears on your screen, you can type a name for it. NetWare will take a Macintosh file folder name and convert it (by eliminating spaces and truncating it) into a form that DOS will accept.

Files can be named and saved directly into a folder that exists on a specific volume. In Figure 7-7 we see that we are given a series of choices for folders into which to save a file. Files can be flagged to give them any of the following special attributes: Read-Only, Shareable, Hidden, Indexed, Modified Since Last Backup, System, and Transaction Tracking.

Security on a Macintosh NetWare Network

The equivalent to NetWare's Parental rights does not exist on an AppleTalk network.

Users on Macintosh networks containing both AppleShare and NetWare file servers will find that files on the AppleShare server have AppleShare privileges whereas files on a NetWare server have NetWare rights. In other words, there is no AppleShare equivalent to NetWare's Parental rights. In this section we'll examine how the Macintosh version of NetWare displays such information as effective rights and trustee rights as well as a number of other security issues.

NetWare's Macintosh version permits users to select a parent folder to view security options. By double clicking, the user's screen changes so that a list of folders nested within the selected parent folder appears below. If we select a folder at this point and click the Folder Info button, we'll see a display similar to that shown in Figure 7-8.

Figure 7-7.
Folders in a Volume

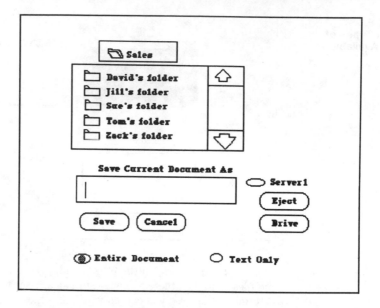

Figure 7-8.
Options for Files

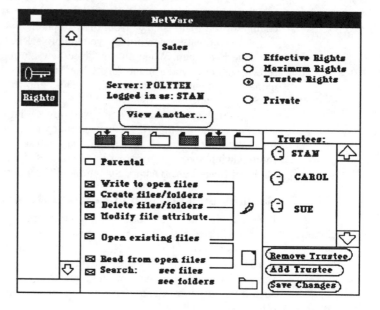

The folder's (or volume's) effective rights displayed in Figure 7-8 are the trustee rights assigned that are included in the maximum-rights mask. Notice that this Macintosh version of NetWare uses the pen, paper, and folder icons already familiar to Macintosh AppleShare users. Although NetWare on the Macintosh offers essentially the same type of rights discussed in Chapter 3 (with some small exceptions), the icon-oriented appearance is striking. Figure 7-9 illustrates how we can view groups and add trustees that we want to assign to a folder.

**Figure 7-9.
Viewing Groups and
Trustees**

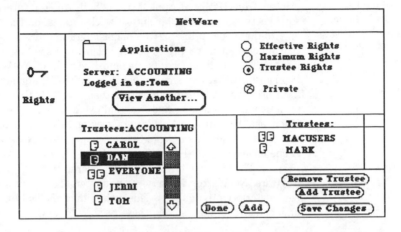

The NetWare Control Center

The NetWare Control
Center contains key
information on users,
groups, servers, volumes,
folders, and files.

The heart of NetWare for the Macintosh user is the NetWare Control Center, where network information concerning users, groups, servers, volumes, folders, and files may be viewed and modified. The Network Control Center probably will appear as an icon on a file server. When you double click on this icon it begins searching for NetWare file servers. If you are not logged on to some of these file servers, you may do so by double clicking on the file server icons as they appear.

The NetWare Control Center menus include the following: Server, Volumes, Folders/Files, User, and Groups. A sample screen appears in Figure 7-10. The Server window is divided into left and right panels. The left panel contains icons for each file server on the network whereas the right panel contains icons enabling you to access appropriate information on users, groups, and volumes linked to that file server. You may access information on only one file server at a time.

**Figure 7-10.
The NetWare Control
Center**

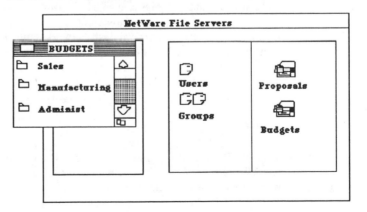

Printing under NetWare for the Macintosh

AppleShare software does not contain a print spooler. Under NetWare, Macintosh workstations print to a print-queue server that in turn spools the files to a printer.

DOS machines on a mixed NetWare network containing computers and printers from IBM and Apple can use both Apple printers and their own non-Apple network printers. Macintosh workstations, on the other hand, can print only to the Apple printers. One major limitation of AppleShare software is that it does not use a print spooler but instead sends files directly to its printers. Novell developed its Macintosh version of NetWare so that Macintosh workstations can spool to an AppleTalk queue server that emulates an Apple printer. This queue server then forwards the files to a NetWare print queue for spooling and eventual printing. The Chooser menu permits Macintosh users to see NetWare queues and the Apple printers attached to the network. Novell suggests that the supervisor create a separate print queue for each AppleTalk printer on the network.

There is one other major consideration when printing under NetWare. NetWare print services do not emulate printer-control codes or page-description languages. This means that application programs running under NetWare must supply these printer drivers.

3COM 3+ SOFTWARE ON THE MACINTOSH

Shortly after the birth of the Macintosh, 3Com was one of the first vendors to offer network software for it in the form of EtherMac. This primitive software (by today's standards) provided disk-server but not file-server capability. Today, 3Com offers 3+Share and 3+ Open network operating systems for IBM microcomputers as discussed in Chapter 6. At present 3Com provides only 3+Share for the Macintosh, but it does plan to offer 3+ Open for the Macintosh sometime in 1990. The 3+ Open version will include support for AFP. Since 3Com software contains support for Ethernet and XNS protocols, it can relieve many companies' concerns about internetwork connectivity.

3+ Services Available for the Macintosh

The standard 3+Share services discussed in Chapter 6 are available on a Macintosh network, including Name, File, Print, Mail, Route, NetConnect, and Backup. Since all 3+Share software uses the same naming convention and file format, it is easy to interconnect 3+Share networks composed of IBM microcomputers and Macintosh networks and then share files and communicate with 3Com's efficient electronic mail program. One can also combine the two types of workstations on a single 3+Share network. 3+NetConnect makes it possible to connect a Macintosh 3+ network with an Ethernet network or IBM Token Ring Network.

Security

The Macintosh 3+Share network provides a number of different access rights including Private, Read Only, Read/Write/Create, Shareable, Write Only, Read/Write, and Write/Create. Figure 7-11 illustrates the rights available when creating a new shared folder.

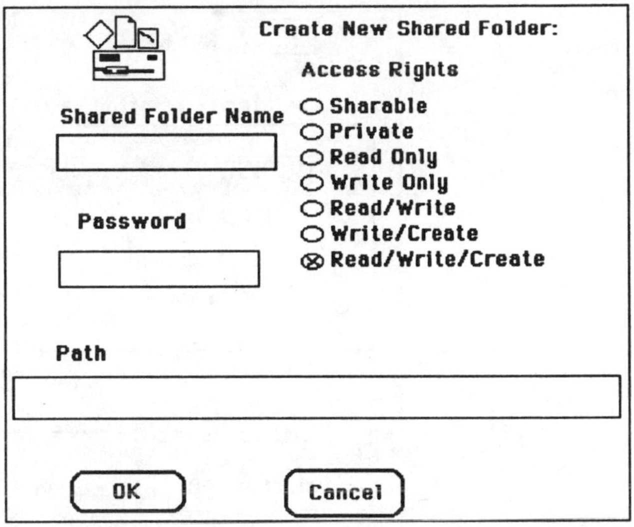

Figure 7-11.
Rights Available When
Creating a Shared
Folder under 3+Share
for the Macintosh

Figure 7-11.
Rights Available When
Creating a Shared
Folder under 3+Share
for the Macintosh

Printing on a 3+Share Network

Printing on a 3+Share network using a Macintosh is virtually identical to printing on the corresponding DOS-based network except for the Macintosh graphics interface. After linking to a specific printer, you send a file to be printed. The file goes to a print queue on the server, where it waits its turn. Figure 7-12 illustrates a typical print-queue screen. Each print job is illustrated with an icon that indicates its status. A picture of a printer means the document is printing, and a clock indicates it is waiting to be printed. A traffic light indicates that the print job has been deferred by the owner until a later time. A piece of paper with the upper-right-hand corner bent means that the document is still spooling. The user has selected a Hold option before sending files to be printed. All files sent by the user are added to this print job until the hold is released. A good example of why you might select this option is if you have several different documents to print during the day and want them to be available together at one time for convenient pickup.

Using 3+Backup on a Macintosh Network

3+Backup requires a 3Com server with a tape unit that has 3+Backup installed. Network administrators can select automatic or manual backups as well as full or incremental backups. A manual backup uses a dialogue box pictured in Figure 7-13 that enables you to select which drive partitions you wish to backup if you do not want a complete backup. The automatic option enables a supervisor to indicate when backups should take place. In Figure 7-14 a supervisor has established the company's weekly backup schedule and will click on the Save button to save this schedule.

Figure 7-12.
A Typical Print-Queue
Screen under 3+Share
for the Macintosh

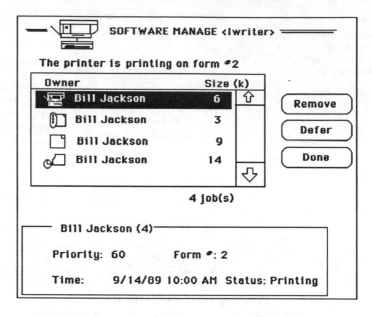

Figure 7-13.
A Manual Backup under
3+Share on the
Macintosh

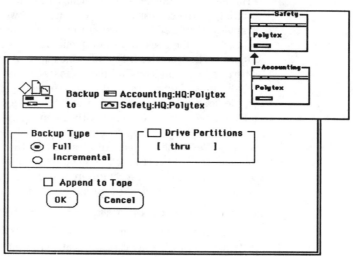

TOPS ON THE MACINTOSH

TOPS is one of the pioneers in Macintosh networking. Its TOPS/Macintosh makes it possible to link Macintosh computers with PCs and Sun workstations. Unlike other networks described in this chapter, which rely on centralized file servers, TOPS uses a peer-to-peer distributed approach in which workstations share resources.

TOPS works with LocalTalk and Ethernet cabling systems. When using LocalTalk cabling, TOPS generally runs on workstations that are daisy-chained together, with a maximum of thirty-two stations per daisy chain. A

**Figure 7-14.
Automatic Backup
Schedule under
3+Share on the
Macintosh**

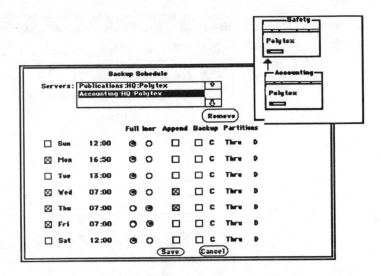

TOPS FlashBox using FlashTalk enables the network to transmit data three
times faster than AppleTalk's 230 kbps. A TOPS Spool program permits
spooling to an Apple LaserWriter, and TOPS NetPrint enables a DOS
workstation running a DOS application to print to an Apple ImageWriter II
or LaserWriter. A TOPS translator program translates PC file formats such
as WordStar, WordPerfect, and dBASE III into common Macintosh formats
and vice versa.

Publishing Resources

You can share your files with others on the TOPS network by publishing a
drive or folder containing your files, which is then called a volume. Figure
7-15 indicates that the user has published a disk, which now has a black icon
denoting its published status. It is impossible to publish an individual file. To
make a file available it needs to be placed in an otherwise empty folder or on
a floppy disk that is then published. Users who wish to make use of a
published resource select the folder or disk by clicking on the particular icon
and then clicking on the Mount button, which is also displayed in
Figure 7-15.

Some Considerations When Sharing Resources under TOPS

When you share your Macintosh's resources with other workstations on a
TOPS network, there are some important facts to keep in mind. It is far more
efficient if you organize your files into folders according to access. In other
words, documents you do not wish to publish can be grouped together as well
as documents that you wish to share only with password restrictions.

Another consideration is the different nature of filenames on
different machines. Whereas a Macintosh file, directory, or folder name can
have up to 31 characters, including blank spaces, a DOS file is restricted to 8
characters with no blank spaces and a 3-character extension. UNIX filenames

**Figure 7-15.
A TOPS Spool Screen**

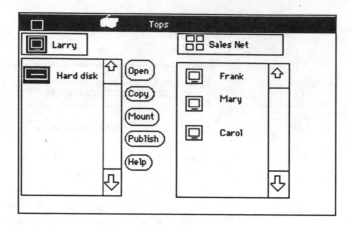

can be up to 256 characters in length. Since names will be truncated when moving to another machine, it is important to select names carefully.

Printing under TOPS

As mentioned earlier, TOPS offers a background print spooler called TOPS Spool. This utility generates a PostScript file when a file sent to the LaserWriter is redirected to a temporary disk file. Figure 7-15 illustrates a TOPS Spool screen.

Translating Files with TOPS Translators

Earlier in this chapter we indicated that TOPS has a utility program that makes it relatively easy to translate from one file format to another. Figure 7-16 displays the TOPS Translators screen. Notice that you also set the direction of the file transfer. Another screen available with this utility indicates your preferences. You can specify whether you want to be notified if there are filename conflicts and whether you want to assign all filenames or let the program assign filenames.

**Figure 7-16.
TOPS Translators
Understand Both the
Macintosh and PC
Worlds**

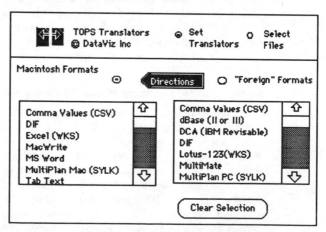

WHAT HAVE YOU LEARNED?

1. LocalTalk describes the physical network hardware Apple offers for its network.
2. AppleTalk describes the family of networking suites offered by Apple.
3. AppleShare is Apple's centralized file-server software.
4. NetWare uses a Service Protocol Gateway to translate AppleTalk commands into NetWare commands and vice versa.
5. 3Com's 3+Share software contains protocols that make it easy to link Macintosh computers with IBM PCs running under Ethernet.
6. TOPS is a distributed network environment in which workstations share resources by "publishing" them.
7. TOPS makes it easy for Macintosh computers to communicate with Sun workstations as well as with IBM PCs.

Quiz for Chapter 7

1. Apple's network hardware is known as
   a. CheapTalk
   b. TinkerTalk
   c. AppleTalk
   d. LocalTalk

2. Apple's major network protocol is called
   a. SpeakEasy
   b. Apple Filing Protocol
   c. Apple Universal Protocol
   d. Macintosh OSI Protocol

3. AppleTalk networks transmit at speeds of
   a. 1 mbps
   b. 4 mbps
   c. 230.4 kbps
   d. 188 feet per second

4. AppleTalk provides link-access protocol for all but one of the following:
   a. LocalTalk
   b. Ethernet
   c. IBM's Token Ring Network
   d. Xnet

5. AppleTalk networks are mapped into a series of
   a. zones
   b. area codes
   c. regional centers
   d. AppleAreas

6. Apple's LaserWriter requires the _____ protocol.
   a. AppleSoft
   b. PostScript
   c. RS-232-C
   d. V.35

7. Security under AppleShare is at the _____ level.
   a. bit
   b. file
   c. folder
   d. document

8. Under Phase 2 of AppleTalk, it is possible to have up to _____ zones per network.
   a. 32
   b. 64
   c. 128
   d. 256

9. To translate AppleTalk system calls into NetWare commands, NetWare uses
   a. SBM
   b. SPG
   c. NETBIOS
   d. SPM

10. Under NetWare on the Macintosh, a 31-character Macintosh filename would be converted into a DOS filename of _____ characters with an extension.
    a. 5
    b. 8
    c. 15
    d. 31

11. Under NetWare, a gray folder is
    a. read-only
    b. create-only
    c. delete-only
    d. unavailable for use

12. Under NetWare, information concerning users, groups, servers, volumes, and folders is found in the
    a. help file
    b. NetWare Control Center
    c. group file
    d. information folder

13. The earliest 3Com network product for Macintosh was called
    a. EarlyMac
    b. EtherMac
    c. 3-Mac
    d. 3dMac

14. Internetworking under 3+Share on the Macintosh is the responsibility of
    a. 3+Name
    b. 3+Share
    c. 3+Link
    d. NetConnect

15. Backup on a 3+Share network for the Macintosh is handled by
    a. Backup +
    b. 3+Backup
    c. 3+Save
    d. Backup 3 Plus

16. TOPS represents a
    a. distributed network
    b. centralized network
    c. centralized file server
    d. centralized workstation

17. To share a resource with another workstation, a TOPS workstation must first _____ it.
    a. publish
    b. mount
    c. copy
    d. delete

18. To increase LocalTalk speed under TOPS, use
    a. TOPSBURN
    b. FLASHBURN
    c. FlashTalk
    d. Flasher

19. To translate from one file format to another under TOPS, use
    a. TOPS Translators
    b. TOPS Convert
    c. TOPS File
    d. MAC-to-PC TOPS

20. To spool a file for printing under TOPS, use
    a. Spool it
    b. PrintSpooler
    c. StorePrint
    d. TOPS Spool

AT&T's Local Area Networks

ABOUT THIS CHAPTER

AT&T's STARLAN is a low-cost bus network that illustrates the company's open architecture philosophy. In this chapter we will take a close look at STARLAN's hardware and software and explore why it might be an ideal solution for a small department or a large company that is considering departmental networks. Because AT&T is committed to linking its DOS-based STARLAN with its UNIX-based minicomputers, we will look at what this connection can mean for a company. We will also examine how STARLAN links to AT&T's powerful Information Systems Network (ISN) and how ISN offers true voice and data integration. Finally, we will look at how ISN supports the new Integrated Services Digital Design (ISDN) standards that will become more and more important in the near future.

STARLAN and STARLAN 10 Hardware

AT&T designed the STARLAN network to be as simple as possible. Up to ten PC workstations can be linked together by installing a Network Access Unit (NAU) in each workstation's expansion bus and then using unshielded twisted-pair telephone wire to daisy-chain these units together. Each NAU has three telephone jacks. The IN jack of one unit is connected to the OUT jack of another unit. The third jack is used for connecting an analog phone to a workstation. One workstation with a hard disk is designated as the file server, and each workstation installs a copy of the STARLAN software. AT&T refers to workstations that use a file server as "clients." Figure 8-1 shows how a small daisy-chained STARLAN network would look with an AT&T 6300 Plus used as a file server. The maximum distance permitted for a daisy-chained STARLAN network is 400 feet.

The Network Access Unit (NAU)

Each network workstation requires a Network Access Unit (NAU) circuit card. STARLAN NAUs transmit at 1 mbps and STARLAN 10 NAUs transmit at 10 mbps. Both networks use CSMA/CD to avoid data collisions.

As we just pointed out, the Network Access Unit (NAU) is required in each network workstation. There are actually three different kinds of NAUs. STARLANs with PCs or PC-compatibles as file servers require the PC NAU. IBM PS/2 microcomputers require an MC 100 NAU designed for this computer's microchannel bus. And AT&T's own 3B2 minicomputers require a 3B2 NI card which is Ethernet-compatible. STARLAN NAUs transmit at 1 mbps whereas STARLAN 10 units transmit at 10 mbps. Each NAU comes with a ten-foot, twisted-pair, modular cable. You can order longer cables from AT&T, but their length cannot exceed 328 feet (100 meters) between any two network devices.

    In addition to the three telephone jacks we have already mentioned,

**Figure 8-1.
A Small STARLAN
Network**

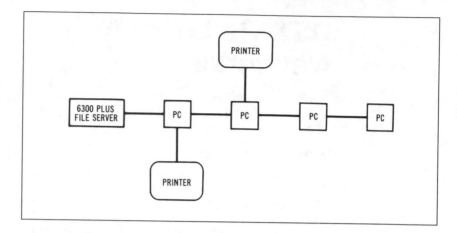

each NAU also contains 8K or 32K of RAM, network-addressable ROM, and a CSMA/CD controller. STARLAN is a baseband contention network that transmits data at 1 mbps using a CSMA/CD approach. The NAU uses a shared memory system that makes it appear that the memory resides in the host's main memory even though it is physically found on the NAU itself. The CSMA/CD coprocessor accesses this memory as do the computer's read and write operations.

Network Hub Units (NHUs)

A Network Hub Unit (NHU) can link eleven workstations directly together in a star topology or can be used as a master unit with eleven secondary NHUs to create a two-tier network with up to 1210 units.

A Network Hub Unit (NHU) expands a STARLAN network beyond ten workstations by enabling a network supervisor to connect as many as eleven workstations up to 800 feet from the NHU in a star topology. One NHU can also act as a master unit and link up to eleven secondary NHUs, each with star topologies, creating what is known as a two-tier star. This arrangement can support up to one hundred active workstations and as many as 1210 physical connections. The NHU also contains one AUI port, which allows connections for existing coax-based Ethernet networks. 3B2 NIs installed in 3B computers can also be attached to the NHU via the AUI. An NHU can be mounted in a telephone wiring closet or in the same room as the workstations. The NHU has one port labeled OUT that is used to connect it to another NHU or to a Network Repeater Unit (NRU). A connector on the NHU attaches to a wall-mounted transformer that provides low-voltage AC. The NHU also amplifies and retimes network signals before transmitting them, detects and isolates jabber conditions caused by a faulty device or connection, and detects the presence of network traffic and collisions and indicates these with its LEDs. Each NHU must be within ten feet of a commercial power outlet that is not switch-controlled. Figure 8-2 shows how an NHU creates a star topology.

An important network design consideration is that STARLAN and STARLAN 10 NAUs and NHUs are not interchangeable. It is possible, however, to bridge the two networks, a subject that will be discussed later in this chapter.

**Figure 8-2.
NHU Linking PCs
Together**

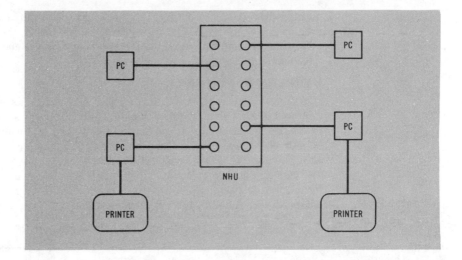

Media

STARLAN can use the new IEEE 10BaseT standard of two pair of
unshielded twisted-pair wire. STARLAN 10 wiring also is consistent with
AT&T's Premises Distribution System 62.5/125 micron optical-fiber cabling.
An AUI adapter is available that provides connections to Ethernet boards. As
mentioned previously, the AUI port on the NHU supports a variety of
connections, including standard thick coax, thin coax, fiber-optic, and
broadband coax cable.

File Servers

Workstations can access applications and share resources from file server
based either on DOS or on UNIX System V. A small group of DOS
workstations can be daisy-chained together and share resources without
needing a dedicated server. AT&T's PC6386 WGS is a PC workstation that
can run UNIX and file-server software, but AT&T also recommends its 3B2
family of minicomputers for this function. These larger computers permit up
to 15.9 gigabytes of disk storage when configured with SCSI Host Adapters.

AT&T offers file-server software for a 1-mbps STARLAN network
that can use the company's own proprietary software, including a 3B2 DOS
Server Program and a PC6300 Network Program. AT&T also markets a 386
Server Program, DOS Server Program, and 3B2 Server Program that run
under OSI protocols. The STARLAN 10 network must use a special version
(3.1) of these programs.

AT&T supplies recommended maximum simultaneous client numbers
as well as the absolute maximum number. Since AT&T's recommendations
are designed to keep the network running optimally, we'll use these values. A
6386 WGS, for example, has a recommended simultaneous client maximum
of thirty-two under DOS, whereas under UNIX this number increases to
sixty-four, illustrating the advantages of a true multiuser, multitasking
operating system. The 3B2 minicomputer can support fifty simultaneous

users. Although the smaller workstations can support only two parallel printers and one serial printer attached to the file server, the 3B2 minicomputers can support up to eleven parallel printers and between forty-five and eighty-eight serial printers.

STARLAN SOFTWARE

STARLAN's network software is consistent with the OSI specifications discussed in Chapter 2. Figure 8-3 indicates the network's different protocol layers. The physical layer is concerned primarily with providing transmission on a baseband network. The medium used is 24-gauge building telephone wiring consisting of two unshielded twisted pairs dedicated to STARLAN. The data link layer regulates this contention network by using CSMA/CD techniques consistent with IEEE 802.3 standards. The logical link control adheres to IEEE 802.2 standards and uses the LLC Type-1 connectionless protocol.

**Figure 8-3.
STARLAN Protocol
Layers** *(Courtesy of
AT&T)*

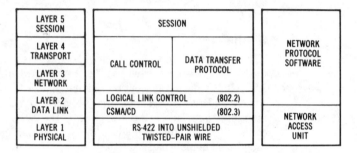

The network and transport layers establish point-to-point connections between two network endpoints, handling flow control, call administration, and error handling. Finally, the session layer uses MS-DOS protocols to establish sessions with application programs. It has a set of additional commands to enable it to establish sessions with UNIX-based computers running under STARLAN.

STARLAN Packet Structure

As pointed out in our earlier discussion of the OSI standards, the packet for one network layer becomes part of the information field of the next lower layer. The MAC sublayer of STARLAN follows the IEEE 802.3 standards. As seen in Figure 8-4, the MAC frame begins with a preamble used to synchronize receiver and transmitter. The start-of-frame delimiter (SFD) lets the hardware know when the synchronization is over and the message begins. The address part consists of both a destination address and a source address. The length field indicates the number of octets in the LLC data portion of the packet. User data is found in the next field, the LLC data area. The final two packet portions are the packet address destination (PAD) and frame-check sequence (FCS). The PAD is used to pad any packets that fall below the acceptable minimum of sixty-four octets of information. Finally, the FCS detects errors so that the MAC layer can discard defective packets.

**Figure 8-4.
MAC Frame**

PREAMBLE	SFD	ADDRESS	LENGTH	LLC DATA	PAD	FCS

Using STARLAN

All STARLAN commands are classified under the following three categories: Administration Services, File-Sharing Services, and Printer-Sharing Services. These commands can be entered four different ways: typing a command string, using command prompts, responding to network prompts, and using menus.

STARLAN's network software is similar to IBM's PC Network Program in that both programs are designed to be easy to use for beginners while allowing experienced network users to access the network with DOS commands and even to customize operations by creating DOS batch files. Both programs also offer beginners the opportunity to perform virtually all major network functions through the use of menus.

All STARLAN commands are classified under Administration Services, File-Sharing Services or Printer-Sharing Services. The Login and Logout commands along with commands to modify passwords, view statistics, and add and delete users are found under Administration (AD). To log on under STARLAN a user simply provides the type of command (AD), the actual command, a DOS path, and a password:

LOGIN AD \\servername \username
/PASS=password

To give several consecutive commands for the same command service, the user can use prompts to avoid typing the command service repeatedly. Typing the command service and pressing <ENTER> yields the prompt (AD, FS, or PS), and the user can then enter the commands. For instance, if the user wants to log in and then get help on how to use the ADDUSER command, he or she would type the following:

AD>login \\servername \user/pass=password help adduser

Rather than using command prompts, the user can choose to respond to STARLAN's prompts by typing a command prefix and the command name and pressing <RETURN>. He or she will be prompted by STARLAN to supply the file-server name, the user name, and a password if needed. By using network prompts a new user can enjoy faster network operation (rather than going through several menus) without needing to memorize all the network command structure.

The fourth way to enter commands is to use the STARLAN menus. These menus can be accessed by typing the command MENUS. Figure 8-5 shows what the STARLAN Main menu displays. Notice that there is a Command Bar displaying the commands available from this menu (Open, Transfer, Close, Window, Quit). The line below this is known as the Subcommand Bar and contains subcommands or, when there are none, descriptions of commands. A Window indicates the items to be selected. The last line contains the screen label keys that indicate which function key to press for a particular command. Notice that only two function keys are active on this Main menu, <F5> and <F8>. The commands on the Command Bar and the items in the window can be accessed by using the cursor arrows <UP>, <DOWN>, <LEFT>, and <RIGHT>. Commands can also be entered by typing the first letter of the command as seen in the Command Bar and then pressing <RETURN>. To open a highlighted file, for example, a user need only type O followed by <RETURN>.

Figure 8-5.
STARLAN Menu

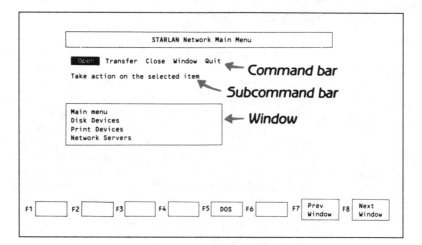

File Sharing

Each user has his or her own personal home directory, which may be protected with a password. Upon logging on to STARLAN, a user needs to establish a link between the workstation and his or her home directory located on the file server. Note that a user can log on to only one file server at a time. STARLAN's FS LINK command establishes this connection in a manner similar to the way workstations are linked to file servers on 3Com's 3+Share network software.

Since one of the major advantages of a network is the ability to share files, STARLAN offers a number of options in this area. You can copy files from your home directory to another user's directory, and you can place a copy of a file you wish to share in another subdirectory. To share files the subdirectory must be shared with other users by using the FS SHARE command. In most cases you would eliminate a password or use a password different from your own personal password. Finally, you can share your own home directory, but with this approach other users will have to know your password in order to link their directories with yours and thus you will lose your security.

Under STARLAN a network administrator can establish four levels of shared access to files on a file server: read, write, create, and exclusive. The exclusive option prevents two users from trying simultaneously to update a file and thus wiping out valuable information. All these options are outlined in Table 8-1.

8

**Table 8-1.
Levels of STARLAN
Shared Access**

Key	Access	Meaning
R	Read	Files in a shared directory can be read
W	Write	Files in a shared directory can be written to
C	Create	Files can be created in a shared directory
E	Exclusive	Only one user at a time can access a shared file

After placing material in a directory or subdirectory so that it may be shared, the user must provide a share name and pathway. Let's assume that Georgia has created a subdirectory called REGMTG in her home directory. This material contains the budget she is developing for a regional meeting. Although Georgia wants to share this information with others in her group, she also wants to keep her working copy from being changed. The solution is to create a subdirectory called REGPROJT using the DOS command MKDIR (make directory):

MKDIR E: \REGPROJT

The next step is to copy the contents of the subdirectory REGMTG to this new subdirectory using the DOS COPY command:

COPY C: REGMTG D: \REGPROJT
C> FS SHARE \REGPROJT

STARLAN will want to know a sharename—a name by which users will access this shared subdirectory. Georgia decides on BUDGET.

Sharename? BUDGET
\\SERVER1\GEORGIA\REGMTG shared as GEORGIA\BUDGET

At the moment, anyone on the STARLAN network can share this file. If Georgia wants to limit access, she can use the FS MOD command and create a password:

FS MOD BUDGET/PASS=password
\\SERVER1\GEORGIA\BUDGET modified

Anyone can always see a list of shared directories on a network by using the FS DIR command:

C> FS DIR
Object list for \SERVER1* . . .
GEORGIA C:\USER/HOME 0 links
TAX C: \TAX/RWC 0 links

Bridging STARLAN and STARLAN 10 Networks

AT&T offers a stand-alone desk bridge unit in two different configurations: the 1:10 bridge, which connects a STARLAN network to a STARLAN 10 network, and a 10:10 bridge, which links two STARLAN 10 networks or a STARLAN 10 and an Ethernet network. A bridge unit contains a motherboard and two LAN circuit boards. The 10:10 bridge contains two AUI ports, whereas the 1:10 bridge contains one AUI port for connection to a STARLAN 10 network and one modular jack for connection to an NHU.

The bridge is compatible with IEEE 802.3 and Ethernet standards and can link a range of media including twisted-pair, 10BASE5 (thick coax), and 10BASE2 (thin coax). It also supports fiber-optic MAU connections.

AT&T's bridges do have some restrictions. Only two networks can be bridged, and they cannot be bridged to a third network. The maximum cable length between hub unit and bridge is approximately 750 feet.

STARLAN Network Management

The STARLAN Network Manager (SNM) is AT&T's management software designed to handle networks with more than one hundred nodes. The program can be run from a host computer, from an RS-232C terminal, or from a PC with terminal emulation. Release 1.0 runs on the 3B2 minicomputer or the 6386 WGS and manages the 1-mbps STARLAN network whereas release 2.0 runs on a 6386 WGS and can manage both the 1-mbps and 10-mbps versions of STARLAN.

SNM uses an INFORMIX-based on-line database called the Network Configuration Database (NCD). This database can be configured to include such information as the building location of each node as well as moves and changes.

The SNM polls nodes to determine their status and provides a network map. The program provides on-line real-time reporting of any network errors as well as traffic data in bytes per second or percent of media capacity utilized. It also can monitor network traffic in terms of packets per second and provide error statistics, including the number of collisions and retransmissions.

ELECTRONIC MAIL ON AN AT&T LAN

PMX/STARMail is the LAN equivalent of AT&T's Mail Private Message Exchange software. In addition to being able to link STARLAN and STARLAN 10 networks, the mail system can also be connected with the public AT&T Mail Service, where messages can be delivered by the U.S. Postal Service, Airborne Express, and Telex as well as electronically. The Mail Service is compatible with the X.400 electronic mail standards, which is a critical consideration for companies desiring future OSI-compatibility. AT&T's Mail Service contains gateways to IBM's DIOSS and PROFS as well as to HP, Wang, and DEC Office Systems through AT&T's Mail Exchange.

PMX/STARMail is a graphics-oriented program that contains a DESK where messages are prepared, an IN BOX that holds incoming mail, an OUT BOX used for outgoing messages, and a WASTEBASKET for messages to be deleted. The program allows users to edit messages and to attach word-processing documents or spreadsheets to mail. What makes this particular mail program so unusual is that it reflects AT&T's ability to make communications between UNIX and DOS transparent to the end user.

STARLAN AND INFORMATION SYSTEMS NETWORK (ISN)

At first glance, STARLAN appears to be an effective network for a department or small business but of limited value for a larger company. AT&T does allow for expansion, however, if companies need more sophisticated network functions. Information Systems Network (ISN) is a high-speed network that can integrate voice and data transmission and provide interfaces to PBXs, IBM mainframes, Ethernet LANs, and its own STARLAN networks. Figure 8-6 shows the ways that ISN can integrate communications for a large company.

Figure 8-6.
ISN Links STARLAN
Networks, PBXs, and
Mainframes *(Courtesy of AT&T)*

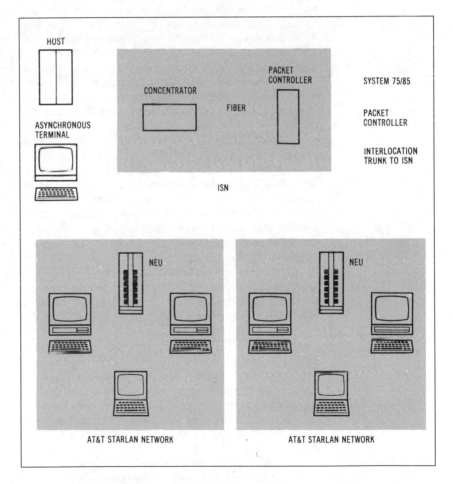

AT&T offers a STARLAN Interface Module (SIM) to connect STARLAN networks via its ISN. This option increases the effective distance for a STARLAN to several thousand feet. Each SIM has two jacks that can either connect workstations together on a STARLAN network or connect them to an NHU located on an ISN concentrator or packet controller. The SIMs come in two versions. The B version provides a bridge between multiple STARLAN networks through ISN, and the C version provides a connection between STARLAN nodes and RS-232 devices not on the STARLAN network but on ISN. So an AT&T DOS workstation on a STARLAN network, for example, could access a 3B2 computer on ISN.

The heart of ISN is a *packet controller* that acts as switch and management center. Concentrators collect data from host computers, STARLANs, and other devices and pass this data to the packet controller through multiplexed channels, each composed of a pair of optical fiber. ISN breaks down messages to very short packets (18 envelopes of 10 bits of data) and interleaves the packets into a sequence of time slots on the transmission bus. The transmission across this short bus is so fast that, in effect, ISN maintains virtual circuits, or direct links, between communicating devices with almost no blocking. An ISN packet controller can support up to 1200 simultaneous virtual circuits, more than enough for most large businesses.

The ISN packet controller contains three buses: the transmit bus, which carries packets from sending modules to the switch; the receiving bus, which carries packets away from the switch to device interface modules; and the contention bus, which determines the order of access to the transmit bus.

As Figure 8-7 illustrates, under ISN all modules that are ready to send data packets compete with each other for access to a time slot on the transmit bus. Each module transmits its own contention code to the contention bus one bit at a time. When a module recognizes that another module has a higher contention code, transmitting results. The winning module accesses the next data-packet time slot on the transmit bus. The data modules that have lost this round have their contention numbers raised at this point and begin competing for the next available time slot. The ISN switch is capable of a maximum switching rate of 48,000 packets per second.

Figure 8-8 illustrates some of the interfaces available through ISN. With the proper protocol ISN users can interface directly with asynchronous hosts or IBM 3270 terminals, thus eliminating the need for costly cluster controllers. Users can establish two sessions per terminal and switch between applications. Each protocol converter on the network contains seven asynchronous ports and one synchronous port. ISN supports Type A coaxial cable at 2.358 mbps as well as IBM 3278/9 and 3178/9 terminals.

A company with several departments might find it cost-effective to tie together several departmental STARLAN networks and use ISN to enable all networks to communicate with distant company IBM mainframes. ISN supports both a BSC and an SNA/SDLC interface. The synchronous traffic can share T1 facilities with an AT&T PBX, thus eliminating expensive long-distance modems.

ISN also offers an Ethernet bridge consistent with IEEE 802.3 baseband network standards. Companies with Ethernet networks that are too far apart to communicate though direct cabling can communicate through ISN. The ISN Ethernet bridge is a 10-mbps CSMA/CD module that

Figure 8-7.
ISN Bus Design
(Courtesy of AT&T)

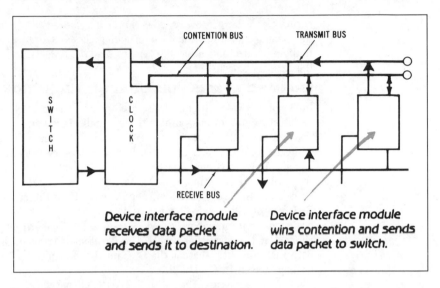

Device interface module
receives data packet
and sends it to destination.

Device interface module
wins contention and sends
data packet to switch.

Figure 8-8.
ISN Interfaces *(Courtesy of AT&T)*

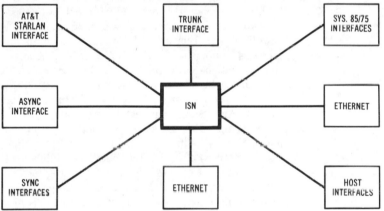

terminates the physical and data link layers of the OSI model. The bridge
supports Transmission Control Protocol/Internet Protocol (TCP/IP) as well as
Xerox Network System (XNS) devices.

ISN AND NETWORK MANAGEMENT

ISN is a star topology just like STARLAN. As we saw earlier, star
architecture networks usually provide excellent diagnostic reports and
management tools. This topology enables ISN to provide detailed traffic and
performance statistics and to add new users simply by assigning a new device
to an unused port and giving this device an address.

The drawback to star topology networks has always been the danger
that the entire network will collapse if the central processor fails. ISN
provides a measure of protection by using nonvolatile memory for storing
configuration and fault data. In the event of a power failure, it uses

automatic system recovery when power is restored. ISN also monitors the functioning of various modules, including the control processor, and reports faulty modules, indicating the type of module, a description of the faults, and the time they occurred.

ISDN AND AT&T'S VOICE/DATA INTEGRATION

In Chapter 3 we examined Integrated Services Digital Network (ISDN) architecture and discussed how these standards would eventually revolutionize office automation. ISDN standards define a digital interface that is divided into B and D channels. B channels carry voice, data, and video signals, and D channels carry signaling and control information to manage the network. Furthermore, ISDN postulates two types of interfaces, the Basic-Rate Interface (BRI) and the Primary-Rate Interface (PRI). Although BRI is designed for small-capacity devices such as terminals and PRI is designed for large-capacity devices such as PBXs, both interfaces carry one D channel and several B channels. The B channels transmit at 64 kbps each for both BRI and PRI whereas the D channels transmit at 16 kbps for BRI and 64 kbps for PRI.

Imagine an office with a STARLAN network and an AT&T System 75 PBX phone system using AT&T's ISN. Let's assume that a network user needs to send a voice message accompanied by a video display and several data files to another user. Using ISDN standards on AT&T's ISN, the user's premises equipment (PBX and data terminal) transmits signals to establish communications with the network. Once the link is established, the video, voice, and data signals are sent in digital form into the network using its B channels. The network in turn sends this information to the addressee.

As the leader in network integration, AT&T is also a leader in following the ISDN guidelines, although its equipment doesn't precisely match all these standards. AT&T's equivalent of PRI is the bit-oriented signaling (BOS) of its Digital Multiplexed Interface (DMI), and its equivalent of BRI is the bit-oriented signaling of its Digital Communication Protocol (DCP). Figure 8-9 illustrates AT&T's approach to integrating its services following ISDN guidelines. An example of ISDN in action, which AT&T likes to cite as an illustration of what we can expect in the future, is its E911 service. When a customer calls the emergency 911 number, the call is routed to an operator who sees the caller's telephone number and address appear automatically on the console screen. A computer has searched a very large database, recovered the key customer information, and transmitted it to the operator's screen while simultaneously routing the voice signal there. In the future, offices will be able to link their networks with several other kinds of networks in a transparent manner to the network user. Figure 8-10 summarizes how ISDN integrates these networks into a coherent system.

Another example of how AT&T is integrating voice and data applications in the modern office is its use of Unified Messaging Systems (UMS). A company with UMS probably also has a PBX system such as AT&T's System 75 and AT&T's AUDIX voice-mail service. Managers in this company might use Office Telesystem (OTS) to link with the UMS.

**Figure 8-9.
AT&T Premises-
Switched ISDN
Architecture** (Courtesy of
AT&T)

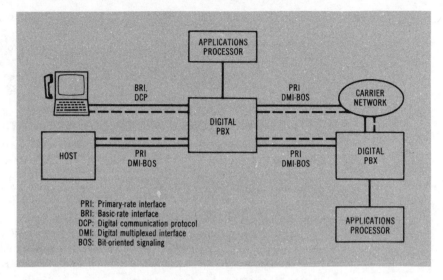

**Figure 8-10.
AT&T Communications
Interexchange Carrier
ISDN Architecture**
(Courtesy of AT&T)

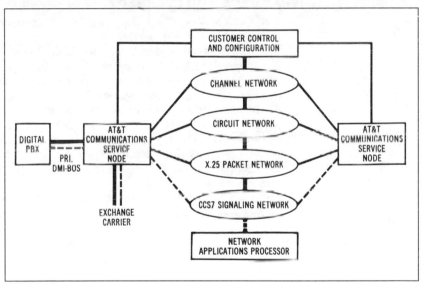

Employees in this office can choose whether to read their messages
on their terminals or hear them spoken. They can reply by voice or by typing
their replies on the keyboard. Let's assume that an employee calls in to
retrieve his or her phone messages. Using such AT&T supplementary
products as Mailtalk or Speak-To-Me, the employee can hear the messages
spoken by a computer.

We indicated that managers at this company might use OTS. OTS
incorporates the same structure as UMS so that it can receive UMS messages
but adds a number of handy management functions. It is available to up to a

hundred users and can provide users of AT&T DOS-based workstations and 3B2 UNIX-based minicomputers with an electronic calendar with resource scheduling. It also improves telephone management by providing multiple directories and speed dialing and enabling users to write telephone memos. Finally, OTS processes text and accesses external databases. AT&T hopes to expand services such as these to provide a truly integrated office where voice and data messages are exchanged effortlessly.

AT&T CONNECTIVITY AND OTHER INTERNATIONAL STANDARDS

Whereas ISDN is standard waiting to be implemented, several other international standards already exist that AT&T has chosen to support by providing LAN interfaces. A TCP/IP UNIX System Interface consists of hardware and software that permits an AT&T 6386 WGS to access TCP/IP networks. TCP/IP WIN/3B software provides TCP/IP links for a 3B minicomputer. The AT&T UNIX System V NFS software enables AT&T users to access computers using this protocol, especially Sun engineering workstations. Finally, AT&T offers an X.25 Packet Assembler/Disassembler (PAD) with software for its 6386 WGS and 3B2 computers.

WHAT HAVE YOU LEARNED?

1. A STARLAN network can daisy-chain up to ten workstations together with one node serving as the file server.
2. STARLAN is a network following the CSMA/CD protocol that transmits data at 1 mbps. STARLAN 10 transmits data at 10 mbps.
3. STARLAN software contains three types of commands: Administration Services, File-Sharing Services, and Printer-Sharing Services.
4. STARLAN network security consists of a login password, password requirements for using a directory or subdirectory, and data encryption.
5. Several STARLAN networks can be connected together using the Information Systems Network (ISN) and the STARLAN Interface Module (SIM).
6. The ISN packet controller uses a transmit bus, a receiving bus, and a contention bus.
7. Under ISDN guidelines a company can transmit voice, data, and video signals simultaneously.

Quiz for Chapter 8

1. STARLAN permits up to ten workstations to be daisy-chained together in what kind of network architecture?
   a. star
   b. bus
   c. ring
   d. token ring

2. The expansion bus of each STARLAN workstation must contain
   a. at least 640K
   b. a Network Hub Unit (NHU)
   c. a Network Access Unit (NAU)
   d. a Network Interface Unit (NIU)

3. STARLAN follows the IEEE 802.3 guidelines for avoiding data collisions by using
   a. CSMA/CD
   b. packets
   c. tokens
   d. one-way communications

4. To connect different offices within the same building, a STARLAN would use
   a. coaxial cable
   b. a wiring closet
   c. Network Interface Units
   d. an analog phone signal

5. A 1:10 bridge links a
   a. STARLAN and a STARLAN 10 network
   b. two STARLAN networks
   c. two STARLAN 10 networks
   d. two Ethernet networks

6. Under STARLAN which of the following can be used as file servers?
   a. AT&T 6386 WGS
   b. AT&T 6300, 6300 Plus, and IBM compatibles
   c. AT&T 3B2
   d. All of the above

7. STARLAN will work only with which version of DOS?
   a. DOS 2.1
   b. DOS 3.0
   c. DOS 3.1 and above
   d. DOS 2.2

8. To connect more than ten workstations in a STARLAN network it is necessary to use a
   a. Network Cable Connection (NCC)
   b. Network Interface Unit (NIU)
   c. Network Repeater Unit (NRU)
   d. Network Hub Unit (NHU)

9. More than one hundred workstations can be connected in a STARLAN network by using a Network Hub Unit connected to
   a. other Network Hub Units
   b. ten daisy-chained workstations
   c. Network Repeater Units (NRU)
   d. Network Interface Units (NIU)

10. The practical limit when daisy-chaining workstations together under STARLAN is
    a. 200 feet
    b. 400 feet
    c. 600 feet
    d. 800 feet

11. Using a Network Hub Unit a STARLAN network can extend a maximum of
   a. 400 feet
   b. 800 feet
   c. 1000 feet
   d. 1200 feet

12. STARLAN workstations are connected using
   a. two twisted pair of unshielded 24-gauge telephone wire
   b. coaxial cable
   c. fiber-optic cable
   d. data-grade cable

13. Under STARLAN a user may log in to
   a. one file server at a time
   b. only two file servers at a time
   c. only three file servers at a time
   d. an unlimited number of file servers

14. To protect files from being destroyed by two people trying simultaneously to write to them, STARLAN lets shared files be
   a. write-only
   b. read-only
   c. create
   d. exclusive

15. The electronic mail program that works on STARLAN is known as
   a. Mail
   b. Electronic Messenger
   c. PMX/STARMail
   d. Postman

16. Two STARLAN networks can be connected together through ISN by using
   a. coaxial cable
   b. STARLAN Interface Module (SIM)
   c. ISN Interface
   d. broadband cabling

17. Under ISDN, control signals are transmitted using
   a. the one D channel
   b. any one of the several B channels
   c. a special C channel for control
   d. a token-passing protocol

18. For limited devices ISDN has established
   a. BRI
   b. PRI
   c. DRIP
   d. SIP

19. For large devices such as PBXs ISDN has established
   a. BRI
   b. PRI
   c. DRIP
   d. SIP

20. The heart of ISN is a
   a. microprocessor
   b. packet controller
   c. analog switch
   d. cardiac coil

Other Major LANs: Arcnet, 10Net, and VINES

ABOUT THIS CHAPTER

In this chapter we will examine three LANs that have captured a significant market share because of the valuable features they offer. Arcnet is a proven technology that illustrates how a token bus works. It provides a hardware platform for virtually all the major local area network operating systems. Though one of the oldest LAN products still on the market, Arcnet now comes in a new 20-mbps version and thus may be a major player in the LAN market for the foreseeable future. 10Net offers several security features that make it a major government contractor. Finally, VINES may offer a preview of the next stage of network connectivity. Its transparent bridges and global directory (StreetTalk) make it the leader in internetwork connectivity.

ARCNET

Arcnet is reliable and inexpensive and uses a media-access approach independent of IEEE standards. It supports a wide range of network operating systems, including NetWare and the PC LAN Program.

Attached Resource Computer Network (Arcnet) was developed in 1977 by Datapoint. Today it is available from a number of vendors, including Standard Microsystems, Acer Technologies, Earth Computers, and Thomas-Conrad. Arcnet provides reliable, inexpensive network hardware that supports a wide range of network operating systems including NetWare. In fact, the Arcnet Trade Association (ATA) has standardized Performance Technology's NETBIOS so that Arcnet users can run virtually any NETBIOS-compatible network operating system on Arcnet, including the IBM PC LAN Program. Standard Microsystems even offers Microsoft's OS/2 LAN Manager software for Arcnet. What makes Arcnet particularly interesting is that, although it does not correspond to the IEEE 802 body of standards, its vendors have exerted a major effort to make it a de facto industry standard. For the most part, in fact, they have succeeded because of Arcnet's low cost, flexibility, and reliability. A new version now offers speed as well, transmitting at 20 mbps in contrast to the 2.5-mbps speed of standard Arcnet.

Topology

Arcnet offers bus, star, and distributed star topologies using thin coaxial cable, twisted-pair wire, or fiber-optic cable. This flexible network permits the intermixing of all these topologies and media.

The star is the most common Arcnet topology. Up to eight workstations can be connected to a central hub with a 2000-foot maximum. A passive hub can be used if distances do not exceed 100 feet. Active hubs can be joined together through an interface found on the back of the hub or through one of the eight ports. The network can stretch up to four miles. Because of the number of Arcnet vendors, a wide range of product configurations are available. Active hubs, for example, can be purchased with anywhere from four to thirty-two ports.

A bus configuration using coaxial cabling can contain up to eight workstations. This bus can be linked to a star-configured Arcnet network if a company's computing needs grow. An Active Link (a repeater) can expand a coax bus network by linking two bus cables and a star network by increasing point-to-point distances. Active Links can be purchased with various combinations of connectors so that twisted-pair, coax, and fiber-optic segments can all be linked into one Arcnet network. Figure 9-1 illustrates a star configuration linked to a coax bus network under Arcnet.

**Figure 9-1.
Star Configuration
Linked to Coax Bus
under Arcnet**

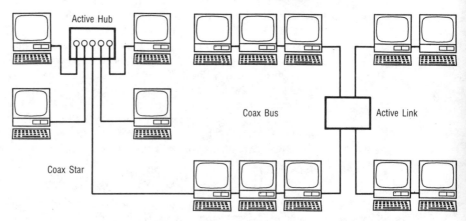

At one time limited to RG-62 A/U thin coaxial cabling, today's Arcnet is popular in part because it can also use existing unshielded twisted-pair wire as well as IBM types 6, 8, and 9. Its star configuration makes it easy for a network supervisor to diagnose cabling problems, since they are localized to particular hubs or node links and reflected on most Arcnet cards by an LED.

Arcnet's Access Method

Arcnet uses a token bus protocol that is a logical ring but a physical star.

Arcnet uses a token bus protocol that considers the network to be a logical ring. The permission to transmit a token is passed in a logical ring according to the workstation's network interface card address, which must be set between 1 and 255 using an 8-position DIP switch. Each network interface card knows its own address as well as the address of the workstation to which it will pass the token. The highest-addressed node closes the "ring" by passing the token to the lowest-addressed node. Figure 9-2 illustrates how this process works.

Arcnet is a character-oriented protocol that has five different types of frame formats: an Invitation to Transmit, which passes the token from one node to another; a Free Buffer Enquiry (FBE), which inquires whether the next workstation can accept a data packet; the Data Packet itself (up to 507 bytes); an Acknowledgement (ACK) indicating a packet has been received correctly; and a Negative Acknowledgement (NAK) used to decline an FBE. Figure 9-3 illustrates the Arcnet packet format.

**Figure 9-2.
Arcnet's Access
Method**

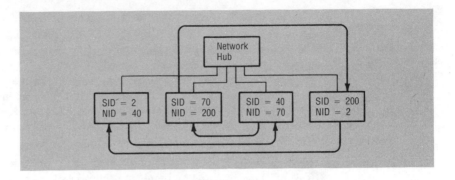

**Figure 9-3.
Arcnet's Packet Format**

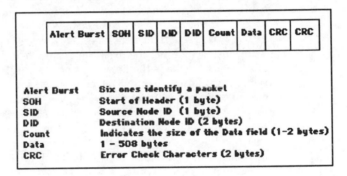

Alert Burst	SOH	SID	DID	DID	Count	Data	CRC	CRC

Alert Burst	Six ones identify a packet
SOH	Start of Header (1 byte)
SID	Source Node ID (1 byte)
DID	Destination Node ID (2 bytes)
Count	Indicates the size of the Data field (1–2 bytes)
Data	1 – 508 bytes
CRC	Error Check Characters (2 bytes)

When node 100 receives the token, for example, it might need to send a packet to node 222. It would first send an FBE to node 222 to confirm 222's ability to receive a message. When node 100 received an ACK as a response, it would transmit its packet. Upon receipt of the packet, node 222 would respond by verifying the error-checking information (CRC) and replying with an ACK. If node 222 were silent, node 100 would know that there must have been an error in transmission. If node 100 received an ACK, it could issue an FBE to the next node to use the token, node 101.

20-mbps Arcnet

The new 20-mbps Arcnet adheres to IEEE standards for packet addressing and logical link control.

Datapoint has developed a 20-mbps product known as Arcnetplus, which remains backward-compatible with existing cable and 2.5-mbps Arcnet. It permits data-packet sizes up to 4224 bytes versus the traditional limitation of 508 bytes and can address up to 2047 nodes versus the historical limitation of 255 nodes.

Perhaps even more important, this new version supports IEEE 802 packet addressing, logical link control, and internet protocol addressing. Chip sets are being built by Standard Microsystems and NCR's microelectronic products division.

DCA'S 10NET AND 10NET PLUS LANS

10Net products have become a major alternative for companies looking for inexpensive LAN hardware and software that still offer a number of communication and security features.

Recently purchased by DCA, the 10Net family of LANs has developed rapidly over the past few years and today offers a wide variety of hardware and software options. 10Net combines flexible, inexpensive hardware with software that is loaded with features not found on far more expensive network operating systems. As a result, it is assuming an increasingly important role as an inexpensive alternative to 3+Share, NetWare, and the PC LAN Program for companies that still need effective LAN communication links and security.

10Net Configurations and Topologies

10Net can be configured in a number of different ways. Its network interface cards and software can be combined to form a 1-mbps bus network topology or a star architecture using the StarLAN approach. The bus can be up to 10,000 feet in length and the StarLAN topology up to 8000 feet in length with a distance of 800 feet between PC and hub. If 10Net is configured with an Ethernet topology, the network supports a distance of 500 meters per segment with a maximum distance of 2.5 kilometers on thick Ethernet coaxial cable and 180 meters per segment with a 900-meter maximum on thin Ethernet coax. A fiber-optic 10Net LAN permits a PC-to-hub or hub-to-hub maximum distance of 1 kilometer (the 1-mbps version) or 3 kilometers (the 10-mbps version) with a total network distance of 6 kilometers. The hardware and software support up to 3 hub levels and a maximum of 392 nodes. Figure 9-4 illustrates how different 10Net topologies can be linked using repeaters.

**Figure 9-4.
Different 10Net
Topologies Linked with
Repeaters**

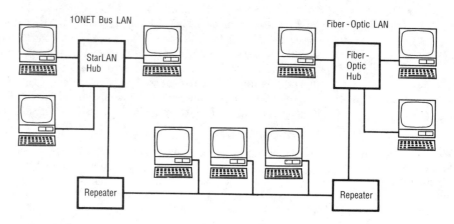

10Net Plus Software

10Net Plus software is NETBIOS-compatible and uses the SMB protocol suites. Because the software requires only 110K (and an additional 20K RAM for NETBIOS), it has become a popular substitute for the PC LAN Program on IBM Token Ring Networks, where it can transmit data at 4 mbps over

Among the methods used by 10Net file servers to achieve greater efficiency are prefetch, write buffering, and disk caching.

unshielded twisted-pair cabling. The program also runs with 10Net's own interface cards and a variety of different cabling and protocol schemes, including IEEE-802.3 10BASE5 STARLAN over twisted-pair wire, thick or thin coaxial cable Ethernet (10 mbps), and fiber-optic cabling (1 mbps or 10 mbps).

In Chapter 5 we discussed some special techniques that NetWare file servers use to enhance performance. 10Net file servers act in much the same way by using such techniques as prefetch, write buffering, and disk caching. Rather than merely fetch a 200-byte record that has been requested, 10Net's server fetches 1000 bytes under the assumption that it will not have to perform another disk access when you request the next record. This prefetch anticipates your next request and thus speeds up network performance. Write buffering is a technique in which the file server writes to a buffer rather than directly to disk and then transmits a larger block less frequently. Finally, disk caching brings an entire track of information into an area of memory known as the cache, where it is available on request.

Some Features That Distinguish 10Net Software

Other features that make 10Net Plus a good value include its pop-up version of the CHAT program, its bundling of The Network Courier electronic mail program, and its menu-driven installation. The Network Courier will be discussed in some detail in Chapter 10's survey of leading electronic mail programs. CHAT is 10Net's program for brief communications between users. A Bulletin Board program enables users to leave messages for everyone on the network, and CB permits users to have multipoint public discussions. A Group Calendaring program makes it easy to schedule meetings by coordinating a number of individual schedules of network users. A TALLYS program lets a network manager examine dozens of network statistics, including the number of packets sent and received over the network, the number of collisions, and the number of bad packets sent.

Sharing Network Resources

A superstation is a 10Net network node that shares its resources with the network.

10Net software works on the assumption that a node that shares its resources is a *superstation* as opposed to a workstation that simply uses its own and other node's resources. As in the case of many MS-Net–based network programs, 10Net uses the NET SHARE command to share a resource and the NET USE command to use a resource. Users provide a short name or alias along with the network name of the device they wish to share. Figure 9-5 illustrates how the NET SHARE command provides information on resources (and their aliases) that have been shared.

10Net's Levels of Security

10Net provides four different levels of security: file security, directory security, user security, and superstation default security. At the file and directory levels, attributes can be defined for files, groups of files, or an entire directory. Similarly, files and directories can be limited to a specific user or to specific groups. A user's security level (0 is the lowest and 255 the highest) must be greater than or equal to the read or write security of the

Figure 9-5.
The NET SHARE
Command

```
┌─────────────────────────────────────────────────────────────┐
│      Network sharing information at NODE SALES                │
│                                                               │
│                                                               │
│    Alias      Access      Devices                             │
│   ─────────────────────────────────────────────────          │
│    PROP        RW          C:PROPOSAL                          │
│    PLAN        R           D:\MRKTPLAN                         │
│    LASER       SYS         LPT1                                │
│                            C:                                  │
│                                                               │
├─────────────────────────────────────────────────────────────┤
│                  Please Enter Selection                       │
│  F1+SHAR F2=STOP F3=HELP F4=QUIT F5=BACK F6=DONE F7=VIEW       │
└─────────────────────────────────────────────────────────────┘
```

file or directory he or she is trying to access. For example, a file with a read security level of 60 and a write security level of 80 would require a user with a security level of at least 80 to have full access to the file. A user with a security level of 70 would be able to read the file but not update it.

10Net Secure LANs

One area where 10Net LANs have proven to be popular is in government installations that require security. The 10Net Secure LAN incorporates 10Net hardware (a 10Net circuit board and encryption board) and 10Net Plus software. The 10Net encryption board provides "single-keyed" encryption of all data written to the PC's hard disk and all data transmitted over the network in conformance with ANSI x9.17 standards.

The hardware and software can function on a single PC or on the entire network. The 10Net Plus software provides multilevel file access as well as a full audit trail of user activity with date-transfer security. Users are required to provide a valid ID and password before the DOS boot. Users can also be restricted from using selected peripherals.

Providing secure systems for the government has become a major revenue source for 10Net, which has more than 10,000 nodes installed. In addition to its 10Net Secure LAN, it also offers a Tempest configuration and, very shortly, a C2 secure system that conforms to the requirements of National Security Agency.

Today, government networks use the Transmission Control Protocol/Internet Protocol (TCP/IP) developed a decade ago under a contract with the Department of Defense. 10Net offers 10Net TCP, a collection of programs that implement a standard TCP/IP protocol family for PCs running under DOS. It functions as a terminate-and-stay-resident program that can be run whenever needed for terminal emulation. The U.S. government has already expressed its intention to move from TCP/IP to Government OSI Profile (GOSIP), and hence there is a need to bridge the two protocols. Because the government represents such a major market for 10Net, the company has been working under a joint agreement with Northern Telecom to implement the Common Management Information protocol (CMIP), which would permit TCP/IP networks to comply with the network-management specifications of the OSI standard.

Token Ring Bridge

The 10Net Token Ring Bridge integrates a 10Net LAN with an IBM Token Ring Network. Using a dedicated node as a bridge PC, the program monitors network traffic and handles the 1-mbps and 10-mbps 10Net transmission speeds with the 4-mbps transmission speed on the IBM network. This software-only product performs bridging at the NETBIOS level.

VINES

Banyan Systems' Virtual Networking System (VINES) is a network operating system based on the UNIX System V that places a premium on internetwork connectivity, security, and transparent operations. The company offers a number of add-on products, including electronic mail and network-management software, which we will discuss later in this section.

VINES also supports a wide variety of hardware platforms, including IBM's Token Ring, SMC Arcnet, Interlan Ethernet, 3Com's EtherLink and EtherLink Plus, and Proteon's ProNET-10. It does require a dedicated file server, which can be one of its own models or an Intel 80286 (VINES/286), Intel 80386 (VINES/386), IBM AT, PS/2, or compatible unit.

All VINES services (naming, file, printer, mail, and so forth) execute as UNIX processes. These services can be stopped and started from the server without disrupting other services. Although computer-industry experts have long extolled the multitasking and multiuser capabilities of UNIX, they have pointed out that its lack of a user-friendly interface would hinder its wide acceptance by the general public. In contrast, the VINES user interface is menu-driven, as illustrated in Figure 9-6. In fact, even though VINES is based on UNIX System V, a user must exit this network environment before he or she can use UNIX.

Figure 9-6.
The VINES Menu

```
    VINES:   VIRTUAL NETWORKING SYSTEM

    1 - Mail
    2 - Catalog of StreetTalk names
    3 - Printer Functions
    4 - File Sharing
    5 - Password Update
    6 - Communications with Other Computers


Use arrow keys to highlight a choice and press ENTER.
Press F1 for HELP. Press ESC to exit this screen.
```

StreetTalk

The key to VINES'
internetwork connectivity
is its distributed database,
StreetTalk, which provides
a global directory for
network communications.

StreetTalk is VINES' distributed database serving as its resource naming service. Resources can represent users, services (such as printers, file volumes, and gateways), and even lists. The StreetTalk name structure is three-fold with each part separated by the @ symbol:

OBJECT@GROUP@ORGANIZATION

Notice how closely this structure parallels the 3Com Name Service described in Chapter 6. As an example, Frank Jones, an account executive in Polytex General's Western regional office might have a StreetTalk name such as the following:

FRANK JONES@SALES@WESTERN

With StreetTalk and VINES a user does not need to know pathways or the location of users or other resources. If Frank needed to send a message to Bill Taylor working in the Southwestern regional office, Frank would need only know Bill Taylor's name, and StreetTalk would take care of the mechanics of finding Taylor's node address and routing the material to him accurately. To make matters even easier, StreetTalk permits the designation of nicknames. Figure 9-7 illustrates a menu a network manager would use for adding a user's nickname. If Frank knew Taylor only by the nickname "BT," he could consult the StreetTalk catalog using a screen similar to the one pictured in Figure 9-8 and find the name corresponding to BT. Similarly, if Frank had proper access, he could request a file without knowing its directory or subdirectory or even the physical location of the file server. Thus, he could request BUDPROJ89 and simply let StreetTalk find and retrieve it, since each file server on a VINES network maintains a StreetTalk directory of all resource known to the network.

**Figure 9-7.
Adding a User's
Nickname under VINES**

```
+------------------------------------------------------------+
|    Use arrow keys to highlight a choice, then press ENTER. |
|                                                            |
|    SELECT from list below    SEARCH for other nicknames    |
|    ADD a nickname            FIND nicknames for a full name |
|    EXIT this screen (ESC)    HELP (F1)                      |
|                                                            |
|    ------------------------------------------------------  |
|                                                            |
|    (There are 5 nicknames in group "Sales@Poly".)          |
|                                                            |
|    1 - cct                                                 |
|    2 - ddw                                                 |
|    3 - hp                                                  |
|    4 - kak                                                 |
|    5 - ss                                                  |
+------------------------------------------------------------+
```

Because of StreetTalk's global naming capability, Frank can access an IBM mainframe in Arizona or an Ethernet network running VINES in New Jersey through an identical procedure. The network operating system handles network addressing and communications with the mainframe running

Figure 9-8.
A StreetTalk Catalog

```
┌─────────────────────────────────────────────────────────┐
│  What would you like to look at?                          │
│                                                           │
│      Users                       Nicknames                │
│      File Volumes                Groups                   │
│      Printers                    Organizations            │
│      Lists                       Servers                  │
│      EXIT this screen (ESC)      HELP (F1)                │
│                                                           │
│                                                           │
│  Use arrow keys to highlight a choice and press ENTER     │
│                                                           │
│  - - - - - - - - - - - - - - - - - - - - - - - - - - - -  │
│                                                           │
│  You are Frank K. Olsen@Sls@Polytex                       │
└─────────────────────────────────────────────────────────┘
```

SNA or the Ethernet network, which uses a different addressing scheme than the Token Ring Network Frank is using. All this work is transparent to Frank, the end user, who in both cases simply selects the name of the resource he wants to communicate with from a VINES menu.

Behind the scenes, the various VINES file servers communicate and exchange StreetTalk information with each other using what are called outbound blasts. These communications occur whenever a new server joins the network, when the administrator adds or deletes group or service information, and every twelve hours from the time the last server came on line.

Security under VINES

VINES provides several different layers of security. A network administrator can require a password for login to the network. He or she can also specify the hours and days permitted for a particular user to log in to the network. As Figure 9-9 illustrates, VINES versions 3.0 and above contain security software known as VANGuard, which makes it possible to require users to change their logins at specified intervals, to limit the number of simultaneous logins, to force users to login from a specific location, and to restrict users to access only a specific file server.

Figure 9-9.
A VanGuard Menu

```
┌─────────────────────────────────────────────────────────┐
│   User: Daniel Schatt@Demo@Poly]                          │
│   [Current Security Settings: None]                       │
│                                                           │
│       1 - Manage Password Security                        │
│       2 - Prevent User Changes                            │
│       3 - Specific Login Settings                         │
│       4 - Specific Logout Settings                        │
│       5 - Specific Login Times                            │
│       6 - Specific Login Locations                        │
│       7 - Delete User Specific Security Settings          │
│                                                           │
│   Use arrow keys to highlight a choice, then press ENTER  │
│   Press F1 for HELP; ESC to exit this screen.             │
└─────────────────────────────────────────────────────────┘
```

Under VINES, each user, service, and communications link has an access-rights list (ARL) that specifies the users who are authorized to use the network. The network administrator can establish the access rights to a file volume, but he or she cannot restrict access to individual files.

Printing under VINES

Under VINES, printers linked to network PCs can be shared in the same way that printers attached directly to file servers can be shared. This eliminates the distance limitation between printer and server and makes printer location much more flexible. The network administrator determines which printers will be available for which users by assigning a virtual connection for each print queue listed in a user profile. The SETPRINT program permits a user to look at jobs in any print queue, use a different print queue, or change printer settings. The Show Print Queue menu in Figure 9-10 illustrates how a user can hold or cancel a print job in a queue.

Figure 9-10.
A Print Queue under VINES

```
+---------------------------------------------------------------+
|                                                               |
|                              Show Print Queue                 |
|                                                               |
|     CANCEL job          HOLD job        REPRINT job           |
|   ----------------------------------------------------------- |
|     There are 4 print jobs in print queue LaserPrinter@Mkt@Poly|
|                                                               |
|    Job     State     Creator          Size   Title  Form Type |
|                                                               |
|    01      Done      Suzie S Marshall@Sa  12033  input  Standard |
|    02      Ready     Stan Schatt@Mk     3237   input  Standard |
|    03      Hold      Bill Bones@Sales   434445 input  Standard |
|                                                               |
|    Use arrow keys to highlight a command and press ENTER.     |
|    Press ESC to exit this screen; F1 for HELP.                |
|                                                               |
+---------------------------------------------------------------+
```

Communicating with Other VINES Users

For intranet communications, VINES includes two standard network packages, SEND and CHAT, and offers an optional electronic mail program. SEND is a command that enables a user to send a one-line message that will appear at the bottom of another user's screen. To use this command, a user types SEND and presses <ENTER>. Prompts then request the message (enclosed in quotation marks) and the name of the recipient. By indicating ALL, a user can send a one-line message to all other users with LANs connected to the sender's server.

The CHAT program creates a window enabling a user to chat with up to four others at one time. The program opens conversation windows for each user. If you are chatting in a private conversation with a user and a second user expresses a desire to chat, you can place the first user on hold. Since CHAT works on all VINES networks, five users at different locations can have a sustained "conversation" on a particular project that is much like a conference call.

Although VINES does come with an electronic mail package, Banyan's Mail program is available as an add-on. A major advantage of this program over others is that it uses the StreetTalk naming convention so that names and nicknames are consistent. It also features a store-and-forward approach that enables it to use high-speed links between servers. The Mail program menu, which is displayed in Figure 9-11, provides most basic mail services, allowing a user to edit text and organize documents into appropriate folders.

**Figure 9-11.
VINES Mail**

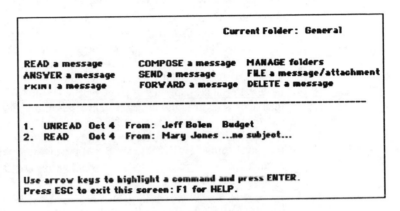

Current Folder: General

READ a message   COMPOSE a message   MANAGE folders
ANSWER a message   SEND a message   FILE a message/attachment
PRINT a message   FORWARD a message   DELETE a message

----

1. UNREAD Oct 4 From: Jeff Bolen   Budget
2. READ   Oct 4 From: Mary Jones ...no subject...

Use arrow keys to highlight a command and press ENTER.
Press ESC to exit this screen: F1 for HELP.

Banyan offers a MacVINES Mail Gateway software option that provides communications between Macintosh and IBM microcomputers. VINES Network Mail in conjunction with CE Software's QuickMail provides the necessary DOS and Macintosh file conversions. VINES Network Mail includes the Listener and Bridge. The Listener runs as a service under VINES and talks to the Bridge using AppleTalk protocols. Figure 9-12 illustrates how Macintosh computers and PCs can exchange mail on a VINES Ethernet backbone network.

**Figure 9-12.
Macintosh Computers
and PCs Exchange Mail
under VINES**

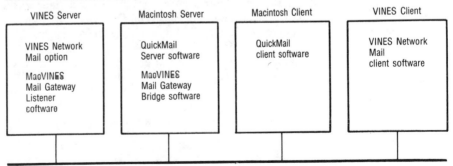

VINES Server

VINES Network
Mail option

MacVINES
Mail Gateway
Listener
software

Macintosh Server

QuickMail
Server software

MacVINES
Mail Gateway
Bridge software

Macintosh Client

QuickMail
client software

VINES Client

VINES Network
Mail
client software

Banyan's Intelligent Communications Adaptor

Banyan's Intelligent Communications Adaptor (ICA) uses an 8-MHz Intel 80286 microprocessor to manage six high-speed serial communication ports. Two ports are configured for 64-kbps synchronous communications. An ICA can support several different protocols, including HDLC, SDLC, and X.25. Because the ICA has its own processor as well as 512K of dual-ported, zero-wait-state RAM, it reduces overhead on a VINES server.

The number of ICAs supported varies according to the VINES file server selected. Banyan's own top-of-the-line Corporate Network Server (CNS), supports a maximum of five ICAs or thirty communication ports, in addition to supporting up to 100 simultaneous network users.

VINES Gateways to Other Networks

The major strength of VINES is its ability to provide transparent access to network resources regardless of where they are or what protocol they happen to be using. Banyan's TCP/IP routing software enables a user to access TCP/IP resources whether they reside on a local or wide-area network without worrying about these physical details. For example, VINES mail can be sent to SMTP mail users using the SMTP Mail Gateway option. VINES mail addresses are automatically converted into the standard SMTP user@host@domain format or UUCP-style address (host!host!host!user). The VINES TCP/IP program encapsulates TCP/IP packets within VINES packets for travel across a VINES network. A server equipped with the TCP/IP routing option strips the VINES headers and sends the packets to an attached TCP/IP host or gateway.

When emulating an IBM 3274/6 cluster controller the VINES 3270/SNA option supports up to ninety-six concurrent sessions per server with up to thirty-two sessions supported by a single communications link. The software permits up to four concurrent host sessions and one DOS session per PC. In addition to providing 3278/79 terminal emulation, the software permits host print jobs, file transfers, and APIs to be performed on local PC printers so that users can build DOS-based applications to communicate with SNA host applications.

The VINES Applications Toolkit

The Banyan VINES Applications Toolkit is an advanced development environment for VINES based on UNIX System V that provides C-language APIs for X.25, TCP/IP, and serial interfaces to support network communications. The Toolkit enables developers to write applications that are media transparent because it provides access to VINES Socket Communications protocols. Also included is a UNIX/DOS Bridge File Service, which enables DOS-based programs to share and interchange source code with the UNIX environment. A Network Compiler implements Remote Procedure Calls, which generate code required for application-to-application communications.

VINES Network Management

Banyan offers network management software that provides detailed information on servers, disk activity, LAN and WAN interface statistics, and overall network performance. Designed to serve as a network diagnostic tool, this software provides network administrators with information on file-server cache size, the percentage of cache hits, the number of times the file system was unavailable, and such overall vital signs of network performance as the total messages sent and received, the number of messages dropped, and the average amount of swapping. Network administrators can simultaneously view activities across multiple servers.

WHAT HAVE YOU LEARNED?

1. Arcnet is a reliable, low-cost LAN that provides a physical star and a logical ring.
2. Arcnet is a character-oriented protocol.
3. Standard Arcnet can transmit at 2.5 mbps, whereas a new version can reach speeds of 20 mbps.
4. 10Net provides a high-security, low-cost LAN.
5. 10Net's file servers use prefetch, write buffering, and disk caching.
6. A superstation is a 10Net node that shares its resources.
7. VINES is a UNIX-based LAN operating system that runs on a wide range of hardware platforms.
8. StreetTalk is the distributed database serving as a resource naming service for VINES.
9. VINES provides effective gateways to TCP/IP networks and IBM mainframes.

Quiz for Chapter 9

1. Arcnet was developed by
   a. Datapoint
   b. Standard Microsystems
   c. Acer Technologies
   d. Earth Computers

2. Under Arcnet, a passive hub can be used if distances do not exceed
   a. 50 feet
   b. 100 feet
   c. 200 feet
   d. 500 feet

3. Arcnet's access method is
   a. polled star
   b. CSMA bus
   c. token ring
   d. token bus

4. The newest Arcnet version provides speeds of
   a. 4 mbps
   b. 16 mbps
   c. 20 mbps
   d. 50 mbps

5. Using a StarLAN approach, 10Net can achieve speeds of
   a. 1 mbps
   b. 5 mbps
   c. 10 mbps
   d. 20 mbps

6. 10Net Plus software requires only _____ of RAM.
   a. 50K
   b. 110K
   c. 500K
   d. 640K

7. 10Net's file server fetches more than the required number of records, through a technique known as
   a. profetch
   b. prefetch
   c. postfetch
   d. fetch

8. 10Net provides network statistics using
   a. Netstat
   b. Record
   c. TALLYS
   d. STAT

9. A network node under 10Net that shares resources is known as a
   a. workstation
   b. sharer
   c. superstation
   d. altruist station

10. 10Net provides _____ levels of security.
    a. 1
    b. 4
    c. 6
    d. 10

11. A 10Net encryption board provides
    a. single-keyed encryption
    b. double-keyed encryption
    c. double-handed encryption
    d. sleight-of-hand encryption

12. A UNIX-based LAN operating system is
    a. Arcnet
    b. 10Net
    c. VINES
    d. NetWare

13. The distributed database serving as VINES' resource naming service is called
    a. ORACLE
    b. SQL Server
    c. TownTalk
    d. StreetTalk

14. A VINES user can communicate with four other users simultaneously with
    a. Mail
    b. Bulletin
    c. CHAT
    d. SEND

15. VINES/3270 SNA software
emulates a
   a. cluster controller
   b. host printer
   c. mainframe
   d. multiplexer

Electronic Messaging on Local Area Networks

ABOUT THIS CHAPTER

In this chapter we'll take a close look at several different electronic messaging systems that are available for the leading local area networks. Since the industry is moving to incorporate CCITT standards in electronic mail packages in order to facilitate internetwork connectivity, we'll examine Action Technology's message handling system (MHS), a product that network software companies and electronic messaging companies are licensing to provide compatibility with the CCITT X.400 set of recommendations. We'll also describe the effects on electronic messaging of the new CCITT X.500 set of standards.

WHAT IS ELECTRONIC MESSAGING?

Electronic messaging includes not only electronic mail (E-MAIL) but also gateways to other networks and to facsimile machines as well as numerous scheduling and organizing features.

Today electronic messaging means much more than simply one network user sending a note to one or more other network users. Many electronic messaging programs allow users to send mail from one network to another local area network or even around the world. Often these programs can also maintain calendars for everyone on the network, schedule meetings, and, in some cases, even send phone messages automatically. More than simply a paperless office mail system, today's electronic messaging programs are designed to handle virtually all intraoffice and interoffice communications, linking network users with each other and with the rest of the world.

CCITT X.400 AND WHAT IT MEANS FOR ELECTRONIC MESSAGING

In Chapter 2 we mentioned the International Standards Organization (ISO) Open Systems Interconnection (OSI) model, which is designed to promote a set of standards for internetwork communications. The OSI model designates the application layer (layer 7) as the location for a message handling system (MHS). An MHS provides a standard for electronic messaging so that different computer networks can communicate regardless of differences in their operating-system environments. In developing its model, the ISO used a set of standards that has been developed by the CCITT (Consultative Committee for International Telephony and Telegraphy), which is usually referred to as the CCITT X.400 set of recommendations. Table 10-1 reflects the scope of these standards. Although much of this material is too complex to cover in this book, it is important that we look at the basic building blocks of an X.400-compliant system, since virtually all LAN manufacturers have announced support for these international standards.

**Table 10-1.
The CCITT X.400
Recommendations**

Standard Set	Application
X.400	System model and service elements
X.401	Basic service elements and optional user interfaces
X.408	Encoded information and conversion rules
X.409	Presentation transfer syntax and notation
X.410	Remote operations and reliable transfer system
X.411	Message transfer layer
X.420	Interpersonal messaging user-agent layer
X.430	Access protocol for teletex terminals

Basic Elements of an X.400 Message Handling System

An X.400 MHS includes
user agents (UAs),
message transfer agents
(MTAs), and a message
transfer system (MTS).

An X.400-compliant MHS includes user agents (UAs), message transfer
agents (MTAs), and a message transfer system (MTS). Figure 10-1 illustrates
the structure of an MHS. The user agent interacts with a message transfer
service in support of a network user. In other words, the UA is that software
part of the MHS that provides the interface or connection between a network
user and an MHS, thus enabling the user to retrieve and send messages.

**Figure 10-1.
A Message Handling
System**

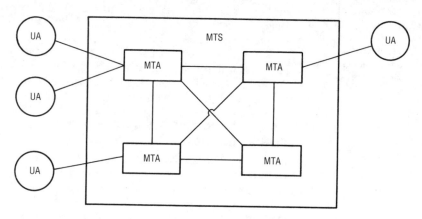

The message transfer agents (MTAs) consist of the messages sent
by users; they provide a number of different store-and-forward services. You
might want to think of MTAs as a post office. Sometimes they store
messages until a requested delivery time and date. Other times they may
have to convert the message into a form a destination user can understand.

The message transfer system (MTS) provides a number of network
and internetwork services to enhance electronic communications. Upon
request it can provide notice of verified delivery or nondelivery (with an
explanation), time and date stamps of submission as well as delivery,

multidestination deliveries, alternate recipients, and even different grades of delivery service, including nonurgent, normal, and urgent.

The P1, P2, and P3 Protocols

The P1 protocol provides rules for routing information between two MTAs.

As part of its X.400 recommendations, the CCITT has developed three key protocols or sets of standards. Protocol P1, as defined in the X.411 recommendation, sets the rules for routing information between two MTAs. Basically, this protocol specifies the format to be followed in packaging information. Information is packaged in an "envelope" consisting of the data to be sent as well as several fields that provide such important control elements as the following:

- A message identifier uniquely identifying where the message originated and the name of the user sending the message
- Information describing how this data should be displayed
- Information describing the destination user and this user's address
- Delivery instructions and instructions for any return receipt information required

Notice that the type of information defined in protocol P1 is very similar to the information that the post office requires when you request any kind of special service.

The P2 protocol defines the types of services requested, and the P3 protocol provides rules for changing existing parameters for electronic mail routing and delivery.

As defined in the X.420 recommendation, protocol P2 enables users to request such services as restricting the sending of certain messages to authorized users and specifying the types of notification requested from the recipient (including requiring an immediate reply to a message). This protocol also defines services that make it easier for companies to receive large volumes of messages by providing subject information and even cross-filing data.

Protocol P3 has been defined in the X.410 recommendation. Perhaps the easiest way to understand this set of standards is to think of it as a set of rules for a user or UA to follow when talking to an MTA, or post office, after a message has been transmitted. Under protocol P3, for example, a user can change existing parameters and conditions. The user may decide that present conditions dictate a need for a password, a need to alter the maximum size permitted in a message, or perhaps a test to see if a message can be delivered before the actual delivery takes place.

CCITT X.500 AND WHAT IT WILL MEAN FOR NETWORK USERS

The CCITT X.500 set of recommendations will facilitate worldwide electronic mail by providing the basis for a common directory.

Though still in the development stage, the CCITT X.500 recommendations will have a major impact on worldwide electronic messaging. This protocol provides a set of rules for a common directory for all electronic mail users. One major problem with the X.400 recommendations is that they do not solve the problem of incompatible electronic mail post office box addresses on different networks. The X.500 recommendations will provide a standard for a global electronic mail directory of users. Sometime in the not-too-distant future a user on a NetWare network in St. Louis will be able to send a message to a user on an IBM mainframe computer in Paris as routinely as we now drop a letter into our mailbox and raise the mailbox flag to indicate that we want the letter delivered.

MHS

MHS provides X.400 control information and a way to connect different electronic mail systems together.

In October 1986 Action Technologies began offering its MHS program to developers, and beginning in early 1988 Novell began to bundle MHS with version 2.1 of NetWare without charge.

When a user requests that a message be sent, MHS takes this message and places it in an "envelope" that contains key X.400 control information. An 18-line ASCII file called a message control block (MCB) accompanies the message and provides such information as the desired destination, a date/time stamp, the priority requested, and return notification requirements. Because an MHS message consists of three parts—a header, the text or message itself, and an associated parcel, which can consist of any binary-encoded data—messages can be sent along with lengthy reports or data files. Other X.400 services include the following:

- User-agent (UA) access management
- Nondelivery alert
- Content type
- Delivery notification
- Multiple destinations
- Relay-and-forward message
- Workgroup addressing
- Dead-letter notification

MHS provides store-and-forward service, which means messages can be sent from one network to another with scheduled delivery dates and times.

Just as important, MHS provides gateways to other networks and even converts messages to the format appropriate for these networks. Since MHS is fully compatible with X.400 recommendations, its "store-and-forward" method of operation means that messages can be sent with delivery dates and times. Companies can schedule noncritical reports for night delivery and even schedule electronic document interchange (EDI).

You must remember that MHS is a utility program that virtually all network users will never see or use directly. It enables programmers to develop application programs and electronic mail/scheduling programs that will work in conjunction with it. Different application programs will share this common interface, so it is reasonable to foresee a time when programs operating on different networks will communicate directly with each other using MHS. As an example, a network supervisor in Phoenix, Arizona, might schedule an accounting program to produce a key management report that reflects sales and profits for that day. This report could be scheduled to be run each evening and then transmitted at a certain time to the company's headquarters in New York so that it could be on the agenda of an 8:00 am executive meeting. Similarly, this same report could be scheduled to be produced at night and then sent immediately to a long list of all important company managers worldwide. Because MHS keeps workgroup addresses on file, mailing reports to distribution lists is very easy. Finally, MHS messages can start executable programs, so it also is possible in our example to have 100 sales branches of our fictitious company compile sales reports at night. Then these branches could submit the reports at scheduled intervals to their corporate New York headquarters, where the information would be received automatically and transmitted to a database program. At a certain time the database manager could compile all this data and produce a report with accompanying graphics. Assuming a printer does not suffer a paper jam, this entire scenario could take place without human intervention.

THE COORDINATOR

Overview

Action Technologies' The Coordinator at one time was sold by Novell as the Netware Electronic Mail System (EMS). Today it is one of the leading electronic mail and scheduling programs. In this section we'll examine many of The Coordinator's features, including how to receive, create, and send electronic mail; how to organize what the program labels "conversations;" and how to operate the program's extensive scheduling functions.

Reading Your Morning Mail Using The Coordinator

The Coordinator organizes all communications on a particular subject and keeps them in sequential order as a "conversation."

Figure 10-2 illustrates the opening menu for The Coordinator. This menu can be customized so that a user's schedule for the day, unopened mail, an uncompleted project, or virtually any other material created with The Coordinator will appear upon accessing the program. This entire process can be automated by including the MAIL command in a user's login script.

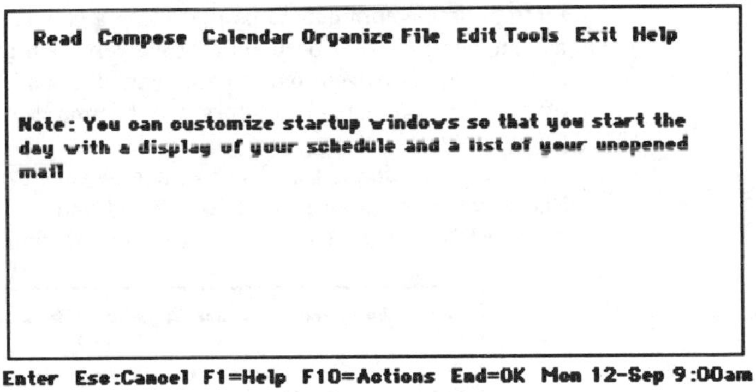

**Figure 10-2.
Opening Menu of The
Coordinator**

```
┌──────────────────────────────────────────────────────────────┐
│  Read  Compose  Calendar  Organize  File  Edit  Tools  Exit  Help │
│                                                                │
│                                                                │
│   Note: You can customize startup windows so that you start the│
│   day with a display of your schedule and a list of your unopened│
│   mail                                                         │
│                                                                │
│                                                                │
│                                                                │
│                                                                │
│                                                                │
│                                                                │
│                                                                │
└──────────────────────────────────────────────────────────────┘
   Enter  Esc:Cancel  F1=Help  F10=Actions  End=OK  Mon 12-Sep 9:00am
```

The Coordinator organizes all communications on a particular subject and keeps them in sequential order as a "conversation." Let's follow Carol Jackson for a couple of moments while she checks her mail. By pulling down the Read menu displayed in Figure 10-2, she will see the Read options displayed in Figure 10-3. When she selects List Unopened Mail, she will see a screen similar to that displayed in Figure 10-4.

The Coordinator lists communications under four different categories: New matters, Ongoing matters, Completed matters, and I am copied. The New matters category includes open conversations in which Carol is a principal participant rather than an observer. This means it includes correspondence to and from her but not correspondence in which she has

Figure 10-3.
The Read Menu

```
┌─────────────────────────────┐
│ List unopened mail   F2     │
│ Open enclosure...           │
│ ─────────────────────       │
│ Read backward        F7     │
│ Read forward         F8     │
│ Read first       Shift+F7   │
│ Read latest      Shift+F8   │
└─────────────────────────────┘
```

Figure 10-4.
Carol Lists Her
Unopened Mail

```
┌──────────────────────────────────────────────────────────┐
│ Read  Compose  Calendar Organize File  Edit Tools  Exit  Help │
│                                                            │
│              Unopened Mail    Subject                      │
│                                                            │
│  New matters                                               │
│  12-Sep Joe    request  -> me     Expense report          │
│  31-Aug Teri   inform   -> me     Lead at ABC Corp         │
│                                                            │
│  Ongoing matters                                           │
│  30-Aug Phil   thankyou -> me     Western region sales figures │
│                                                            │
│  I am copied                                               │
│  10-Sep Joe    inform   -> sales  New expense report format │
└──────────────────────────────────────────────────────────┘
  Enter  Del F1=Help  F3=Reply  F10=Actions  L:4 Mon 12-Sep 9:00 am
```

merely received a copy (cc). Ongoing matters refers to new communications
in ongoing conversations in which Carol is an principal participant. Completed
matters lists communications that close a conversation and any
communications that occur in that conversation after it closes. After a
conversation is closed, participants can still send comments about it to each
other. The I am copied category lists communications in which Carol is simply
an observer (cc).

Since Joe is Carol's boss, she decides to open mail from him first.
She moves her cursor to that item listed under New matters and presses
<ENTER>. Figure 10-5 illustrates a screen similar to what Carol will see.

Figure 10-5.
Carol Reads Her Mail

```
┌──────────────────────────────────────────────────────────┐
│ Read  Compose  Calendar Organize File  Edit Tools  Exit  Help │
│                                                            │
│  To       Carol Jackson (cjackson @ at4)                   │
│  Subject  Expense report                                   │
│  Enclosure K:\LOTUS\expenrpt.wk1                           │
│  When     Please reply by Tue 13-Oct-89                    │
│                                                            │
│  Carol, I'll need a bit more explanation on the $200 lunch listed │
│  for Dallas. Is the figure in R22 a typo or did you take the entire │
│  company out for lunch? Please get back to me immediately. │
│                                                            │
│  Joe                                                       │
└──────────────────────────────────────────────────────────┘
```

Now that Carol has opened this correspondence, it will no longer be
listed under unopened mail. Under NetWare, Carol can use the memory-
resident component of The Coordinator to check for new mail periodically and
alert her when any mail arrives using an Activate/Set Mail Alert Option.

Notice that Carol could select the Open enclosure option and actually view the expense report that she sent Joe. With this option she would be offered the opportunity to view, edit, file, or discard the enclosure. Only text files can actually be viewed. If Carol wanted a hard copy of her enclosure, she could select Edit and then select Print window from the Print menu under Tools.

Types of Communication Available with The Coordinator

The seven types of conversations available with The Coordinator include Note, Inform, Question, Offer, Request, Promise, and What if.

Carol's day has not started very well. When she read Joe's note and then viewed the enclosure, she discovered that she had made a serious mistake in her expense report. She needs to write Joe a note correcting this mistake. Her note will become part of the ongoing conversation The Coordinator maintains on this particular topic. To begin, Carol selects the Compose option from the Main menu.

Figure 10-6 illustrates the Compose options available to Carol. She can choose from seven different types of conversations, including Note, Inform, Question, Offer, Request, Promise, and What if. Note is used to prepare a communication that opens a conversation and posts it for delivery. This option should be used when you don't need or want a response and don't need a record of the conversation.

Figure 10-6.
The Compose Menu

Inform is used to convey information when you want an acknowledgment that your message has been received. When you send an important report or a memo that announces a new policy, you probably want an acknowledgment. Question is used when you want to ask a simple question or make a simple request. Carol could use this option if she wanted to ask Joe for the address of the Tokyo sales office or ask him if she could use her comp time next Tuesday.

Carol would select Offer if she wanted to offer to teach a training class or offer to represent the company at an upcoming trade show. If Joe accepts Carol's offer, then The Coordinator will treat it as a Promise, a type of conversation we'll examine shortly. Request is used to ask one or more people to perform one or more actions. The Coordinator works more efficiently if you limit yourself to one request per conversation. The Request format can be used during any kind of negotiation, and The Coordinator will keep a running record of requests and counteroffers.

Carol could select Promise if she wanted to promise to perform a specific action or confirm that she had agreed to perform a specific action. The Coordinator will keep track of her progress on this particular project.

The What if option is used to explore a possible course of action or solicit suggestions and opinions about it. If Joe asked Carol to provide information on what effect a 10 percent cut would have on her budget, she would reply using the What if option.

The Coordinator requires that the person opening a Question, Request, or What if conversation also close that conversation, since presumably that person has to decide if requests have been fulfilled or questions answered. Similarly, only the person to whom an Offer or Promise has been made can close that conversation. The Coordinator considers all options except Note to be "managed conversations" and actually suggests the correct protocol or rules for ending the conversation. Figure 10-7 illustrates the protocol acceptable for an Offer.

**Figure 10-7.
The Protocol for Making
an Offer**

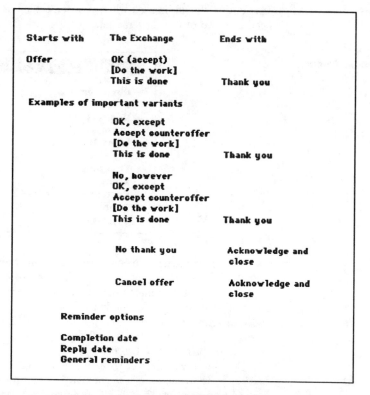

Starts with	The Exchange	Ends with
Offer	OK (accept) [Do the work] This is done	Thank you

Examples of important variants

	OK, except Accept counteroffer [Do the work] This is done	Thank you
	No, however OK, except Accept counteroffer [Do the work] This is done	Thank you
	No thank you	Acknowledge and close
	Cancel offer	Acknowledge and close

Reminder options

Completion date
Reply date
General reminders

Addressing Communications with The Coordinator

Carol composed a brief message to her boss pointing out the mistake in her expense report and correcting it. She now needs to decide how to handle her communication. From the Compose menu she may select several options, including Envelope, Reply, Forward, Send, and Utilities. The Envelope option is used to address an envelope for a communication that starts a conversation or establishes reminder dates for a conversation so that your calendar will automatically be updated. It also is used if a file needs to be enclosed with a communication. Figure 10-8 illustrates the information required under the Envelope option. The "Cc" option includes the capability to send a blind courtesy copy (bcc), a copy that will go to a designated person without the knowledge of person addressed in the communication. The Category item allows you to include one or more categories associated with the topic on which you are composing a communication. The Coordinator uses these categories to organize conversations. Since several categories can be used with a single communication, a memorandum explaining an unexpected telecommunications expense concerning the XYZ project might contain the categories XYZ, BUDGET, and TELECOM. Up to 64 different categories may be defined at any time.

**Figure 10-8.
Addressing an
Envelope**

The When option under the Envelope menu is used to set one or more reminders. Figure 10-9 illustrates that you may indicate a project's completion date and a "reply by" date. These two items are included in the headers of communications and distributed to all participants in a conversation. The Remind me option sets a personal reminder, and The Coordinator will remind you on a date that you specify. With a conversation you can use as many personal reminders as you wish, each with its own text. Figure 10-10 indicates how Carol might want to include several personal reminders in conjunction with a memo she has drafted regarding a meeting she is planning.

**Figure 10-9.
Using the When Option**

**Figure 10-10.
The Coordinator
Permits Personal
Reminders**

```
Mon  27-March-89   Order Buffet for Sales Meeting
Wed  29-March-89   Send out final agenda
Fri  01-April-89   Complete slides
```

The Reply, Forward, and Send Options Using The Coordinator

The only possible reply to a note under the Coordinator is a note. In other situations, though, this program will prompt you for the type of reply you wish to select. Figure 10-11 illustrates several different options regarding a request that has been received.

**Figure 10-11.
Reply Options**

```
Reply options
after CJefferson's request
-----------------------------------------------
A   YES                          (promise)
B   OK, except                   (counteroffer)
C   No, however                  (counteroffer)
D   Delegate it
E   *This is done                  (report)
F   *Can't, Won't or No           (decline)

G   Postpone responding
H   Comment
I   Acknowledge receipt
```

The Forward option permits you to include the text of one communication in that of another. If, for example, you receive a request or question that you need to delegate to another person, you probably would want to send that person a short memorandum and forward the original request as part of the communication.

Once a communication has been written and an envelope, a reply, or forwarding information have been provided, it's time to post the mail. The Send option transfers the communication to MHS for routing and delivery.

The Coordinator's Calendar

The Coordinator comes with a calendar feature that can make appointments for any date up to the year 2048 and keep detailed notes on each day's appointments.

What distinguishes The Coordinator from some other electronic mail programs is that it has the added dimensions of any good office coordinator: it keeps detailed calendars for all network users, provides reminders, and organizes all office files. Figure 10-12 illustrates the options available under the Calendar menu. The program can make appointments for any date up to the year 2048. If we select "Show Calendar," we'll see a screen similar to that in Figure 10-13, which provides a detailed listing of our day's schedule, including reminders, appointments, conversations that need replies, and any material we need to work on this day. The reminders listed are general reminders and not reminders specific to a particular conversation. The "Carry forward" category includes any unfinished actions up to two weeks after their due dates. A Print window option in the Printing window enables you to print any daily calendar you wish.

One calendar feature that can make any executive more effective is the Repeat/appt/rem option that enables a repeat appointment to be

**Figure 10-12.
The Calendar Menu**

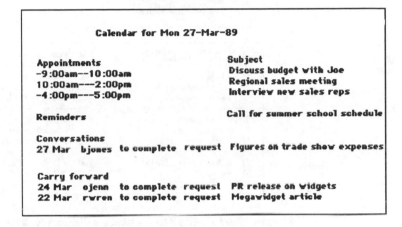

**Figure 10-13.
The Calendar Provides
Details**

```
          Calendar for Mon 27-Mar-89

Appointments                    Subject
-9:00am--10:00am                Discuss budget with Joe
10:00am---2:00pm                Regional sales meeting
-4:00pm---5:00pm                Interview new sales reps

Reminders                       Call for summer school schedule

Conversations
27 Mar   bjones  to complete  request  Figures on trade show expenses

Carry forward
24 Mar   ojenn   to complete  request  PR release on widgets
22 Mar   rwren   to complete  request  Megawidget article
```

scheduled daily, weekly, biweekly, monthly on a date, monthly on a day, yearly on a date, or yearly on a day. This certainly makes it easy to set up standing appointments.

The Coordinator's Organizing Features

If you select Organize from The Coordinator's pull-down menu, you'll see a screen similar to that pictured in Figure 10-14. Figure 10-15 displays the options you have when reviewing your communications and conversations, and Figure 10-16 shows your options on the By type submenu under the Review menu. You could review all the promises you made to your boss, all the conversations with a prospective customer, or even all the offers on a specific system that you made to a prospective customer after July 1. In other words, you can select all the options simultaneously if you need them to define a particular review. Since many conversations specify future actions, you can use the Review option to identify and organize conversations with due dates for actions you must carry out or for communications to which you must reply.

**Figure 10-14.
The Organize Menu**

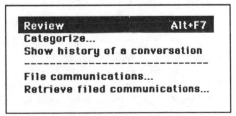

Figure 10-15.
Options for Reviewing
Communications

```
    * By type              All conversations
    * By dates             Any date
    * By categories        Any category
    * With                 Anybody


      Save settings

   OK - build list
```

Figure 10-16.
Reviewing
Communications by
Type

```
A  All open matters          K  Enclosures
   ----------------------        ----------------------
B  All promises              L  All missing replies
C  My promises               M  Missing my replies
D  Their promises            N  Missing their replies
   ----------------------        ----------------------
E  All requests              O  When I'm copied
F  My requests               P  Closed matters
G  Their requests            Q  Marked for deletion
   ----------------------        ----------------------
H  Other offers/informs      R  All conversations
J  Notes                     S  All communications
```

Some Other Valuable Features Found in The Coordinator

The Coordinator contains a word-processing program as well as a built-in gateway to other messaging systems, including those found on IBM, DEC, and Hewlett Packard computers.

From the Edit menu of The Coordinator you can access a word-processing program that produces standard ASCII text files. It permits text to be cut and pasted, moved in blocks, searched and replaced, and printed on most popular printers. The program's menus can be customized so that novices do not have to deal with so many different types of conversations. The Coordinator can update both the sender's and recipient's calendars automatically, build distribution lists, enclose any type of file (including a spreadsheet), and send conversations on specified dates. This last feature is a characteristic of MHS's store-and-forward method of routing information. A memorandum can be written well ahead of time but not delivered until a certain date.

Because it uses MHS, The Coordinator has built-in gateways to other messaging systems, including IBM's PROFS and DIOSS, DEC's All-in-1 and VMSmail, Wang Office, HP-DESK, CompuServe's InfoPlex, FAX, TELEX, and MCI Mail.

THE CC:MAIL PROGRAM

Reading Your Mail with cc:Mail

We'll return to our example of Carol Jackson, who previously used The Coordinator to read and send mail. Let's assume that she now works for a company running cc:Mail on its local area network. Carol has logged in, which resulted in her login script executing a batch file that brought her to the cc:Mail Main menu illustrated in Figure 10-17.

The Inbox is the place where you receive messages from other cc:Mail users. Carol currently has four messages in her Inbox; as she opens and reads each message, the New count will decrease by one each time. As Carol files some of these messages, the folder count will adjust to include these new folders. The program permits a user to have up to 200 folders at any time. If Carol simply does not want to deal with one of the new messages in her Inbox, she can leave it there and it will remain as part of the Msgs total.

The cc:Mail program provides bulletin boards that all users can access to read messages. Only the administrator may delete messages, however. Carol could read a bulletin board message and then copy it to a personal folder for her own personal copy.

After selecting the Read Inbox messages option in Figure 10-17 and pressing <ENTER>, Carol will see a screen similar to that pictured in Figure 10-18. Since Joe Blow happens to be Carol's boss and since she is nervous about her expense report, she selects his message and presses <ENTER>. Figure 10-19 illustrates how cc:Mail displays a message. After Carol has read her message, she presses <ENTER> to bring up an Action menu, displayed in Figure 10-20, which appears over the message text.

**Figure 10-17.
The cc:Mail Main Menu**

**Figure 10-18.
Selecting a Message to Read**

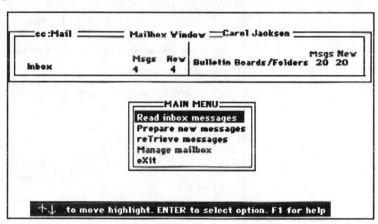

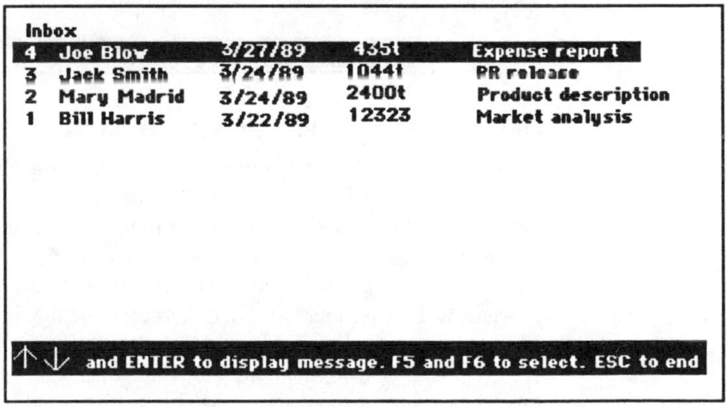

Figure 10-19.
Reading a Message

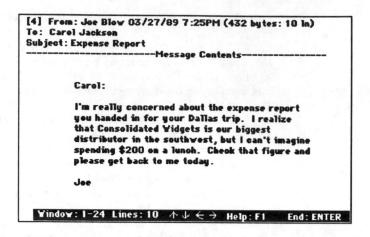

```
[4] From: Joe Blow 03/27/89 7:25PM (432 bytes: 10 ln)
To: Carol Jackson
Subject: Expense Report
------------------------Message Contents---------------


        Carol:

        I'm really concerned about the expense report
        you handed in for your Dallas trip.  I realize
        that Consolidated Widgets is our biggest
        distributor in the southwest, but I can't imagine
        spending $200 on a lunch.  Check that figure and
        please get back to me today.

        Joe


Window: 1-24  Lines: 10  ↑↓ ←→   Help: F1    End: ENTER
```

Figure 10-20.
The Action Menu

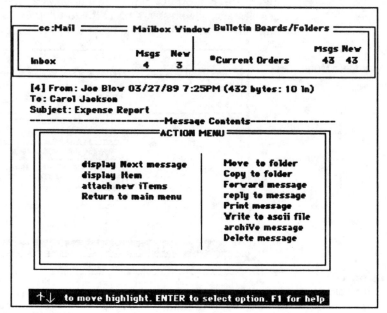

```
══cc:Mail ══════  Mailbox Window Bulletin Boards/Folders ═══
                          Msgs New                 Msgs New
Inbox                      4    3    *Current Orders  43  43

[4] From: Joe Blow 03/27/89 7:25PM (432 bytes: 10 ln)
To: Carol Jackson
Subject: Expense Report
------------------------Message Contents---------------
═══════════════════════ACTION MENU═══════


    display Next message        Move  to folder
    display Item                Copy to folder
    attach new iTems            Forward message
    Return to main menu         reply to message
                                Print message
                                Write to ascii file
                                archiVe message
                                Delete message



↑↓  to move highlight. ENTER to select option. F1 for help
```

Replying to a Message with cc:Mail

We'll assume that Carol wants to reply immediately and let Joe know that there's a mistake in her expense-account report. She selects the Reply to message option and sees a screen similar to that displayed in Figure 10-21. While replying, Carol can use the resources of cc:Mail's full text editor. She can enter up to 20,000 characters in a text item and use such word-processing features as word wrap, reformatting, block movement of text, find and replace text, ASCII file creation, and printing to most standard printers.

Once Carol has completed her message, she can press the <F10> key to bring up a Send menu, which is displayed in Figure 10-22. If Carol had wanted to send a courtesy copy (cc) or even a blind cc to another user she could have selected the Address menu. Figure 10-23 illustrates the other options available here, which include a request for a receipt.

Figure 10-21.
Writing a Quick Reply

```
From: Carol Jackson
To:  Joe Blow
Subject:  Correction to Expense Report
-------------------------------Message Contents----------------

    Joe,

    I've looked over the expense report, and you're right.
    Consolidated Widget may be my biggest distributor,
    but the lunch in Dallas ran $20 and not $200. Believe
    it or not, $20 still buys a hamburger feast in Texas.

    I hope this clears up the any questions or concerns you
    have about the report.


L:10  C:37  %Full: 0  Highlight(^^^^): AltF1  Help: F1  End: F10
```

Figure 10-22.
The Send Menu

```
From: Carol Jackson
To: Joe Blow
Subject: Expense Report
------------------------Message Contents----------------

                    SEND MENU
                   Send message
                   attach copy of dos File
                   attach new iTems
                   display Message
                   edit sUbject
                   Address message
                   display Next message
                   Return to main menu


  ↑↓ to move highlight, ENTER to select option. F1 for help
```

Figure 10-23.
The Address Menu

```
From: Carol Jackson  3/27/89  3:33PM (459 bytes: 10 ln)
To: Joe Blow
Subject: Expense Report
-------------------------Message Contents----------------

                    ADDRESS MENU
   eNd addressing            Copy to person
   Address to person         Copy to mailing List
   address to Mailing list   Blind copy to person
   address to bboard/Folder  reQuest receipt
   Return to main menu       Delete address list


  ↑↓ ←→  to move highlight. ENTER to select option. F1 for help
```

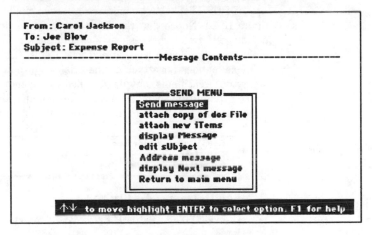

One of the options available under cc:Mail's Main menu is Prepare new messages. The screen for writing new messages will look exactly like the screen displayed earlier for replying to messages. When Carol creates a new message, she has the option of including any kind of file with the message as well as copying the message to a personal folder so she can keep this material on file with other related items. She can also send her communication to public mailing lists available to all cc:Mail users or to one of her own mailing lists. Notice how practical this feature is for a human resources department, which might need to communicate with employees by position (all managers), by payroll designation (all nonexempt employees), or by sex or race. Similarly, the bulletin board option under cc:Mail permits companies to post general announcements, job vacancies, and other companywide information without having physically to mail notices to everyone.

Attaching Files to Your Mail with cc:Mail

Virtually any kind of file can be attached to a cc:Mail communication.

Any type of DOS file may be attached to a cc:Mail communication, even executable programs (.COM or .EXE files), as long as they are not copy-protected. By selecting the appropriate option from the Send menu, "attach copy of DOS File," Carol would see a screen similar to that displayed in Figure 10-24. Notice that the directory shows a variety of different files including electronic spreadsheet files and picture files. By selecting another option from the Send menu, attach new Items, Carol would be provided with additional options for attaching material, as displayed in Figure 10-25. Up to twenty different items may be attached to a communication, and each item can be given a title such as "Agenda for Annual Retreat" for a text item or "Map showing directions to annual retreat" for a graphics item.

**Figure 10-24.
Attaching a DOS File**

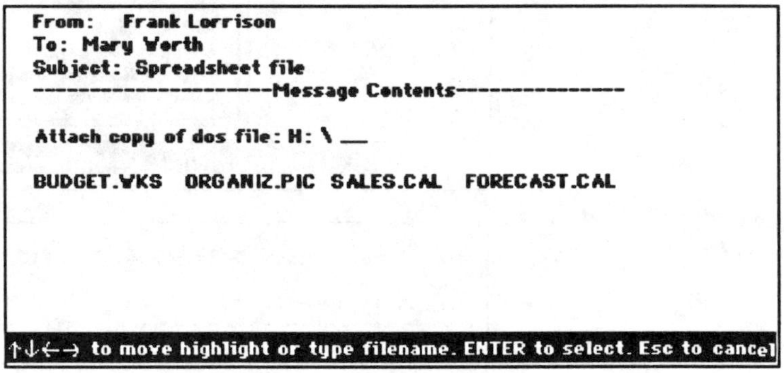

```
From:   Frank Lorrison
To:  Mary Worth
Subject: Spreadsheet file
--------------------Message Contents--------------

Attach copy of dos file: H: \ __

BUDGET.WKS   ORGANIZ.PIC  SALES.CAL   FORECAST.CAL




↑↓←→ to move highlight or type filename. ENTER to select. Esc to cancel
```

The Snapshot Utility Program with cc:Mail

The Snapshot utility program enables you to take snapshots of virtually any screen and then attach these pictures to any communication.

Using the Snapshot utility program included with cc:Mail, you can import information from other application programs and include them with mail communications. When you run the SNAPSHOT.COM program, a small resident kernel (around 20K) remains in RAM as a terminate-and-stay-resident (TSR) program. Since the Snapshot program permits display of previous snapshots taken, it is possible to generate a "slide show" on any network workstation.

**Figure 10-25.
Attaching an Item to a
Message**

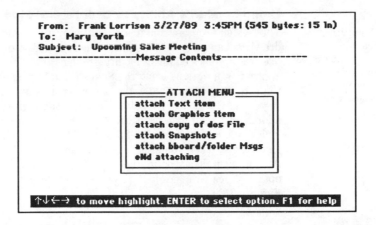

```
From:  Frank Lorrison 3/27/89  3:45PM (545 bytes: 15 ln)
To:  Mary Worth
Subject:  Upcoming Sales Meeting
------------------Message Contents------------------


                    ┌─────ATTACH MENU─────┐
                    │ attach Text item           │
                    │ attach Graphics item       │
                    │ attach copy of dos File    │
                    │ attach Snapshots           │
                    │ attach bboard/folder Msgs  │
                    │ eNd attaching              │
                    └────────────────────────────┘


   ↑↓←→ to move highlight. ENTER to select option. F1 for help
```

The Snapshot program permits you to select a key to be used to take a snapshot but defaults to <ALT>-1. Figure 10-26 illustrates the Snapshot menu that appears when you press the appropriate key while running an application program. Figure 10-27 reveals that, if you select the Take and store snapshot option, you'll be given the opportunity to indicate under what name you wish to store the file.

**Figure 10-26.
The Snapshot Menu**

```
┌─────────────cc:Mail Snapshot─────────────┐
│                          │                │
│ ▐Take and store snapshot │ Display stored snapshot │
│                          │                │
│                          │                │
└──────────────────────────┴────────────────┘
   ↑↓←→ and ENTER to select. Esc to cancel
```

**Figure 10-27.
Taking and Storing a
Snapshot**

```
┌─────────────cc:Mail Snapshot─────────────┐
│                                           │
│   Take snapshot and store in file: C: __  │
│                                           │
│                                           │
└───────────────────────────────────────────┘
 Type the filename and press ENTER. F1 for directory. Esc to cancel
```

The procedure for taking a Snapshot of a graphics screen is slightly different. When you press the designated snapshot key, the screen displayed is captured and then automatically saved in the current drive and directory under a filename that is generated automatically. The files are named SNAP followed by the letters EGA, CGA, or HGC, depending on the type of graphics adapter in use on the workstation. These files are numbered consecutively so that the second EGA snapshot would carry the name SNAPEGA.002.

Using cc:Mail's Ability to Create and Modify Graphics

The cc:Mail program contains a built-in graphics editor that can be used to create original graphics or modify graphics created with other programs.

The cc:Mail program contains a built-in graphics editor so that original drawings can be created and then incorporated into a message. You can also use this graphics editor to modify graphics that have been captured from application programs using the Snapshot utility program. Let's first examine the way we would create a graphic to accompany a short note.

After you have written your message, given it a subject, and addressed it, you may press the <F10> key to bring up the Send menu, which you saw in Figure 10-22. One of the options under this menu is attach new iTems. When you select this item and press <ENTER>, you'll see the Attach menu displayed in Figure 10-28, from which you can choose the option attach Graphics item to bring up the graphics menu displayed in Figure 10-29.

**Figure 10-28.
Select Attach Graphics
Item from the Attach
Menu**

```
══════ ATTACH MENU ══════
    attach Text item
    attach Graphics item
    attach copy of dos File
    attach Snapshots
    attach bboard/folder Msgs
    eNd attaching
```

**Figure 10-29.
The Graphics Menu**

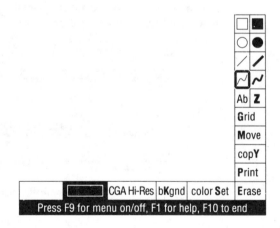

With this graphics menu it is possible to select different color sets as well as background colors, thick or thin free-drawing lines, empty or solid circles, letters, and grids.

One very useful feature of cc:Mail is that it is possible to share snapshots taken from selected application programs with users who may not have access to these programs. The cc:Mail program enables you to treat one of your snapshots as if it were a photocopy of a screen. You can also treat your snapshots like text and simply add this text to whatever messages you wish to send. Your recipient will see the database report or spreadsheet screen without having to run the appropriate application program.

Viewing the cc:Mail Mail Directory

One of the NetWare network supervisor's responsibilities if cc:Mail is installed is managing the network mail directory. As Figure 10-30 illustrates, the location status of a mailbox is identified with an L for a local user, an R for a remote (stand-alone) user, an r for a remote network user on another post office, a P for a remote post office that connects directly to your post office, and by a p for a remote post office that can be accessed through another remote post office (hub).

Figure 10-30. Managing the Mail Directory

Name	Loc	Last Checked In		Comments
Albert, Charles	L	3/28/89	2:54PM	VP Sales
Bush, George	L	3/28/89	9:00AM	President
DeBaugh, Francis	R	3/28/89	7:00AM	Miami
Jackson, Andrew	r			Phoenix
Peoples, Paul	L	3/28/89	10:09AM	Sales
TUCSONPOST	P	3/28/89	1:04PM	Tucson post office
Zaslow, Ziggy	L	3/24/89	3:45PM	Accounting

Remote users have mailboxes in the post office just as local network users do; unfortunately, these remote users must access their mailboxes from outside the local area network. They can use a stand-alone PC running cc:Mail Remote software for direct access or they can access their post offices indirectly from another post office. These remote users can send and receive messages but cannot use the local bulletin boards.

When a cc:Mail Remote user directly accesses a cc:Mail post office, the post office checks to see if the user has a mailbox there (that is, whether the person is registered in the mail directory). If the user is not listed, he or she can only send messages to specific mailboxes but cannot receive mail. Other post offices running the cc:Mail DIALin utility program can directly access a remote post office if it is running cc:Mail Gateway. The cc:Mail administrator must provide these remote users with a post office name and a telephone number to which the cc:Mail DIALin utility program is connected.

Since we may need to see the mailbox address for remote users, we can use our <Right> cursor key to move to the right of the Comments column and see a screen that will resemble the one pictured in Figure 10-31.

Figure 10-31. Viewing cc:Mail Addresses

Name	Loc	cc:Mail Address
Albert, Charles	L	
Bush, George	L	
DeBaugh, Francis	R	1-612-444-3232
Jackson, Andrew	r	PHOENIXPOST
Peoples, Paul	L	
TUCSONPOST	P	1-602-443-4343
Zaslow, Ziggy	L	

Compiling and Analyzing Mailbox Statistics

The Chkstat utility program provides the cc:Mail administrator with detailed statistics on individual mailbox usage as well as on total post office usage.

The cc:Mail program provides several key utility programs to help the administrator manage a network's electronic mail efficiently. A directory function of the cc:Mail Chkstat program provides a listing of information on each individual mailbox, including the mailbox name, the location, the time the user last checked in, and any general comments. This information is displayed as follows:

Mailbox Name	Locn	Last Checked in		Comments
Alpert, Harmon	L	03/08/89	2:15 pm	Sales Mgr
Boris, Barbara	R	03/10/89	10:00 am	LA Office
Smith, Sylvester	L	03/10/89	9:53 am	Account Exec

A Users function of the Chkstat utility program provides detailed information on mailbox users that includes their mailbox name, location, USR file number, and the number of bytes in their file. Since remote users and post offices have a remote post office as their cc:Mail address for indirect access, they do not have an individual USR file number and hence no file bytes will appear when users are listed.

Mailbox Name	Locn	USR File #	File Bytes
Alpert, Harmon	L	00007	672
Boris, Barbara	R	00003	
Smith, Sylvester	L	00010	974

The Messages function of the cc:Mail Chkstat utility program provides the administrator with information on how messages are dispersed on the mail system by mailbox and by bulletin board. For example, he or she can examine the total number of stored messages by typing the following command, which will produce the information displayed on the next page.

cc:Mail Post Office: LOCALPOST

The Messages function also provides detailed statistics on the distribution of messages to individual mailboxes, including how many messages (in bytes) are shared and how many are not shared (are unique to a particular mailbox or bulletin board). An administrator can also request reports regarding

```
Message Statistics 04/15/89
Number of stored messages:              50
Total bytes in messages:            143356
Total bytes remaining:              272772
Reclaimable bytes:                   16772
Additional bytes:                   512000
```

specific groups of messages, such as those in Carol Jackson's mailbox dated on or before February 21 that have already been read.

Gateways from cc:Mail to the Rest of the World

The cc:Mail program provides gateways to IBM and DEC electronic mail users.

The cc:Mail program provides a number of gateway connections to other computer mail systems. The cc:Mail program ProfSLINK provides electronic mail exchange between a NetWare LAN running cc:Mail and any VM computer running IBM Professional Office System (PROFS). Users on this IBM mainframe system may also send mail to cc:Mail users on the local area network. There is also a cc:Mail DEClink program to link a NetWare LAN to a DEC computer so that ALL-IN-1 and VAXmail users can communicate directly with LAN users.

Other major cc:Mail gateways for interconnectivity of electronic mail include cc:Mail for the Macintosh and cc:Mail FAXlink. The cc:Mail for the Macintosh provides a convenient way to transfer Macintosh and IBM PC files between networks, since these files are placed in cc:Mail envelopes which use the same format on both computers. The cc:Mail FAXlink program permits PC and Macintosh cc:Mail users electronically to create, send, receive, and view text and graphics-oriented messages using facsimile machines. Fax messages can be viewed prior to printing, replied to, forwarded to other destinations, and stored in electronic files. Only one facsimile board is required for each network.

USING THE NETWORK COURIER

Functions of The Network Courier Administrator

The Network Courier administrator is responsible for setting up a post office, providing mailbox names and privileges for users, establishing communications with other post offices, and defining the times and frequency of calling other post offices.

The LAN supervisor serves as The Network Courier's administrator. An Administrator program enables the supervisor to set up a post office, provide mailbox names and privileges for users, establish communications with other post offices, and define the times and frequency of calling other post offices. During installation, the administrator will use a Courier Administrator menu to specify a network name and post office names associated with it as well as IDs. An External-Admin menu includes a Setup option so that the administrator can specify such items as baud rate, parity, data bits, stop bits, dialing mode, and type of line (full-duplex or half-duplex). A Config option under Setup enables the administrator to specify hardware communications parameters for each external post office to be linked.

The Network Courier comes with four major programs: The Administrator, The External Mail program, The Mail program, and The Mail Monitor program. Before we look specifically at how a network administrator establishes network parameters for external communications, let's follow a network user and observe how he performs his routine daily work using this program.

Reading Your Mail with The Network Courier

We'll assume that John Smith is an average user on a Novell NetWare network running The Network Courier. John may have his login script written so that it automatically checks for new mail when he logs in and then allows him to look at this mail. Assuming he has not written such a script, John would type MAIL at the network prompt and see a screen similar to that in Figure 10-32.

Figure 10-32.
Mail Summary Screen

```
Network Courier                              New mail: 6  Unread mail: 4

Alias Read Compose Delete Forward  Storage  Print  Options  Login  Update
Read toggled items of mail, or all unread mail if nothing toggled

   ┌──────────────────────────────────────────────────────────────┐
   │  FROM      SUBJECT              DATE      TIME       PRI       │
   │                                                                │
   │  VPSales   Expense Report       03-27-89  15:57      4         │
   │  KarenC    Upcoming Presentation 03-27-89 13:45      3         │
   │  BillR     Question on PO #33443 03-27-89 08:30      2         │
   │  MaryCr    Printer Question      03-27-89  11:34     1         │
   │  DickG     New Vacation Policy   03-23-89  10:34               │
   │  PaulineC  List of References    03-22-89  12:34               │
   │                                                                │
   └──────────────────────────────────────────────────────────────┘
```

Notice in this example that John's mail has automatically been arranged in order of priority, with the highest priority item (priority 4) listed first. A network administrator may also provide certain users with the privilege of sending urgent mail (priority 5). Notice also that John can see the date and time each message was sent as well as a corresponding subject. Messages that are unread are shown in bold or enhanced video on monochrome monitors and in yellow on color monitors.

John has four new messages that he has not yet read and two items he has read. We'll assume that he wants to read his highest priority message first, so John presses the <R> key for the Read option and then uses his cursor to highlight the first item before pressing <ENTER>. Figure 10-33 displays the Read mail message screen John will see. Notice that the mail in John's queue has decreased by one, since one less letter is left to read.

If the message is lengthy, John can use his <UP> and <DOWN> keys or even his <PgUp> and <PgDn> keys to scroll through the document. At the top of the Read screen are several options that he can take, including Delete, Hold, Forward, Print, Reply, and Storage.

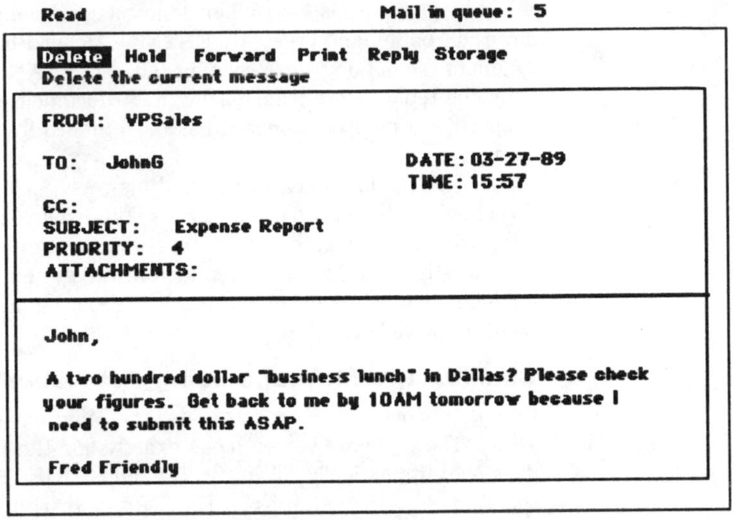

Figure 10-33.
Reading Mail with The
Network Courier

```
Read                              Mail in queue:  5
─────────────────────────────────────────────────────

 Delete  Hold   Forward   Print   Reply  Storage
 Delete the current message
┌───────────────────────────────────────────────────┐
│                                                     │
│  FROM:  VPSales                                     │
│                                                     │
│  TO:   JohnG                       DATE: 03-27-89   │
│                                    TIME: 15:57      │
│  CC:                                                │
│  SUBJECT:    Expense Report                         │
│  PRIORITY:   4                                      │
│  ATTACHMENTS:                                       │
│                                                     │
├───────────────────────────────────────────────────┤
│                                                     │
│  John,                                              │
│                                                     │
│  A two hundred dollar "business lunch" in Dallas? Please check │
│  your figures. Get back to me by 10AM tomorrow because I       │
│  need to submit this ASAP.                          │
│                                                     │
│  Fred Friendly                                      │
│                                                     │
└───────────────────────────────────────────────────┘
```

Replying to a Message with The Network Courier

We'll assume that John believes in the management principle of dealing with
a piece of paper (or electronic message) only once. He thus replies
immediately to this first message before dealing with any other item. After
selecting the "Reply" option and pressing <ENTER>, he sees a screen
similar to the one pictured in Figure 10-34.

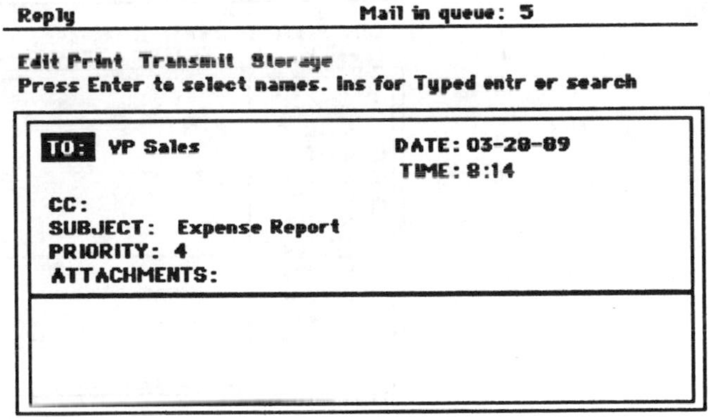

Figure 10-34.
Replying to a Message

```
Reply                             Mail in queue:  5
─────────────────────────────────────────────────────

 Edit Print  Transmit  Storage
 Press Enter to select names. Ins for Typed entr or search
┌───────────────────────────────────────────────────┐
│                                                     │
│  TO:  VP Sales                     DATE: 03-28-89   │
│                                    TIME: 8:14       │
│  CC:                                                │
│  SUBJECT:  Expense Report                           │
│  PRIORITY: 4                                        │
│  ATTACHMENTS:                                       │
│                                                     │
├───────────────────────────────────────────────────┤
│                                                     │
│                                                     │
│                                                     │
│                                                     │
│                                                     │
└───────────────────────────────────────────────────┘
```

The Reply screen comes preaddressed to the sender of the current
message, and the subject and priority fields of the current message are copied
automatically into the address section of John's reply. John can use pop-up
windows to display lists of mail users to determine who he wants to cc in this
reply. The Network Courier provides a simple text editor that has word wrap
and overwrite and insert modes. The <F5> key gives John the option of
including a DOS text file in his reply wherever the cursor happens to be

when he presses this key. When John has completed his reply, he selects the Transmit option and presses <ENTER> to send his reply. The program will give him the option *before* sending (OK TO TRANSMIT? YES NO) to save or print the reply before transmitting it. A document transmitted is like a letter dropped in a mailbox—once it has been mailed it cannot be copied or stored away.

After John has transmitted his reply, he's returned to the Read screen where the original message is still displayed. John must decide at this point whether he wants to delete it, print it, store it, or simply hold it. A message that is held will be retained in the system and appear in the future on John's Unread mail screen, but it will not be prioritized or appear in boldface or yellow.

Composing a Message Using The Network Courier

Compose is one of the options under the Main menu we examined in Figure 10-32. The Compose screen looks exactly like the Reply screen except that it does not automatically fill-in the TO and SUBJECT fields. With the cursor in the TO field, John can press <ENTER> and see a pull-down window that displays a list of all addressees available on the mail system. He may scroll through this list, select the desired person, and then press <ENTER>. Figure 10-35 illustrates how this process works. The CC field contains the very same pull-down window listing possible addressees to be copied. The SUBJECT field may be up to forty characters in length, and the PRIORITY field may be any number between 1 and 4 or even 5 if John has been given the privilege of sending urgent messages.

**Figure 10-35.
Selecting a Message
Recipient**

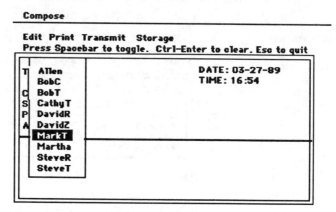

The ATTACHMENTS field can be used to attach virtually any kind of files. By placing his cursor over this field and pressing <ENTER>, John can view the PATHNAME: prompt and the current drive and path. If he presses <ENTER> at this point, he'll see a files window where he can locate whatever file he needs to attach. John can attach files existing in different directories and even on different volumes. After he has selected all the files he wants to attach, he simply presses <ENTER>.

One useful feature of The Network Courier's ATTACHMENTS field is that portions of files can be attached to a message that is being composed. If John had saved a spreadsheet as a print file, for example, he could use the Storage/View option to view the print file, mark the section of the spreadsheet needed, and copy the information from a paste area to the location of his cursor in the message he is composing. He would use function keys to accomplish this marking <F6>, pasting <F7>, and copying <F8>.

Some Key Options of The Network Courier

With The Network Courier a user can set and change passwords, stamp communications with the date and time, sort communications a number of different ways, and establish a "useful-life" for communications.

The Options menu under the main Mail menu consists of five key utilities: Password, Date/Time, Sortkey, Headers, and Useful-Life. The Password option allows you to change your user password and requires you to verify the new password before making the change. The Date/Time utility lets you set the time and date so that you may time/date stamp all mail you send. You will not have to use this utility if your computer has a built-in clock and calendar. The Sortkey utility enables you to decide how you want your mail sorted.

John's mail was sorted according to priority, but there are four additional methods available for sorting:

DATE: in the order received
FROM: by sender name
SUBJECT: by subject name
PRIORITY: by priority (top priority first)

The Headers utility is provided because normally The Network Courier displays only 50 notifications of mail or headers at a time. You can change this number to reflect your particular needs (let's say 200), and the new number will remain in the system until you decide to change it. With the Useful-Life option you can specify how long you want to send mail to another post office in order to cut the costs of external mail delivery after the mail's useful purpose has been eliminated. You can set the number of hours from 0 to 999. Selecting zero means that the mail's life expectancy is unlimited, and mail will not be eliminated even if undelivered. The manufacturer recommends that you leave the default value of zero (unlimited) for regular mail but put a limit on urgent mail, because it declines in value rapidly.

The Mail Monitor Program

The Network Courier's Mail Monitor program is memory resident and permits the mail program to run in the background and alert you that mail has arrived while you are running an application program.

The memory-resident Mail Monitor program permits the mail program to run in the background and alert you that mail has arrived while you are running an application program. It permits you to interrupt the application program temporarily, read the message, store the message, and even reply to the message, and then return to your application program's screen.

To load The Mail Monitor program a user types MONITOR followed by a space and your mailbox ID, which is followed by a space and -P and your password. For example, John logs in as follows:

M:MONITOR JOHNS -PPLAYBOY

John can then load and use any application program such as Lotus 1-2-3 or dBASE IV. Whenever he wants to use The Mail Monitor, John simply presses the <ALT> and <F1> keys. This key combination can be changed if another application program already uses it.

The Mail Monitor program contains the options Silent, Beep, and Notify. When you select the Silent option The Mail Monitor will not inform you when mail arrives but will store the message. You can still view the mail at any time by pressing the hot keys. The Beep option provides a beep when mail is delivered, and the Notify option beeps to announce the arrival of mail and also displays a notice at the bottom left-hand corner of your screen that resembles the following:

Message From: Frieda
Esc to Ignore, Enter to Read

Displaying a notice such as this halts other I/O operations such as printing, so you are given the option when selecting Notify to limit the number of minutes you wish to have a notice displayed on your screen. Setting the value at 0 indicates that you wish the message to stay on the screen until you acknowledge it, no matter how long it takes.

The External Mail Program

The Network Courier's External Mail Program is used to send and receive external mail (messages transferred between post offices).

As we indicated earlier in this chapter, The Network Courier's External Mail program is used to send and receive external mail, which includes messages transferred between post offices. If a Modem Mail option is installed, external mail then includes mail sent to and received from modem mail users.

One of the mail administrator's responsibilities is to establish a calling schedule under the Administrator program to be used by The External Mail program. Figure 10-36 illustrates a typical calling schedule. If a specific time interval is not listed, only priority 5 calls (urgent) will be made during that time period. When mail is sent that needs to be routed to another post office, the External Mail program checks the network clock to see if it is authorized to transmit at that time. If not, it holds the messages an appropriate time and waits to begin transmitting them. The program will track any costs listed in the calling schedule and print these costs in report form. If you wish, you can dedicate a computer to running The External Mail program and send and receive external mail 24 hours a day.

**Figure 10-36.
A Typical Calling
Schedule**

Times

Regular   `Intervals`
Define/Modify intervals dial time

Interval	From	To	First minute (cents)	Additional Minutes (cents)
1:	00:01	07:59	20	45
2:	12:00	12:59	35	65
3:	13:00	17:00	35	50
4:	17:01	20:59	20	50

RUNNING CONETIC SYSTEMS' HIGGINS

Reading Your Morning Mail with Higgins

The Higgins program is invoked by typing HIGGINS from a directory immediately above the HIGGINS subdirectory. A NetWare supervisor can write a batch file or login script that will check for new mail upon login and then send the user directly to this program. The login script or batch file should be set up to access the appropriate monitor driver (monochrome or color) for the particular user.

A Higgins screen containing a greeting and copyright information is then displayed and the user is asked to type an identification code. There are actually two passwords for each identification code, a public code to allow access to your Higgins data and an optional private code to restrict access to more sensitive information.

Let's assume that Mary Brown is the sales manager for Polytex General, a company that is using Higgins as its electronic messaging system on a NetWare network. Mary logs in with her ID and password and sees a screen similar to the one pictured in Figure 10-37. Notice that she sees a calendar for the month and the current active date. To the left of the calendar is her appointment bar graph, with bars representing her appointments and activities for the day. Each fifteen-minute block within normal business hours is displayed.

Figure 10-37.
The Main Calendar Menu

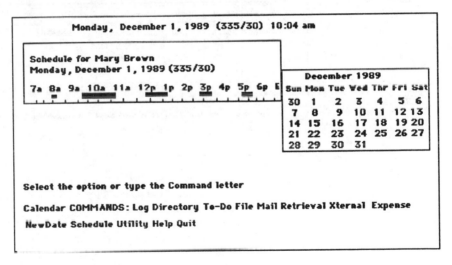

Special Higgins functions include a scratch pad with which to take quick notes, a calculator, a stopwatch, and a Hide the Display option.

Any time while Mary is working she may use any one of several interrupt keys to invoke special Higgins functions, including a scratch pad with which to take quick notes, a calculator, a stopwatch, and a Hide the Display option that will clear the main portion of Mary's display until she presses her space bar. This particular function is designated so that a user can hide confidential information when someone enters her office without having to exit a program.

Notice that there are several options available to Mary on the bottom of the screen. She selects Mail by moving the cursor with the <SPACE BAR> and then presses <ENTER>. This command initiates the Higgins Electronic Mail System and brings up an In-Basket window that lists all incoming memos as well as memos Mary may be working on or memos she may have copied to herself.

Figure 10-38 illustrates the In-Basket window. Notice that phone messages are included in Mary's in-basket list. The V status indicates that a message has been viewed. Under In-Basket COMMANDS at the bottom of the screen are the following options for messages: View, Telephone, Send Correspondence, Delete, Print, Extract, and Finished. If Mary selects Telephone with the phone message highlighted, Higgins automatically calls the number of the person who left this message. Mary selects a message she wants to view and presses <ENTER>.

Figure 10-38. Examining Your In-Basket

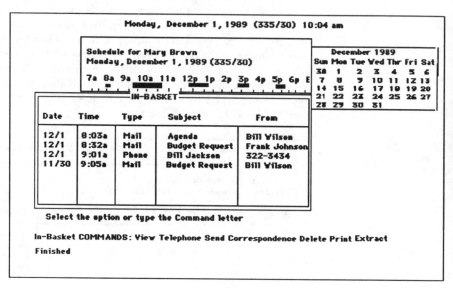

The View command enables Mary to read and take action on her memos, including answering them, forwarding them, filing them, or deleting them. The Higgins program differentiates between attachments (a memo set or history built around when a memo was first answered or routed) and enclosures (files including text files and spreadsheet files mailed along with the memo). Figure 10-39 illustrates the information available to Mary.

She can use the <PgUp> and <PgDn> keys to move through this message. Among her options at this point are Note (use the cursor keys to move through the memo), Save (save this memo), Route (forward the memo to other people), Answer (respond to the memo), and Delete (delete the memo from the in-basket). Other options include Browse (view the next memo in the in-basket), Enclosures (examine a list of the enclosures or view the files), History (examine a list of all attachments associated with viewing a memo

Figure 10-39.
Viewing Your Mail

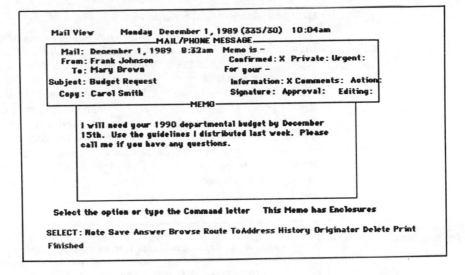

Figure 10-39.
Viewing Your Mail

that has been answered or routed at least once), and Originator (view the E-mail address of the person sending this memo).

Writing a Memo with Higgins

We'll assume that, after reading her mail, Mary realizes she really needs to write a memo. She selects SEND from her menu, and a Mail Send screen appears similar to the one displayed in Figure 10-39. Pull-down windows are available under the To and Copy fields to display all users who may receive electronic mail. If the network is also running the Higgins Exchange program, then the list will contain names of people in other mail domains who can also receive electronic mail. After filling in the memo's heading and writing her note, Mary has several options available to her as indicated on the bottom of her screen. Mary's BlackBook contains her own E-mail address list, whereas the PrivateList contains the addresses of specific individuals from different groups brought together to form a mailing or distribution list. The NotListed option prints a hard copy of a memo for someone who is not listed in the mailing address list. By selecting Enclosures, Mary may add enclosures to her memo. An Enclosures window appears and requests a filename, directory, and description.

Using Higgins MailCall

Higgins MailCall is a terminate-and-stay-resident program that looks for mail and phone messages and then alerts the user, who may be working on other application programs.

MailCall is a terminate-and-stay-resident program that looks for mail and phone messages and then alerts the user, who may be working on other application programs. When new mail arrives, MailCall alerts the user with a beep and a screen message. The messages and beeps reoccur until acknowledged. The user can specify how frequently (in minutes) MailCall will check for mail by using a number between 1 and 9, with 0 representing 10 minutes.

Higgins Calendar Commands

Now that Mary has read her mail and sent a memo, she returns to her Higgins Main menu pictured earlier in Figure 10-37. The Log command displays Mary's appointment log window, which is illustrated in Figure 10-40. By choosing Select, Mary can view any item in her log. Other options permit Mary to Add an item to the log, Extract events from her schedule for a specific period of time by using keywords and a data range, Print her log, move to a NewDate, quickly add a log entry (QuickAdd), or view her Week at a glance. In Figure 10-41 Mary has selected a log item and is viewing it in more detail. Higgins provides a feature called Appointment Call, which, once installed in a batch file or activated by typing APPTCALL, permits Higgins to sound an alarm and remind you about an appointment even while you are using another application program.

Figure 10-40. Sending Mail

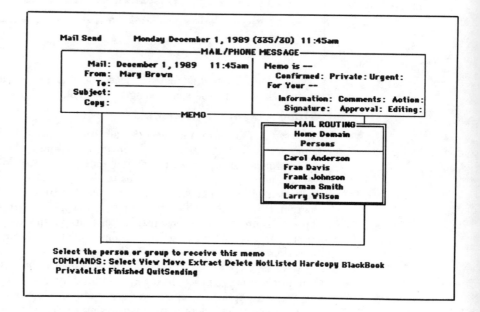

Using The Higgins Directory Command

The Directory command is one option under the Higgins Main menu. In Figure 10-42 Mary has selected the Directory option and now sees a summary window of names, companies, and telephone numbers. When she highlights a particular name and selects View, she'll see a screen similar to the one pictured in Figure 10-43. If Mary wants to write a note running several pages, she can use the ATTACHED command and then use the ADD command to add this material to her directory.

Using a To-Do List with Higgins

The To-Do command produces a To-Do List window similar to the one pictured in Figure 10-44. The list is organized as follows:

According to project alphabetically
Within a project, according to status with Open before Done
Within status, according to priority with priority 1 first
Within a priority, chronologically from the oldest date

If Mary wants to create a new item on her To-Do list, she selects the Add option, which allows her to describe the item and categorize it by project name. The project name associated with the item is useful when

**Figure 10-41.
Using the LOG
Command**

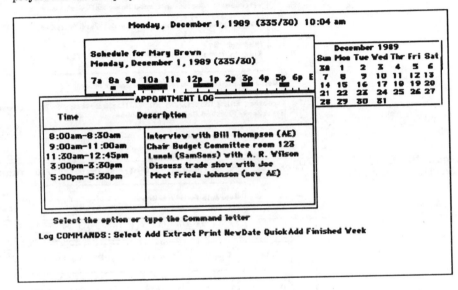

**Figure 10-42.
Viewing the Directory**

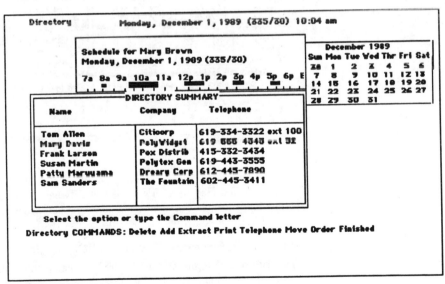

**Figure 10-43.
Viewing a Directory
Entry Description**

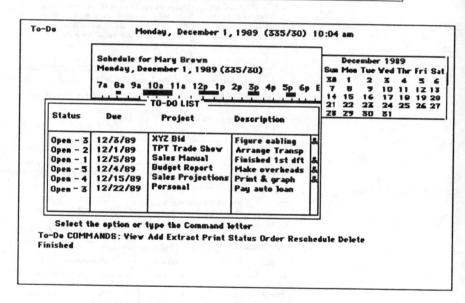

**Figure 10-44.
Viewing a To-Do List**

searching by keywords. To-Do tasks may be designated as having Open or Done status and may have priority levels between 1 and 5. A private field enables Mary to hide this item from someone else who might view her schedule in order to arrange a meeting.

Maintaining Expense Records with Higgins

One very useful Higgins feature is the Expense command. The Expense command maintains automated expense reports; expense items may be entered in the log, where they are associated with an event and a directory entry. Higgins classifies expenses as those already submitted on a report and those not yet submitted on a report.

Higgins permits twelve different expense categories, which need be named only once (when the program is first installed). An Assemble command enables you to assemble new expenses for a new report, enter new expenses for a new report, or simply enter new expenses. Figure 10-45 illustrates an expense report being assembled. Notice that Mary can include details on the purpose of her business lunch and the people entertained— precisely the facts necessary to keep the IRS happy.

**Figure 10-45.
Keeping an Expense
Log**

```
Log          Monday December 1, 1989 (335/30)    1:45pm
                   LOG ENTRY FOR:  December 1, 1989

    From:11:30am   Alarm:        |-----ENTRY ALSO APPEARS ON THESE LISTS-----
     To: 12:45pm   Flag:         | DIRECTORY: A.R. Wilson
    Description:                 |
     Lunch at SamSons            | TO-DO: Open  Priority:2
    Private: No   Source:Log     | EXPENSE: Yes  PROJECT:XYZ POLYWIDGET SALE
           |-----EXPENSE SUMMARY-----|    |-EXPENSE DETAIL-|
           |  Expenses for this item |    | Date:12/1/89 Log:Yes
           |                         |    | Item: Lunch-2
           |  Item    Category  Amount|   | Categry: Entrtain
           |                         |    |  Number: @
           |  Parking  Trans    7.50 |    | Amount: 26.00
           |  Lunch-2  Entertain 26.00|   | Purpose: XYZ Sale
           |                         |    | Where: Samsons
           |                         |    | Who: A.R. Wilson
           |                         |    |      of:
           |                         |    | XYZ Corp

           Select the option or type the Command letter

           Associate Expense COMMANDS: View  Add Finished
```

An Expense Summary window can provide a very effective expense report. Figure 10-46 illustrates such a typical report, which can be printed by selecting the Print option.

Higgins Exchange and Higgins Gateways to Other E-Mail Systems

Higgins Exchange provides routing between two networks running this program. Higgins Gateways provides connectivity with non-Higgins networks.

Each Higgins network requires only a single Higgins Exchange program to provide mail routing and a single Higgins Gateways program to connect with non-Higgins mail systems. Higgins Exchange takes responsibility for automatically distributing any directory changes that have taken place on another network. If copies of a memo have to be distributed to several people at a different location, the program sends one copy and a distribution list to which the information is routed by the Higgins Exchange program running at the remote location.

The Higgins Gateways program provides connectivity with other systems, including MHS, 3+Mail, SNADS, and PROFS. Higgins Exchange has a built-in asynchronous modem program, but you can also use X.25

**Figure 10-46.
An Expense Summary
Report**

```
┌──────────────────────────────────────────────────────────────────┐
│ Expense      Monday December 1, 1989  (335/30)  2:34pm             │
│                     ─EXPENSE SUMMARY─                              │
│   Expense Report for Period Ending: 11/30/89                       │
│   Date        Item      Category    Amount                         │
│ ┌──────────────────────────────────────────────────┐              │
│ │11/01/89  │ Hotel   │ Lodging  │   75.00           │              │
│ │11/01/89  │ Air Fare│ Trans.   │  225.00           │              │
│ │11/01/89  │ Parking │ Trans.   │   25.00           │              │
│ │11/01/89  │ Cab     │ Trans.   │   12.00           │              │
│ │11/01/89  │ Lunch   │ Meals    │    8.50           │              │
│ │11/01/89  │ Dinner  │ Meals    │   12.50           │              │
│ └──────────────────────────────────────────────────┘              │
└──────────────────────────────────────────────────────────────────┘
```

Trans.	Lodging	Meals	Teleph	Incdntl	Auto	Travel Total
237.00	75.00	21.00	0	0	25.00	262.00

Entrtain	Shipping	Supplies	Asoction	Software	Other	REPORT TOTAL
0	0	0	U	0	0	375.50

Select the option or type the Command letter
Expense Report COMMANDS: View Add Print Omit Finished

communications by adding appropriate software. Conetic Systems offers Higgins To:FAX software designed to be used in conjunction with an Intel Connection CoProcessor board installed on the workstation running Higgins Exchange. A special module of Higgins To:FAX software uses the Intel board rather than an existing standard modem to provide 9600-bps mail transfer; file transfer takes place in the background to make the system even more efficient.

Users of portable and stand-alone computers can send and receive Higgins electronic mail using Higgins Remote and a modem in conjunction with Higgins and Higgins Exchange. One very nice feature of this program is that it also supports direct peer-to-peer mail service between remote users.

SELECTING THE RIGHT ELECTRONIC MESSAGING SYSTEM FOR YOUR NETWARE NETWORK

We've examined four major electronic messaging programs in this chapter, all of which are commonly used on NetWare networks. The programs range from those that solely run electronic mail (cc:MAIL and The Network Courier) to those that offer a variety of extra scheduling and organizing functions (Higgins and The Coordinator). When selecting a program for your network there are several different issues that you must consider.

One major issue is whether the program works on all the different networks you have as well as on gateways to your company's minicomputers and mainframe computers. Some of these programs do not offer Macintosh versions at this time (Higgins, for example), whereas others already have DEC gateways available (cc:MAIL).

The gateways will not do you much good, however, if the electronic messaging system does not have the features your company needs. The material in this chapter was written to make you aware of the major features these leading programs offer. The following list summarizes many of these features that may prove necessary for your company's effective electronic messaging.

- Connections to other networks' electronic mail
- Transmissions to distribution lists or multiple distribution lists
- Placing restrictions on users' sending and receiving of mail
- Auto-filing of messages that are sent or received
- On-line help
- Automatic billing of users sending mail
- Uploading of PC files to accompany messages sent
- Prioritizing of messages
- Enclosures in the form of files
- Attachments of related documents

WHAT HAVE WE LEARNED?

1. Electronic messaging can encompass far more than just electronic mail. It can include gateways to other networks and facsimile machines as well as scheduling and organizing functions.
2. An X.400 message handling system (MHS) includes user agents (UAs), message transfer agents (MTAs), and a message transfer system (MTS).
3. The P1 protocol provides rules for routing information between two MTAs. The P2 protocol describes types of user services requested, and the P3 protocol provides standards for changing existing mail parameters.
4. The CCITT X.400 recommendations cover electronic messaging whereas the X.500 recommendations cover a worldwide common directory.
5. The Coordinator organizes all communications on a subject and keeps them in sequential order as a "conversation."
6. The Coordinator offers seven types of conversations, including Note, Inform, Question, Offer, Request, Promise, and What if.
7. One of cc:Mail's unique features is its ability to take snapshots of any screen and add them to any messages.
8. The cc:Mail program is a graphics editor that can be used to draw graphics or modify graphics taken from other programs.
9. The Network Courier allows you to sort user mail by date, sender, subject, and priority.
10. Higgins provides many features besides electronic mail, including sophisticated scheduling and organizing features.
11. Higgins Exchange connects two networks running this program; Higgins Gateways is used to communicate with non-Higgins networks.

Quiz for Chapter 10

1. Electronic mail and the CCITT X.400 set of recommendations are handled by which layer of the OSI model?
   a. network
   b. presentation
   c. application
   d. data link

2. Which item is *not* part of an X.400 message handling system?
   a. a file server
   b. a user agent
   c. a message transfer agent
   d. a message transfer system

3. The basic approach of MHS is
   a. first in, first out
   b. store-and-forward
   c. last in, first out
   d. transfer-and-process

4. A request for an immediate reply to a message is described by which protocol under X.400?
   a. P1
   b. P2
   c. P3
   d. P4

5. Standards for a worldwide common directory are provided in
   a. X.300
   b. X.400
   c. X.500
   d. X.600

6. The electronic mail program once included with NetWare is
   a. The Coordinator
   b. The Network Courier
   c. cc:Mail
   d. Higgins

7. The program that organizes all communications into "conversations" is
   a. Higgins
   b. cc:Mail
   c. The Coordinator.
   d. The Network Courier

8. Which is *not* a type of conversation available under The Coordinator?
   a. Promise
   b. Request
   c. Memo
   d. What if

9. The Coordinator has a built-in gateway to other networks because it has
   a. LU 6.2
   b. APPI
   c. MS
   d. MHS

10. A special snapshot feature is available only on
    a. The Coordinator
    b. The Network Courier
    c. cc:Mail
    d. Higgins

11. Under which program do you receive information in your inbox?
    a. The Coordinator
    b. The Network Courier
    c. cc:Mail
    d. Higgins

12. The electronic messaging program that permits graphics to be attached directly to a document is
    a. cc:Mail
    b. The Coordinator
    c. The Network Courier
    d. Higgins

13. The Chkstat utility program providing detailed information on mailbox users is available with
   a. The Coordinator
   b. The Network Courier
   c. cc:Mail
   d. Higgins

14. The Network Courier allows you to sort users' mail by all of these methods *except*
   a. by date
   b. by sender's name
   c. by subject name
   d. by size

15. The program that permits other users to see your To-Do list but gives you the ability to hide certain items is
   a. The Coordinator
   b. Higgins
   c. The Network Courier
   d. cc:Mail

16. The program providing a calculator, stopwatch, scratch pad, and a Hide the Display option is
   a. Higgins
   b. The Network Courier
   c. The Coordinator
   d. cc:Mail

17. The program that can use a coprocessor board to provide facsimile service is
   a. Higgins
   b. The Network Courier
   c. The Coordinator
   d. cc:Mail

18. The control information and data comprising an MHS message is enclosed in an
   a. MJB
   b. MTC
   c. MCB
   d. MIT

19. The External Mail program is a feature of
   a. Higgins
   b. The Coordinator
   c. cc:Mail
   d. The Network Courier

20. The NetWare command that permits users to connect with a different file server in order to access an external post office is
   a. ATTACH
   b. LINK
   c. CONNECT
   d. MAIL

A Guide to Networkable Software

ABOUT THIS CHAPTER

Many companies have found that installing a local area network also meant selecting new software written specifically for their network. The development of MS-DOS and, more recently, MS-OS/2 has provided some uniformity in network software. Because the network hardware and software offered by IBM, 3Com, Novell, and AT&T all adhere to DOS standards, software publishers have found it much easier to write generic network editions.

In this chapter we will examine network features such as record locking found in all versions of MS-DOS since 3.1 and the options companies have if their single-user software cannot be upgraded to DOS 3.1 standards. We'll survey the most desirable features found in word-processing, spreadsheet, database manager, and accounting programs and see how they function in a network environment.

MS-DOS

MS-DOS versions since 3.1 have provided true multiuser operations with their Share program, which provides different levels of access, and with their "byte-locking" function.

As Figure 11-1 shows, MS-DOS resides in the presentation layer of the OSI model along with the Redirector program. This operating system acts as an interface between the application programs and the NETBIOS, which resides between the presentation and session layers. Multiple users can access files on a network through the MS-DOS Share program, which enables a programmer to grant greater levels of access to the first workstation to use a file than to subsequent workstations. For example, a key accounting data file used by several different workstations can be designated as read-write for the first user to request it. While this user continues to write to this file, other users can only read the file under Share's Read-Write with deny-write sharing mode. MS-DOS versions 3.1 and above have a *byte-locking* function that enables a programmer to write a program so that a range of bytes is locked; other users cannot write to this area until the first user "unlocks" the area. The result of the Share program's different access rights and MS-DOS's byte-locking is that a file will not be destroyed by two users simultaneously writing over each other's data.

Programs written prior to the release of MS-DOS version 3.1 are unable to use this multiuser feature. They can be installed on a network so that one user can write while other users can only read a file, but such manipulation is of limited value in most office environments.

The Redirector program acts as a "traffic cop."

In addition to MS-DOS's multiuser capabilities, programmers have begun to use its Redirector program. This program acts as a "traffic cop"

**Figure 11-1.
The Role of MS-DOS
3.1 in the OSI Model**

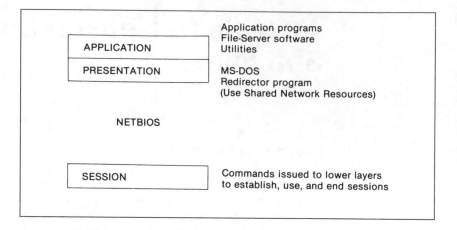

that directs requests for shared network resources. Because of the way the program works, future network software will be file-server oriented rather than disk-server oriented.

CLIENT/SERVER APPLICATIONS UNDER OS/2

In Chapter 1 we examined some of the features that distinguish MS-OS/2, the operating system that IBM, Microsoft, and 3Com see as the foundation of larger future LANs. OS/2 heralds a new level of distributed network computing because of the true multitasking nature of this operating system. Before OS/2, most file servers handled a workstation's database query by sending the entire database file across the network to that workstation. When the workstation completed sorting the database and making whatever changes it needed to make, it returned the information to the file server.

This traditional LAN method of sharing a database program and its files leads to several problems, however. Network congestion increases as more and more workstations request that the program and its files be sent and then send information back to the file server. Network overhead can also become a problem with this approach, since a database program may need to create several different processes to permit multiuser operations. Finally, data integrity may be compromised with so many files traveling through the network.

Microsoft and Ashton-Tate have developed a structured query language (SQL) server program called SQL Server. SQL Server running on a file server under OS/2 can provide database management service to applications running on network workstations.

When a workstation queries an SQL database, the SQL Server *back-end* program receives the request, finds the information desired on a database, and then forwards the specific information requested (not the entire database file) back to the workstation processing. The end user's *front-end* application program uses APIs to make these queries and requests in a manner transparent to the user, so it really does not matter where the database is physically located. Figure 11-2 illustrates this process.

**Figure 11-2.
The Client-Server
Model** *(Courtesy of
Microsoft Corporation)*

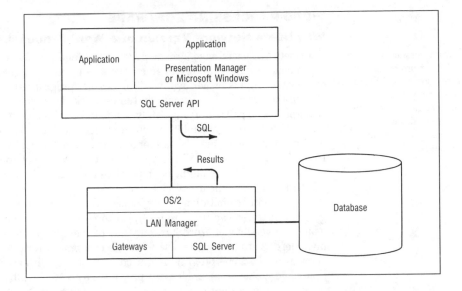

This type of distributed processing is called client/server computing. A front-end client application program accesses a back-end server, in this case a database server. Several different types of client front-end applications (spreadsheets, accounting programs, project management programs, and so forth) can access the back-end server. The front-end application program processes the information it requested and displays it on its screen. Meanwhile, the back-end server program maintains the database's integrity and ensures that the network functions with optimum efficiency.

NETWORK SOFTWARE AND THE LAW

Most single-user software is licensed for one user or one machine. To use software on a network it is necessary to buy a network version of the program, sign a site licensing agreement, or negotiate a volume purchase from the software manufacturer.

Most single-user software packages specify that the program may be used only on a single machine or by one user at a time. Use of such programs under network conditions is clearly illegal.

Thus, a major consideration in selecting network software is the software vendor's policy toward network use of its product. Many companies have developed special network versions of their products that are licensed for specific sizes of user groups. A network supervisor might select WordPerfect, for example, and then license a certain number of copies to run on his or her network. The customer pays for the initial package and then pays an additional fee per user. Besides the basic program, WordPerfect Corporation supplies extra network features (such as some laser-printing utilities) that make it advantageous for a customer to purchase this edition.

For a negotiated fee, the other companies provide a site licensing agreement that specifies that the product may be used at that site by an unlimited number of users. Unfortunately, many major software companies simply offer discounts if their single-user products are purchased in large volumes. This solution is not acceptable for most companies.

WORD-PROCESSING SOFTWARE

Why Use a Network Version of a Word-Processing Program?

Network versions of word-processing programs provide some assurances of file compatibility, printer compatibility, and the standardized appearance of company documents.

Most network users have already developed a fondness for a particular word-processing program and prefer to continue using it. One problem with everyone using his or her own word-processing program and then simply storing the processed documents in the network file server is that not all word-processing files are completely compatible. Different programs have different formatting capabilities, which makes it difficult to provide uniformity in a company. Bill's proposals might look completely different from May's, for example. When they work on a document together and try to exchange data files, it might be impossible for either of them to determine what the final document will look like.

Another limitation to single-user word-processing software is that program features can vary from version to version. If two employees are using two versions of WordStar, only one of them might be able to perform a mail merge with a customer file to create customized form letters. Different versions of the same program might contain slightly different printer drivers that could create some unpleasant printing surprises. Finally, single-user word-processing programs do not offer file-locking capabilities. This feature is extremely important on a network because it means that several individuals can use the same word-processing program without worrying about inadvertently destroying a particular document file.

Word-Processing Features

Although hundreds of word-processing features are available on some of the major network versions, we'll concentrate on those features of particular value to network users. We'll assume that a company with a local area network prints dozens of types of documents, including some material on preexisting forms. Further, the company has several hundred customers that it wishes to communicate with on a regular basis. To achieve these word-processing objectives, a company would have to examine programs that offer certain formatting, editing, and file-managing features and a number of utility programs. Let's look at some key formatting features.

Page-Oriented and Document-Oriented Word Processing

Page-oriented word-processing programs display one page at a time whereas document-oriented word-processing programs display a page break and paragraphs on both sides of the page break.

Perhaps the single most significant word-processing program feature is whether the program is page-oriented or document-oriented. A *page-oriented* program displays one page of a file at a time much as a secretary would edit a typed manuscript by working on one page at a time. Page-oriented programs do not display page breaks on a screen. If you add new material to the bottom of a page, a line count shows that you have added the material displayed on the screen, but you will not see a page break. With some of these programs, you need to repaginate after adding material to see which material will appear on a particular page. Since dedicated word processors are page-oriented, software writers emulated this orientation when developing many early MS-DOS word-processing programs.

As Figure 11-3 illustrates, a *document-oriented* word-processing program enables users to see the end of one page and the beginning lines of the next page on their screens simultaneously. Usually these programs enable users to move from one page to another by using cursor keys to scroll up or down across the screen. Since a great deal of editing is based on such issues as how a paragraph looks in the context of the paragraphs preceding and following it, how consistent verb tense usage is, and how effective transitions are in linking paragraphs, a document-oriented program makes it much easier to edit longer documents.

**Figure 11-3.
Document-Oriented
Word Processing**

```
                 These are the last couple of lines on
                 page one. Now we will begin page two.

         P _____ P

                 Since this is the second page, we
                 can see the page break as well as
                 the last couple of lines on the
                 previous page.
                    A document-oriented word
                 processing program is very useful
                 for a professional writer because it
```

Network users who write memos and letters that rarely exceed one page will find little difference between a page-oriented program and document-oriented program. There is a significant difference, however, for those writers who need to produce long reports or multipaged memos.

Seeing Is Believing

A second major formatting feature that distinguishes some word-processing programs is their ability to display information exactly as it will appear when printed, so that what you see is what you get. This feature is particularly important in a network program because networks frequently use the economy of scale gained from sharing resources to share laser printers. Microsoft Word has a network version that takes advantage of the IBM Enhanced Graphics Adapter to display a number of fonts as they will appear when printed. The network version is specifically designed to work with a laser printer to produce typesetlike quality. For those network users who need actual typesetting, Microsoft offers the Linoword interface between Word and the Linotron laser typesetting machine. Although few programs can match Word's ability to display different fonts, at minimum most network users need only boldface, underlining, and overstrikes displayed on the screen, features that WordPerfect performs admirably.

Style Sheets

Style sheets enable word-processing users to format documents after writing them by linking the document to a set of specifications for a particular style sheet.

Companies large enough to support a local area network usually require specific formats for their various types of documents. A company might stipulate, for example, that all top-level headings in its proposals be uppercase and boldface and all subheadings be lowercase and underlined. Company policy might also dictate that all memos use a specific font with the headings in boldface. Research reports might require still another company-dictated format with footnotes placed at the bottom of the relevant page.

Microsoft Word offers several styles for creating footnotes, headings, and subheadings. A network user writing a letter, memo, report, or proposal selects the appropriate style sheet and Word automatically formats it correctly. This feature is especially valuable on a network, since it ensures that all company correspondence and reports are uniform in style and format.

Forms Processing

Certain word-processing programs can design forms and then place information into these forms.

One frustrating aspect of using a word-processing program rather than a typewriter is that with a computer it is difficult to print information precisely where a standard form requires it. This ability to define and print fields anywhere on a preexisting form is known as *forms processing*, and it is particularly valuable on a company network in which several different forms are used on a regular basis. Samna's Word program is a program that has this capability.

Editing Multiple Documents

A LAN user might need to view two documents simultaneously in order to compare certain passages. Some network word-processing programs such as WordStar 2000 and Word enable users to view and edit different documents simultaneously as they are displayed in screen windows. With Word, for example, you can view up to a maximum of eight windows.

Mail Merge

Some word-processing programs can merge names, addresses, and other information found in a database program with a letter to produce individualized form letters.

One of the major word-processing functions on a local area network is the *mail merge*. Companies frequently merge customer information (name, address, etc.) contained in database files with a form letter produced on the word-processing program. Beyond that, the merge often permits key individualized information to be inserted within the letter if certain conditions are met. For instance, Widget Corporation might write a form letter to all its customers, but it might include a paragraph about an upcoming megawidget seminar only in those letters addressed to customers who recently purchased this product.

If mail merging will be a major network function, a network administrator must address two key questions: what form the customer data will take and how easily this information can be merged with a particular word-processing program. Some word-processing programs offer the capability to merge with several types of files, including dBASE, ASCII, and SYLK formats.

Word-Processing Program File Formats

For many companies data communication is a major network concern. For example, a company might have its local area network connected with its mainframe computer through a gateway PC and perhaps also with remote branch locations. Because PC communications programs are usually designed to transmit ASCII files without word-processing control codes, it is important to consider which kinds of word-processing file formats are available. WordPerfect, for example, can both produce standard ASCII files and import ASCII files that were produced by other word-processing programs. For network users who wish to incorporate Lotus 1-2-3 worksheets within their word-processing documents, WordStar 2000 can read Lotus files directly.

Printer Support

To use all the features of a laser printer, a word-processing program should have a printer driver written specifically for that printer.

A principal advantage of a local area network is its ability to share valuable resources such as laser printers. A network administrator might discover, however, that proliferation of microcomputers and accessories has resulted in some serious problems with incompatibility within the company's network. Since software programs require *printer drivers* in order to print documents, a company with incompatible printers offers a real challenge for a network administrator. Perhaps the administrator's central question when selecting a network word-processing program is, Does the program support all of our printers? Programs such as WordPerfect and Word are particularly strong in this area. Because network programs normally are installed to run with a specific printer, the administrator usually writes batch files under DOS that enable a user to access the word-processing program with the specific printer driver needed. In other words, a novice network user will normally access a network version of Word or WordPerfect that is already installed with the printer needed for a specific application, and thus he or she won't have to worry about specifying the printer.

Because laser printers have assumed such a major role on most local area networks, a major consideration in selecting word-processing programs is whether or not the program supports proportional spacing fonts on the laser printer. Proportional spacing eliminates those gaping spaces found in most documents when a word-processing program justifies the left and right margins.

A second consideration for global companies with local area networks is whether or not they must write in other languages. WordPerfect offers editions in French, German, Spanish, Finnish, Swedish, Norwegian, Dutch, and Danish. Perhaps the most specialized of such foreign-language oriented word-processing programs is the Interword program by Computers Anyware, which works in Arabic, English, and French. The program comes with an EPROM chip that permits the use of multiple languages when installed in the motherboard of a PC. Interword also includes keyboard overlays identifying the letters in each language. The program permits simultaneous display of the three languages in multiple side-by-side columns. Computers Anyware also offers word-processing programs in several other languages, including Russian, Dutch, and Icelandic.

If network users need to print in any foreign language or print special mathematical and specific symbols, it is imperative that the administrator select a laser printer that can download fonts, such as the Hewlett Packard LaserJet Plus.

Other Desirable Word-Processing Features

Among the more advanced word-processing features are macros, mathematical functions, multiple columns, and graphics capabilities.

All the major networkable word-processing programs offer the standard, expected features, such as the ability to search and replace text, the ability to move and replace block paragraphs, and the ability to format text. Other word-processing features are not standard yet might be desirable on a local area network: macros, glossaries, mathematical functions, dictionaries, and searches of documents by key words.

Some programs such as WordPerfect can produce macros, a list of instructions that the program will perform when a specific combination of keys is pressed. For example, if a company needed certain documents to be formatted in ways that required several complicated steps, a network administrator could write a macro that incorporated these steps and enabled the novice user to accomplish the formatting by pressing two keys.

Many companies use what are called *boilerplate* letters consisting of a series of form paragraphs that are organized according to a customer's individual request. For example, a customer who wanted to know about the availability of a superwidget and the training classes associated with it might receive a letter with paragraphs describing the company, the superwidget, and the training classes available, as well as a stock concluding paragraph offering immediate service. Some programs, such as Microsoft's Word, provide glossaries that can be written and then stored. A network user who needs to insert a paragraph about the superwidget's specifications checks the list of glossaries and selects the appropriate superwidget glossary. This material, which can range from one paragraph to several pages, can then be inserted into the letter at the desired location.

Using mathematical functions can also save network users valuable time. A salesperson can draw up a contract and have the word-processing program line up the numbers in appropriate columns and perform all the mathematical operations before providing the final cost to the customer on the appropriate contract line.

Equally valuable is a program's inclusion of a dictionary and even a thesaurus. Programs such as Microsoft Word and WordPerfect offer sophisticated dictionaries that help guide spelling accuracy. If a word-processing program does not offer an internal dictionary, the administrator should determine whether the program's files can be read by one of the major dictionary programs on the market such as the Random House Dictionary and Thesaurus programs.

Because of the sheer number of document files found on many local area networks, a word-processing feature that proves just as advantageous as a dictionary or thesaurus is the ability to identify documents by certain key words. A company might routinely use its word-processing document summary screen to list the document's recipient (ABC Supply Company), the type of correspondence (sales-order confirmation), and the salesperson involved (Frank Wilson). With a program such as Ashton-Tate's network version of MultiMate Advantage, a user can create a document library and search it for a list of correspondence that matches specified criteria. This particular program also offers other special network features for individual users, including a customized dictionary and public and private document files.

Many of the significant word-processing features we have not discussed, such as the ability to produce columns side-by-side and to incorporate text and graphics on the same page, are related to desktop publishing. The network administrator needs to be aware of this aspect of word processing because it is becoming a major network function for many companies.

Desktop Publishing

Desktop publishing refers primarily to the ability to perform a series of closely related functions, including combining text and graphics on a single page and designing a page with multiple columns and multiple typefaces. With programs such as Ventura Publisher and Aldus's PageMaker and a laser printer attached to the network, users can construct a newsletter with graphics and multiple columns and then produce typeset-quality copies.

SPREADSHEET FEATURES FOR NETWORK USE

Generally most network administrators will create templates for types of users. Salespeople, for example, might have a bid form whereas financial analysts might have a budget form. These templates can be in a public area of the file server so that everyone can use them. Network users who need to share information generally place a copy of their completed spreadsheet data in the public area.

Macros

Because levels of sophistication among network users vary so widely, macros provide an easy way for network administrators to enable novices to use complicated spreadsheets such as Excel, Lotus 1-2-3, or SuperCalc. Macros represent programs written to execute specific commands within a spreadsheet so that a user can perform very complex operations by pressing two keystrokes.

Special Financial and Mathematical Considerations

Some companies select a spreadsheet because of particular financial or mathematical functions. One such feature is *goal seeking*, which allows a user to name a target value and have the program calculate the required variable value to reach that goal. If a company wants to achieve a certain profit level, for example, the spreadsheet will indicate the sales volume necessary to achieve this level. SuperCalc offers this highly desirable feature. Some programs have built-in functions to handle amortization and depreciation. A network of financial analysts would want to use a program that offered built-in functions for net present value, internal rate of return, payment, future value and present value.

DATABASE MANAGEMENT

Database programs on a network must have record locking as well as the ability to provide customized reports in order to meet the range of needs of network users.

Although word processing might be the function used most often on a local area network, the LAN's very heart and cost justification are likely to be its database management program. An insurance office might have several agents accessing a central database to identify customers whose policies are about to come due. Similarly, a mail-order business might have several people processing phone orders, checking current inventory, and determining customer credit history, all dependent on a central database program on a local area network.

Because many network users will need to use the database program simultaneously, it is essential to select a network version of a program so that it will have record locking, which permits several people to use the same file (such as a list of customers) as long as they don't try to view the same record (a customer's history) simultaneously. The program permits only one user to revise a specific record at a time. Most of the major network programs are *relational database programs*. This means that users can create a number of files or tables and then produce reports that reveal the relationships among various fields. Ashton-Tate's dBASE IV is an example of this type of program. Although today's database management programs have hundreds of features, we'll examine only the few key ones for a network.

Customized Reports

Since a network must serve many different user needs, it is essential that the database management program have a sophisticated report generator that can create customized reports. Network administrators with unusual reporting needs might want to consider such issues as whether the program can create reports that are column-oriented or row-oriented, handle time and date stamping, and provide custom borders and footers.

Record and Field Limitations

Because of the scope of many network database management files, it is imperative that the network administrator determine the maximum number of records and fields that might be needed and determine unusual field requirements so that the company will not outgrow the program. For example, a salesperson who wants to keep detailed records of conversations with each customer might want a memo field that can hold an entire page of comments.

Procedural, Programming, and Query Languages

Some companies might find that even the most sophisticated database program cannot meet their needs. In such cases, you must choose a program that offers programming interfaces, so that database information can be manipulated by a customized program. Some programs permit data tables to be manipulated from C programs. Many of the network-version programs offer procedural language capabilities, which means that they permit you to write short programs within the database itself. Finally, many network users do not need a programming or procedural language so much as they need the ability to ask complicated questions based on data relationships. For example, a police department with a network database program containing the characteristics of thousands of criminals might ask to see a list of all the red-headed male burglars between 20 and 35 who are left-handed and walk with a limp. A query language would permit the user to phrase this question in English.

IBM has made it clear that it supports its structured query language (SQL) as the future standard for relational database programs. If companies want file compatibility in their future minicomputer and microcomputer network software, they would be wise to look at programs that support SQL.

File Formats

Because a network might be linked to a mainframe computer or another LAN, it is advantageous to have a database program that can import and export data files in a variety of formats. In addition to the dBASE format that has become a standard at some companies, other useful formats include ASCII, DIF, and SYLK.

A second major consideration is whether the company already has a multiuser computer system and wishes to move database information back and forth between the network and the operating system. Informix-SQL is an example of a powerful database management program available under both DOS and UNIX. Since the file structure is identical under both operating systems, data can be imported and exported quickly.

NETWORK ACCOUNTING SOFTWARE

Network accounting programs must have record-locking capabilities as well as a set of integrated modules that provide adequate network security.

Like a database program with record locking, an accounting program must also enable several users to access the same module simultaneously. A large company with hundreds of payments arriving the first week of each month might need several accounts receivable clerks to update its accounting program. Although these clerks wouldn't need to examine the same customer record simultaneously, they all would need to use the accounts receivable module. Similarly, a computerized retail store must have an accounting program that enables several clerks to perform order entry or point-of-sale processing while the program instantly updates the store's inventory information.

In addition to record-locking capabilities, the network administrator and company accountant should consider a number of other accounting-program features. We'll examine some of the more pressing issues that must be addressed.

The Scope of Integrated Accounting Modules

Network accounting programs offer a variety of *integrated modules*. This means that a customer chooses whether such program modules as order entry, point-of-sale, fixed assets, and job costing are needed to supplement the standard general ledger, accounts receivable, accounts payable, and payroll modules. Many network programs offer integrated modules for specific industries. PROLOGIC, for example, links its financial modules and its distribution modules through accounts receivable and accounts payable modules. As Figure 11-4 shows, the relationships between integrated modules can be quite complex. A wholesale distributor might have several different prices for various customers. The customer order processing module creates an invoice using information from the bill of materials and inventory modules and sends the invoice to the accounts receivable module, where a record of the customer's invoice amount is maintained along with any payments made. A network administrator who needs specialized accounting modules may have to compromise some basic accounting-program features in order to enjoy the advantages of integrating specialized information into the general ledger.

Program Security

Because of the nature of accounting, simple network security such as a login password is not sufficient. Most accounting departments need different security levels within a module. A payroll clerk might need security access to

Figure 11-4.
Data Flow within a
Financial and
Distribution System
(Courtesy of PROLOGIC
Management Systems,
Inc.)

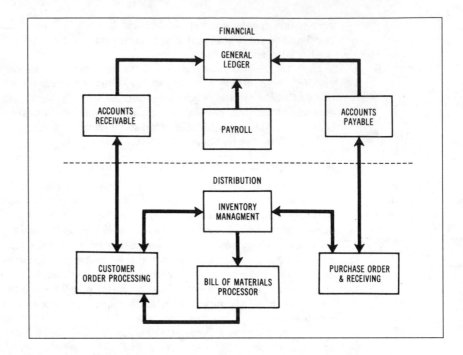

produce a payroll but definitely not to change pay rates or view confidential
salary information. Many of the more sophisticated network accounting
packages such as PROLOGIC enable the network administrator to limit
access to portions of a particular module. An employee might be able to enter
inventory when it is received but not see the screen listing the actual cost of
the items. (Some companies don't want their employees to know what their
profit margin is.)

Closely related to this security issue is the accounting program's
ability to produce a clear *audit trail* of all transactions. Most of the better
programs will produce a report listing all inventory transactions, for example.
An employee cannot simply reduce an item's inventory total by one and then
take the item home. The audit trail report will identify the employee from the
password used when he or she logged on to the system and indicate that on a
certain date at a certain time the employee reduced the inventory value by
the specified amount.

Specific Requirements

Although many companies keep track of their inventories using a FIFO
approach (first in, first out) or a LIFO approach (last in, first out), most
accounting programs don't compute inventory in this fashion but instead use
a weighted average approach. Some powerful programs such as Solomon let
the network administrator and accountant specify which type of cost method
to use: LIFO, FIFO, average cost, specific identification, standard, or a user-
defined approach.

Companies often have specific field requirements. They may need a twelve-digit general ledger account number or inventory part numbers of fourteen digits, for example. The network administrator and accountant should use their present accounting reports as a model and ask perspective software vendors to provide a demonstration that proves their programs can meet these requirements. The demonstration should also provide evidence of how easy it is to enter information and move from one menu screen to another. Figure 11-5 illustrates the amount of information provided on typical menu screens in the Solomon accounting program.

Figure 11-5.
Solomon II Inventory
Menus *(portions of this work have been copyrighted by TLB, Inc., and have been used in this work with the consent of TLB, Inc.)*

```
     01-82-0009        INVENTORY MENU        Screen 10.00

        DATA ENTRY              PROCESSES
     01 Receipts            50 Compute Cost of Goods Sold
     02 Sales               51 Revise Sales Price
     03 Adjustments
     04 Transfers              OTHER
                            90 Reports
        INQUIRY             95 Inventory Setup
     20 Inventory Items     99 Master Menu

        MAINTENANCE
     25 Inventory
     26 Sales Price
     27 Unit Conversion
     28 Product Class
     29 Price Level
     30 Inventory Substitute

            Enter Number of Selection: _
```

```
     01-82-0009      INVENTORY INQUIRY      Screen 10.20

       Inventory ID    Inv Acct Sub    COGS Acct Sub

                     Inventory Description

  Prod Class Id ____  _____  Suplr 2 _____  Qty On Hand _____
  Stock Item(Y,N) _____  Item 2 _____   Qty Uncost _____
  Val Mthd(F,L,A,S,T,U) _____ Ord Point _____  Per Beg Bal _____
  Repl Mthd(Q,C,O) _____  Reord Qty _____  Inv Bal _____
  Comp Sales(Y,N) _____  Max On Hand _____  PTD Qty _____
  Disc Pricing(D,P) _____  Std Cost _____  PTD Sales _____
  Stock Unit _____    Lst Cost _____   PTD Gross _____
  Base Price _____     Avg Cost _____   YTD Qty _____
  Revised Base _____    Qty On PO _____   YTD Sales _____
  Deft Whse-Loc _____    Qty On BO _____   YTD COGS _____
  Weight _____     Qty On SO _____   Pr YTD Qty _____
                                                    Pr YTD Sales _____
                                                    Pr YTD COGS _____
```

Report Capabilities

Many accounting programs offer dozens of standard reports, but what happens if a company needs a certain report that doesn't follow the conventional pattern? One answer is to choose a program with built-in financial report writers. Some companies, such as MBA, offer accounting software with this feature, which permits some choice in selecting which lines will be printed in a balance sheet.

What if a company needs a report comprising information from two or three modules? In this case, the company could either pay thousands of dollars for a customized program or, if the accounting program is written in COBOL, it could consider Snow Software's qPLEX IV, which might present a viable solution. This program can generate reports from various files and then perform mathematical operations within the reports. Moreover, qPLEX IV works with accounting programs such as Real World and database management programs such as DataFlex and dBASE IV.

Customization

It's unlikely that one program will satisfy all the accounting needs of a company. Some programs permit user customization whereas others require users to purchase a source code or pay standard programming rates for customization. In contrast, Open Systems Accounting software allows users both to customize menus by rewriting menu entries and changing the order of a menu and, if more elaborate programming changes are needed, to acquire the source code free of charge. The company also publishes a list of software developers familiar with its source code.

Other Major Accounting Features Worth Considering

Because the implementation of an accounting program on a network is supposed to make the accounting more efficient, a number of program features that can help achieve this goal are worth considering. One such feature is the ability to handle recurring entries automatically, rather than manually. Another feature is the ability to provide help screens. Since a network frequently adds users, on-line help screens reduce training time and make new users more productive. Finally, networks are as prone to power failure as single-user systems. Some accounting programs provide frequent backups and even update their master file with each transaction. This approach ensures accurate on-line data queries and minimizes data loss in the event of power failure.

WHAT HAVE YOU LEARNED?

1. MS-DOS version 3.1 and above permit multiuser operations on a local area network because they feature byte-locking.
2. Single-user software lacks the record-locking feature desirable on a local area network. Using such a program on a network also violates its licensing agreement.
3. Document-oriented word-processing programs offer many advantages over page-oriented programs.
4. A query language can make it much easier to use a powerful database management program.
5. Network accounting programs often consist of a number of sophisticated integrated modules.
6. Some software vendors encourage customers to customize their packages in order to meet individual needs.

Quiz for Chapter 11

1. For multiuser operations, use a version of MS-DOS that is at least
   a. 3.0
   b. 2.1
   c. 3.1
   d. 1.1

2. The program that acts as a "traffic cop" to direct requests for shared network resources is called
   a. Master Manager
   b. IBM PC Traffic Manager
   c. the Director
   d. the Redirector

3. A word-processing program that displays only one page at a time is
   a. page-oriented
   b. document-oriented
   c. paragraph-oriented
   d. style-sheet–oriented

4. Writing a customized form letter using a list of names and addresses is known as (a)
   a. "Dear John" letter
   b. boilerplate letter
   c. mail merge
   d. shopping-list processing

5. A series of form paragraphs linked together in a word-processing function is known as
   a. mail merge
   b. boilerplate
   c. mail link
   d. paragraph meld

6. A feature that enables an electronic spreadsheet user to program several spreadsheet functions so that they may be performed with a couple of keystrokes is known as a
   a. micro
   b. macro
   c. BASIC interface
   d. firmware chip

7. A spreadsheet feature that allows a user to name a target value and have the program calculate the required variable value to reach that goal is known as
   a. circular reasoning
   b. target variables
   c. micro justification
   d. goal seeking

8. IBM supports which query language?
   a. Clout
   b. SQL
   c. ADL
   d. QUESTION

Local Area Network Selection and Management

ABOUT THIS CHAPTER

A company must make many decisions before it purchases a local area network. In this chapter we'll examine how a company can do an initial needs analysis, factoring in company information needs, existing resources, and plans for future growth. Of course, most companies will still need to talk with data communications and telecommunications consultants. But this analysis will provide a basis for discussion and prevent the consultants from selecting a system that meets *their* needs instead of the company's.

We'll look at the steps necessary to develop a request for proposals (RFP) and follow-up procedures. We will also consider the problem of multiple vendors and hardware and software maintenance and training.

Local area network management is a major responsibility. Therefore, we will examine some of the duties of a network administrator and the type of record keeping required to prevent network downtime. Finally, we'll address network access, security, and software integration and survey the types of information and reports necessary for effective network management.

SOLVING PROBLEMS WITH LOCAL AREA NETWORKS

Once problems are identified, the question to ask is, "Will a local area network help solve these problems?"

For companies that already have data communication and telecommunication equipment, the first question generally asked in a LAN needs assessment is, What problems do we have that might be solved if we implement a network? When interviewed, employees from several departments often describe similar problems. These might include:

Too much duplication of effort (several salespeople typing form letters, for example)

Too much paperwork (Why can't we eliminate most of the memos and use electronic mail?)

Loss of data integrity because people working on the same project need to swap disks frequently

Mounting hardware and software expenses because departments don't share resources but build "kingdoms"

Inability to obtain data from other departments

Security concerns over use of computerized information

Growing hardware and line expenses for departments that need to use public information networks

Problems such as these suggest a need for a local area network. The next step is to inventory existing hardware and software resources to determine if they are compatible with a local area network.

SURVEYING YOUR DATA COMMUNICATIONS AND TELECOMMUNICATIONS RESOURCES

Telecommunications Equipment

In some small companies the survey might take one minute and consist of looking around the office to conclude that the company has a simple telephone system with four lines and eight telephones and two IBM PS/2 workstations that are used respectively for word processing and accounting.

Companies need to survey their data communications and telecommunications equipment to learn the most effective way to improve the flow of information.

In larger companies, with much more equipment, the survey must be formalized and an instrument developed to ensure that all answers are standardized. Assuming the company has a PBX telephone system, some of the questions that should be asked include:

1. Has a traffic study been done to determine peak periods of phone system usage?

2. If the PBX were to be used for data as well as telecommunications, how much surplus capacity does the system have at present? People are used to a brief delay when accessing a computer, but they expect instant telephone response. You must therefore determine the degree of degradation that would result if telecommunications and data communications were combined. Since some older PBX systems require two dedicated data lines for a single voice line, it is essential to estimate the number of terminals that the company will need for the future.

3. If the company currently now uses modems to transmit data over telephone lines, would it save money if these transactions could be tracked and perhaps recharged to the departments using a PBX call-accounting system?

4. Is there a need to integrate voice and data communications or significant interest in doing so?

5. If the PBX represents a possible local area network, is there any redundancy built into this switch? What happens if the PBX fails?

6. Is a mainframe computer located at the same location? Is it feasible or even desirable for the microcomputers comprising a local area network to communicate with the mainframe computer through the PBX?

7. What kinds of private networks must be accessed by the local area network? Do these networks require speeds that are possible with a PBX?

8. Does the company need to tie a number of asynchronous PC terminals to its synchronous mainframe? (Because a PBX is an excellent way of linking synchronous and asynchronous devices and providing protocol conversion, a company that already has a PBX should consider this question very carefully.)

9. What kind of information needs to be shared and transmitted through a network? This is perhaps the most critical question of all. If the information consists of lengthy files, it might well be that the PBX isn't fast enough to accommodate the network.

In most cases a PBX will prove to be inadequate to handle all data communications because its speed cannot approach that of a dedicated computer system with data-grade cabling. Most major PBX companies such as AT&T and Northern Telecom offer local area network interfaces to their digital PBX systems, however, so a company with a PBX might well consider the advantages of using the interface for modem pooling and automatic route selection while handling heavy data communication over a computer-based local area network.

Surveying Present Hardware and Software and Desirable Additions

The next step in a needs analysis is to inventory available hardware and software and assess company information needs. A marketing department's inventory of current hardware and software might look like this:

1 IBM PS/80 with 4 megabytes (Mb) of RAM
2 IBM ATs with 640K of RAM and a 40-Mb hard drive
1 Compaq 386 with an 80-Mb hard disk
1 Dell 12-MHz 286 model with dual floppy drives
1 HP Vectra 286 model with a 40-Mb hard drive
1 Hewlett Packard Laser Jet Plus IID printer
3 Epson LQ model 24-pin dot matrix printers

The department currently uses a word processor, a spreadsheet, and a database manager program. Its list of present computer activity as well as its "wish list" for the future with a local area network might look like this:

Lotus 1-2-3 worksheets for forecasting future sales
dBASE IV customer list that everyone could access
dBASE IV customer sales histories
WordPerfect sales form letter
Ability to merge form letters with customer lists
Ability to print sales contracts
Lotus 1-2-3 commission worksheets
Ability to access MRP manufacturing information (from mainframe)
Electronic mail
Ability to inquire on product availability from a remote location
Ability to input an order on-line
Ability to track salespeople's phone expenses
Ability to switch salespeople to least expensive long-distance carrier
Ability to share resources such as laser printers and dot matrix printers
Ability to print envelopes as well as letters
Ability to track salespeople's performance and produce graphs available only to the salesperson involved

After having each department compile such a list, you will need to discover whether the present software can be networked. If the Accounting department has a single-user program that is not upgradable to a networkable version with record locking, buying a new program might be prohibitively expensive. Even if the present accounting program uses ASCII data files, extensive programming is needed to format this data so that it corresponds to a new program's field and record parameters. And this assumes that you can obtain the source code of the new accounting program.

The Marketing department's desire to have remote access to the local area network is understandable. Salespeople would like to be able to view current inventory levels and perhaps even place their orders over phone lines. If the company decides that remote access is essential for its LAN, it must specify this requirement in its request for proposals (RFP). Not all major local area network software can support remote entry. Even those networks that can may have their own requirements such as a dedicated gateway workstation.

The Marketing department also expressed an interest in being able to access (or at least view) manufacturing data currently residing on a mainframe computer. Before deciding that a micro-mainframe network connection is desirable, the network administrator must consider the following questions. Is this mainframe information important enough to Marketing's performance to justify a micro-mainframe connection? What programming would be necessary to download the information directly into one of the network's programs? Do departments that will be linked by the local area network have sufficient reason to view mainframe information to warrant the security problems that could result from establishing the link?

A major concern in many companies is the variety of computer models within departments. Not all IBM compatibles are actually compatible enough to use network adapter circuit cards. As we will see shortly, any proposal for a local area network needs to address this issue and place the burden of proof on the network vendor to guarantee that its network will work with all present equipment.

Nature of Data Transmission

When contemplating a LAN, a company must consider what type of data will be transmitted and address geographic and security concerns.

Before selecting the media and network hardware and software, it is necessary to examine the work that will be done on the network. We just saw what the Marketing department has in mind, but we need to know how large the dBASE IV customer lists and Lotus 1-2-3 worksheets are. Very large dBASE IV file transfers will consume valuable network time and may suggest that the company eliminate from consideration some of the slower LANs (1–2 mbps) in favor of a faster network (6–20 mbps). Once this determination has been made, the company can look at related issues such as geographic considerations and security requirements.

Geographic Considerations

Once a company has an idea of the software it plans in its network and a clear picture of its present resources, it next needs to determine the geographic parameters of the network. For example, will the network encompass several departments, a single building, or multiple buildings? Since many of the local area networks use a bus topology that is limited to 1000 feet (300 meters), a network in a large building might require another architecture such as a token ring.

Media Selection

The network medium might be directly related to the company's geographic requirements. If the network will be installed in an environment where there is a good deal of interference, fiber optics might be required. If the building already has twisted-pair unshielded telephone wire installed, it might be cost-effective to determine whether a network could handle the data transmission requirements using this medium. If the company wants simultaneous voice and data transmission, then it must select a medium capable of such transmission.

Security Considerations

Local area networks vary in the degree of security they offer. As a rule, star topology networks offer the means to monitor all workstations and record the files and programs that they access. Software such as Novell's NetWare establishes several levels of network security beyond simple password protection including the ability to set file attributes. It is also important to consider whether you can quickly change user access. Novell's conception of user groups is beneficial in situations where people's assignments change frequently, requiring changes in network access. Finally, there needs to be some concern for the security and integrity of data. What happens if a user turns off the workstation without properly closing his or her files? Sophisticated network software will prevent files from being damaged in such situations.

Another security consideration is the ease with which the network topology and media allow unauthorized entry. For example, anyone can connect a tap with relative ease via a small isolation transformer hidden behind a termination panel. It is then child's play to connect this transformer to another line and dial-in from another location to access the network. Fiber-optic cabling offers the optimal protection against such intrusions.

If security is a great concern, the network administrator should consider incorporating additional security measures in the RFP. One such measure is the purchase of terminal locks to protect unattended workstations from unauthorized entry. Another safeguard is the use of *callback modems*. In this system, a remote user must provide a password that the network checks against its list of authorized passwords. If there is a match, the network hangs up and calls the remote user back using a telephone number that is stored next to the authorized password. This practice ensures that only authorized users can access sensitive network files, and, with the use of inexpensive WATS lines, it offers substantial savings. Unfortunately, not all networks permit this security measure. IBM's asynchronous communications server, for example, is not designed to handle callback modems.

DEVELOPING A REQUEST FOR PROPOSALS (RFP)

A request for proposals to implement a local area network must solicit vendor information on network hardware, software, and applications programs.

We have seen that before a company can begin the process of inviting vendor proposals, the company must take several steps in order to analyze needs. In our example, the company first determined which software was currently being used and then which software it planned to use under network conditions. To ensure complete compatibility, the company also surveyed its present computer workstations and printers.

Because of the limitations inherent in many networks, the company also determined the maximum size of the network, the potential for expansion, and the type of information and size of files that it wanted to transmit over a network. It also examined the security measures it might want to require to ensure only authorized access. Now the company can develop a formal RFP.

To aid viable vendor proposals, we will provide information in a logical order. Here is an outline for the heart of an RFP:

I. Hardware
   A. Microcomputers
      1. Currently on hand (brand, configuration)
      2. Additional workstations required for the network
         a. IBM compatibility to be able to run which programs?
         b. RAM required
         c. Number of disk drives required
            1. For security reasons, do you prefer no disk drives and an autoboot ROM chip?
            2. If disk drives are required, do you want half-height or full-height?
            3. Do you want 360K, 1.2-Mb, or 1.4-Mb disk drives?
         d. If hard disk is required
            1. What size (in megabytes)?
            2. Mounted in what kind of micro-computer?
            3. Formatted in which version of DOS?
         e. Monitors and monitor adapter cards required
            1. Color or monochrome
            2. Resolution
            3. Size
            4. Other features required
            5. Dual mode
            6. Ability to run certain graphic programs
         f. Other I/O cards required
            1. Parallel or serial cards and cables
            2. Additional RAM cards
            3. Multifunction cards
            4. Accelerator cards
            5. Others
   B. File Servers
      1. Size required
      2. Processing speed of file server

    3. System fault tolerance (if required)

    4. Other features required

    5. Number of tape backup units

C. Bridges to other networks

    1. Other networks to be connected

    2. Adapter cards and cabling required

    3. Software required

D. Backbone networks required to connect multiple bridges

    1. Description of bridges to be connected

    2. Processing speed required

E. Gateways to minicomputer and mainframe environments

    1. Local or remote connections

    2. Protocols required

    3. Number of concurrent sessions required

    4. Terminal emulation required

    5. Local printer emulation required

    6. Amount of activity to be handled

F. Minicomputers

    1. Currently on hand (brand, configuration)

    2. Need to integrate information with LAN

G. Mainframe Computer

    1. Currently installed (brand, configuration)

    2. Need to integrate information with LAN

H. Printers

    1. Currently on hand (brands, buffers, accessories)

    2. Additional printers needed for the LAN

        a. Speed required

        b. Type (laser, dot matrix, etc.)

        c. Compatibility with major printer drivers

        d. Type of connection (parallel, serial)

        e. Length of distance from workstations

        f. Other special printer features

    3. Special language fonts or downloadable fonts

    4. Near letter-quality and fast dot matrix modes

    5. Workstations or areas that will need to access specific printers

    6. Unusual printing requirements (color, multiple copy, specific accounting forms, etc.)

    7. Software packages on the network that require a specific printer

I. Modems

    1. Currently on hand (brand, speed, special features, etc.)

    2. Need for additional units with the LAN

    3. Transmission mode required (simplex, half-duplex, full-duplex)

    4. Interconnections required (point-to-point, multiple drops)

    5. Special features needed

        a. auto-dial

        b. auto-logon

        c. auto-answer

        d. other

J. Plotters
   1. Presently on hand (brands, configuration)
   2. Additional units required
      a. Speed
      b. Number of colors
      c. Compatibility with major brands
      d. Programs to drive plotters
K. Optical scanners
   1. Currently on hand
   2. Additional units required
      a. Speed
      b. Fonts to be scanned
      c. Programs that will need access to this data
L. Other hardware required
   1. Cash registers (for retail environment)
      a. Type of connection (serial, parallel)
      b. Compatibility with point-of-sale accounting programs
   2. Badge readers (for manufacturing environment)
      a. Will employees clock in and out of several jobs for the same day?
      b. Does this information have to be interfaced with an accounting program's payroll module?
   3. Multiplexers
      a. Devices to be attached
      b. Location of these devices
      c. Type of transmission required
      d. Speed required
   4. Protocol converters
      a. Devices to be attached
      b. Protocols involved (SNA, BSC, ASCII, etc.)
   5. Power protection required
      a. Voltage regulation
      b. Elimination of sags and surges
      c. Prevention of common-mode noise
      d. Battery backup

II. Software
A. Operating system and utility programs
   1. DOS
      a. Which version for the root directory?
      b. Are there multiple versions on the network?
   2. Electronic mail
      a. Menu-driven
      b. Help screens
      c. Display messages
      d. Distribution lists possible
      e. Notification when a message arrives
      f. Ability to forward messages
      g. Ability to define multiple user groups

       h. Ability to print and file messages

       i. Ability to attach files including graphics

       j. Other features desirable

    3. Network calendar

       a. Degree of workstation access to calendar features

       b. Ability to schedule rooms and hardware resources

B. Network Management

    1. Ability to perform diagnostics

    2. Ability to add and delete user groups

    3. Password protection

    4. Maintenance of user statistics

    5. Ability to handle remote dial-in users

    6. Ability to handle multiple operating systems

    7. Ability to handle bridges to other networks

    8. Ability to add and delete printers easily

    9. Security provided

       a. Login level (password required)

       b. Directory level

       c. File level

       d. File attributes

   10. Menu-driven with ability for sophisticated users to bypass the menu and use commands

   11. Login scripts or other facilities such as batch files permitted to make it easier for novice users to log in

   12. Print-server software

       a. Number of printers permitted on the network

       b. Number of share devices

       c. Printer queues

          1. Size

          2. Ability to change printing priority

       d. Commands available to network users

          1. For setting parameters for specific printing jobs

          2. For disabling printers for routine servicing

       e. Print-spooling software

       f. Types of printers supported

          1. Parallel

          2. Serial

          3. Laser

          4. Line printers

   13. File-server software

       a. Size of volumes permitted

       b. Access speed

       c. Network drives (logical drives) permitted

       d. Virtual drives (transparent to users)

       e. Restore tape to disk capability

       f. Directory hashing

   14. Network communications server software

       a. Protocols supported

        1. ASCII asynchronous
        2. 3270 BSC
        3. 3270 SNA
        4. X.25
     b. Speed supported
     c. Ability to handle callback modems
     d. Automatic dial-out
     e. User statistics provided
  C. Current software that the network must support
     1. Word-processing
     2. Spreadsheet
     3. Database management
     4. Accounting
     5. Other application software

Trying to Avoid Starting Over

It is unlikely that the company's current software will be supported by a new local area network. Your RFP should detail which programs are currently being used and the nature of their current file structure. If the word-processing program permits files to be saved in ASCII format, it probably will be possible to use the data files with the new network program. Many of the most popular programs (WordPerfect, for example) have network versions of their programs. Selecting a networkable upgrade would ensure that there would be no training necessary for this portion of network activity.

Accounting is a far more complex area. Some programs have networkable upgrades. A company fortunate enough to be using a single-user version can upgrade to a network version without having to worry about file transfers or training. In most cases, however, as we saw earlier, moving from a single-user accounting program to a network accounting program means starting over. In this case, the company probably will choose to run the single-user program until the fiscal year's accounting cycle is complete while gradually adding more and more customer information to the network software. After running both programs concurrently for a couple of months to ensure the accuracy of the new program, a company can switch to the new system.

Software Licenses

Virtually all software packages restrict their usage, sometimes to one user and sometimes to one machine. The RFP should include provisions for software licensing for the network site ("site licensing") or a network version licensed for a specific number of users.

  D. New application software required
     1. Word-processing
        a. Compatibility with current software
        b. Features required
        c. Training to be provided
     2. Spreadsheet/financial analysis
        a. Compatibility with current software
        b. Features required

      c. Training to be provided
   3. Database management
      a. Compatibility with current software
      b. Features required
      c. Training to be provided
   4. Accounting
      a. Compatibility with current software
      b. Features required
      c. Training to be provided
   5. Custom software required
      a. Compatibility with current software
      b. Features required
      c. Training to be provided

VENDOR REQUIREMENTS

Vendors replying to an RFP must match benchmarks for hardware and software.

In order to complete this outline of information in our RFP, we need to examine the relationship between companies and LAN vendors. A number of questions need to be asked of prospective vendors before a network is purchased and installed. It is an excellent idea, for example, to require that vendors demonstrate their networks' ability to run the software your company plans to install. Often companies will require a benchmark showdown of sorts in which competing vendors are asked to perform under similar conditions.

Even if a vendor's equipment can provide a LAN that meets your company's speed and compatibility requirements at a reasonable cost, the equipment may not prove to be sufficiently reliable. Therefore, it is imperative that you request references to vendor customers with installations similar to yours. You also need to secure information about the equipment's reliability, including a mean time before failure (MTBF); maintenance contracts; and response time.

Frequently network vendors will offer a variety of maintenance options, including a guaranteed response time, a repair-or-replace designation, and even a guarantee to provide a file server on loan if they cannot repair the network within a given length of time. Before issuing an RFP, your company must determine how long it can afford to be without network services and then require vendors to meet a response time that suits your needs.

Because a local area network includes computer hardware, network hardware and software, and third-party software, it is common for vendors to "pass the buck" and not accept responsibility when a network problem arises. Part of the RFP should require the principal vendor to take overall responsibility for the network's maintenance. If a software problem suddenly develops, for example, the principal vendor should act as a liaison with the software company to solve your problem.

Often you may discover to your horror that none of the vendors have practical experience installing the precise network configuration that your company requires. At that point, you may insist on serving as a "beta" site for the vendor (and perhaps the manufacturer). For so doing, you should receive a substantial discount in price in exchange for the experience and referral you may later provide.

Other safeguards that your company might want to insist on include a performance bond to be posted by the vendor and a payment schedule phased to correspond to the completion level of the network (including software and hardware). Your safeguards should be linked to a minimum level of performance that you specify in your RFP. If you fear serious degradation in response time with heavy activity, you might require a minimum response time for each of a certain number of workstations when all are involved simultaneously in a certain procedure. Several major network software companies including Novell and 3Com provide excellent benchmark tests that you can require your vendors to duplicate.

Since the maximum distance of local area networks is directly related to their topology and media, be sure to include in the RFP a diagram indicating where workstations will be placed and their approximate distances from each other. Also—and this is essential—indicate where future growth will take place and whether these future workstations will require additional file servers and other peripherals.

III. Vendor Requirements
    A. Experience
        1. Company history (length at present location)
        2. Experience installing local area networks
        3. Customer references for similar installations
    B. Service
        1. Number of factory-trained service technicians
        2. Ability to provide on-site service
            a. Repair or replace service within 24 hours
            b. Ability to respond 24 hours a day
            c. Ability to respond within 2 hours
            d. A sufficient inventory of parts to provide adequate service
    C. Ability to provide a LAN demonstration
        1. Software to be identical with ordered software
        2. Hardware to be identical with ordered hardware
        3. Benchmark tests to be conducted
    D. Training
        1. Ability to provide basic user training
        2. Ability to provide training on all purchased software
        3. Degree of training provided with installation
        4. Charge for additional training
        5. Phone support included in purchase price
        6. Kind of training for the network administrator
        7. Possibility of training others
    E. Responsibilities if multiple vendors are required for this network
        1. Hardware training and network familiarization
        2. Hardware service
        3. Software training
        4. Software service

NETWORK MANAGEMENT

After a network has been installed and the network supervisor has been trained, he or she assumes full responsibility for network management. There are three major areas of responsibility when managing a local area network: security, efficiency, and maintenance. Network security responsibilities include providing user passwords, setting up user groups, and developing a set of reports on network usage. This last task is essential because supervisors need to be able to identify who has been accessing a directory. Since some network software permits "hidden" files and directories, network supervisors often use this technique to remove potential temptations from employees. Network software that permits remote dial-in workstations presents many opportunities for security breaches. One way to minimize security risks after hours at a remote network link is to restrict access from that workstation to certain file servers. Callback modems are also useful if the network communications software permits them.

Network Efficiency

Network management also includes maximizing the system's overall efficiency. Since new and occasional users may have trouble with such routine network functions as the login, network supervisors must help them by establishing routines to follow. In the case of IBM's network software, these are customized batch files that need to be written only once. Novell's NetWare includes login scripts that may take a supervisor only a few minutes to write but that can save novices hours and eliminate a good deal of frustration.

Another aspect of network efficiency involves monitoring network traffic statistics. By examining printer usage statistics, for example, the supervisor might determine that certain log reports need to be spooled and printed after peak hours. Heavy usage of certain accounting programs that place a premium on file-server access can slow the entire network. The supervisor might decide to add a separate file server for the Accounting department in order to speed up the rest of the network.

Finally, all network supervisors need to develop a carefully planned schedule for network backups. Some network areas, such as accounting, might require backups twice a day. The entire system, of course, should be backed up on a daily basis. Most software can time-stamp files, requiring backup only of those files that have been modified since the last backup. The supervisor should perform backups of all files every two weeks and place the six-week-old backup in a safe, off-site location.

Network Maintenance

Network maintenance includes maintaining network efficiency, making regular backups of files, and keeping accurate maintenance records.

The third major management responsibility of a network supervisor is network maintenance. This doesn't necessarily mean physically repairing defective network components, although most supervisors of large systems do keep an inventory of basic components such as network adapter cards. Since many network software packages include diagnostics, a defective adapter card can often be identified and replaced immediately.

Figure 12-1 illustrates a sample hardware documentation sheet. By keeping key information on all workstations, interface boards, printers, and other devices in this format, the network supervisor can organize network resources more efficiently. Figure 12-2 illustrates a similar profile that can be maintained for all software installed on the network. By placing the key information on a sheet like this and then keeping it in a log book, the network supervisor avoids having to search for a manual or box cover when problems arise.

**Figure 12-1.
A Hardware
Documentation Sheet**

Hardware Network Documentation

Type of Equipment: _____
Serial Number: _____
Location: _____
Date Purchased: _____
Warranty Expiration Date: _____
Vendor: _____ Contact: _____
Telephone: _____
Service Contract #: _____
Vendor: _____ Contact: _____ Tel: _____
Problems:
Date   Problem   Solution

**Figure 12-2.
A Software
Documentation Sheet**

Software Network Documentation

Name of Program: _____ DOS Version: _____
Publisher: _____ Tel: _____
Purchased From: _____ Date: _____Tel: _____
Warranty Expires: _____
System Requirements:
RAM Required: _____
Hard Disk/Floppies: _____
Software Maintenance/Support:
Vendor: _____
Telephone: _____
Problems:
Date   Problem   Solution

A network log book should provide clear audit trails of all network changes. Password changes, alterations in user access, software updates that have been installed, and program additions or deletions should be noted and dated. Such a log book should be kept under lock and key when not being used. Without such an administrative tool, the network represents a disaster waiting to happen.

The Network Supervisor's Tools

A network supervisor would be well advised to have a number of tools and materials on hand, including both straight and Phillips screwdrivers as well as needlenose and diagonal cutters pliers. A voltameter or digital voltmeter is useful for cable testing.

Workstations suffer hardware failure most often because of a bad interface board, a defective floppy disk drive, or some bad memory chips. Although large companies will probably have in-house technicians to handle these problems, a network supervisor might find it expedient to keep some of these hardware materials readily available, as well as an ample supply of printer ribbons, printer paper, extra formatted tapes for file-server backups, toner cartridges for network laser printers, and, certainly, at least one box of *formatted* floppy disks.

The Protocol Analyzer

A protocol analyzer analyzes the frames traveling across a network and provides valuable information on the performance of network interface cards, file servers, and software.

The protocol analyzer provides the key to understanding why a network is not running at top efficiency. Protocol analyzers analyze the packets of information flowing across a network and provide valuable statistics. Although there are several major protocol analyzers on the market, we'll focus on one of the major contenders, Network General Corporation's The Sniffer.

When The Sniffer is attached to a network as if it were a workstation, it listens to every transmission that goes by it. Although it focuses primarily on the data link layer of the OSI model discussed in Chapter 2, it also displays information used by applications up to the session layer.

The Sniffer is a self-contained computer with its own network adapter card, hard disk, operating system, and software. Once you exit from The Sniffer program, the machine becomes a standard Compaq AT model running Compaq DOS. While running The Sniffer, however, the machine has two major functions: to capture frames and to display information.

Because of the amount of information passing through a protocol analyzer, a supervisor usually filters it by establishing parameters. For example, he or she can choose to analyze the network by station address, by protocol, or by particular frame pattern. The Sniffer provides a traffic-density bar graph that displays traffic as kilobytes per second, frames per second, or as a percentage of the network's available bandwidth. Information can be displayed in linear form or logarithmic scale.

The Sniffer uses counters to reveal the number of frames seen, the number of frames accepted, and the percentage of the capture buffer used by the program. It also displays pair counts for each pair of workstations communicating information.

Figure 12-3 illustrates both a summary and a detail display of an exchange between two stations. Notice that The Sniffer identifies the two stations communicating from its own name table. Apparently, a user named Dan is communicating with the NetWare file server. The conversation we are eavesdropping on consists of a response from the NetWare file server regarding its LOGIN file. This protocol analyzer also provides some detailed file directory information regarding the file being accessed, including the file's length, its creation date, the last access date, and the last update of the date and time.

Figure 12-3. A Report from The Sniffer *(Reprinted with the permission of Network General Corporation)*

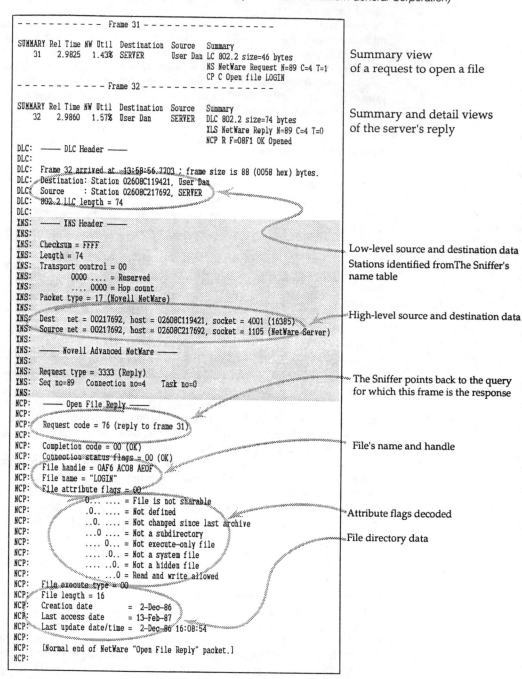

```
- - - - - - - - - -  Frame 31  - - - - - - - - - - - - - - - -

SUMMARY  Rel Time NW Util  Destination  Source   Summary
   31     2.9825   1.43%   SERVER       User Dan  LC 802.2 size=46 bytes
                                                  NS NetWare Request N=89 C=4 T=1
                                                  CP C Open file LOGIN
- - - - - - - - - -  Frame 32  - - - - - - - - - - - - - - - -

SUMMARY  Rel Time NW Util  Destination  Source   Summary
   32     2.9860   1.57%   User Dan     SERVER    DLC 802.2 size=74 bytes
                                                  ILS NetWare Reply N=89 C=4 T=0
                                                  NCP R F=08F1 OK Opened
DLC:  ---- DLC Header ----
DLC:
DLC:  Frame 32 arrived at 13:58:56.7703 ; frame size is 88 (0058 hex) bytes.
DLC:  Destination: Station 02608C119421, User Dan
DLC:  Source     : Station 02608C217692, SERVER
DLC:  802.2 LLC length = 74
DLC:
INS:  ---- INS Header ----
INS:
INS:  Checksum = FFFF
INS:  Length = 74
INS:  Transport control = 00
INS:        0000 .... = Reserved
INS:        .... 0000 = Hop count
INS:  Packet type = 17 (Novell NetWare)
INS:
INS:  Dest  net = 00217692, host = 02608C119421, socket = 4001 (16385)
INS:  Source net = 00217692, host = 02608C217692, socket = 1105 (NetWare Server)
INS:
INS:  ---- Novell Advanced NetWare ----
INS:
INS:  Request type = 3333 (Reply)
INS:  Seq no=89   Connection no=4    Task no=0
INS:
NCP:  ---- Open File Reply ----
NCP:
NCP:  Request code = 76 (reply to frame 31)
NCP:
NCP:  Completion code = 00 (OK)
NCP:  Connection status flags = 00 (OK)
NCP:  File handle = 0AF6 AC08 AE0F
NCP:  File name = "LOGIN"
NCP:  File attribute flags = 00
NCP:         0... .... = File is not sharable
NCP:         .0.. .... = Not defined
NCP:         ..0. .... = Not changed since last archive
NCP:         ...0 .... = Not a subdirectory
NCP:         .... 0... = Not execute-only file
NCP:         .... .0.. = Not a system file
NCP:         .... ..0. = Not a hidden file
NCP:         .... ...0 = Read and write allowed
NCP:  File execute type = 00
NCP:  File length = 16
NCP:  Creation date      = 2-Dec-86
NCP:  Last access date   = 13-Feb-87
NCP:  Last update date/time = 2-Dec-86 16:08:54
NCP:
NCP:  [Normal end of NetWare "Open File Reply" packet.]
NCP:
```

Summary view
of a request to open a file

Summary and detail views
of the server's reply

Low-level source and destination data
Stations identified from The Sniffer's
name table

High-level source and destination data

The Sniffer points back to the query
for which this frame is the response

File's name and handle

Attribute flags decoded

File directory data

As this brief discussion of The Sniffer illustrates, protocol analyzers have proven to be invaluable tools for network managers. With some practice, their reports can be read and analyzed with relative ease to reveal a good deal of information about a network's general health.

WHAT HAVE YOU LEARNED?

1. The first step in developing a request for proposal (RFP) is to analyze the company's needs.
2. The geography of a company's proposed local area network will determine what kind of network topology and media are feasible.
3. Some network workstations should use autoboot ROM chips and not have any floppy disk drives in order to ensure network security.
4. Most software generally is licensed for one user. Network applications require special network versions designated for a certain number of users or software site licensing.
5. The three major network management responsibilities of a network supervisor are network security, efficiency, and maintenance.
6. To maintain network efficiency, it is essential to monitor traffic statistics.

Quiz for Chapter 12

1. The first step of a company LAN needs analysis is to
   a. examine currently existing problems that could be solved with a local area network
   b. inventory all current software
   c. inventory all current hardware
   d. write a request for proposal

2. The variety of microcomputers found in most companies creates a potential LAN problem because of
   a. different costs for components
   b. service needs
   c. NETBIOS incompatibility
   d. different disk drive speed

3. If a needs analysis reveals that several programs on the network will include large databases, this could mean that
   a. you will need a disk server rather than a file server
   b. there might be a problem with file-server access speed
   c. the database software better be able to handle long field names
   d. the operating system cannot be DOS

4. The geography of the company's building, including where it will need workstations, has a direct effect on
   a. the network topology
   b. the network's medium
   c. the network's cost
   d. all of the above

5. For security purposes, a network workstation might include
   a. a lock
   b. an autoboot ROM
   c. no disk drives
   d. all of the above

6. In order to have the entire network use a specific software program, the company must obtain permission from the software company. This is known as
   a. site licensing
   b. software permission
   c. multiple network copies (MNC)
   d. workstation access to software help (WASH)

7. The major problem with multiple vendors in a network environment is
   a. the expense
   b. the lack of quality
   c. the lack of clear responsibility
   d. network efficiency

8. To help novice users, network supervisors should provide
   a. their own set of manuals
   b. a keyboard template
   c. training at the manufacturer's home plant
   d. login scripts and batch files

9. Network supervisors use traffic statistics in order to
   a. monitor network efficiency
   b. avoid network data collisions
   c. prevent network users from having accidents
   d. produce reports that will improve automobile traffic safety

10. In order to maintain control of a network, network supervisors must
    a. keep a log book
    b. have excellent memories
    c. be excellent politicians
    d. have advanced degrees in computer science

Directory of Local Area Network Vendors

Apple Computer, Inc.
20525 Mariani Avenue
Cupertino, CA 95014

AT&T Information Systems
1 Speedway Avenue
Morristown, NJ 07960

Banyan Systems
135 Flanders Road
Westboro, MA 01581

Datapoint Corporation
9725 Datapoint Drive
San Antonio, TX 78784

DCA (10Net)
1000 Aldermann Drive
Alpharetta, GA 30201

IBM Corporation
P.O. Box 1328
Boca Raton, FL 33429-1328

IEEE*
10662 Los Vaqueros Circle
Los Alamitos, CA 90720

Novell, Inc.
122 East 1700 South
Provo, UT 84601

Sun Microsystems
TOPS Division
950 Marina Village Parkway
Alameda, CA 94501

3Com
3165 Kifer Road
Santa Clara, CA 95052-8145

*Source of information on IEEE standards

Glossary

Active Token Monitor: The workstation that assumes responsibility for network management in IBM's Token Ring Network.

Apple File Protocol: The suite of protocols associated with Apple's local area network.

AppleShare: Apple's file-server software for its local area networks.

Application Layer: The layer of the OSI model concerned with application programs such as electronic mail, database managers, and file-server software.

Arcnet: A local area network featuring a physical bus and a logical star.

ARM: Asynchronous Response Mode. Stations send messages whenever they desire to transmit without waiting for a poll bit.

ASCII: American Standard Code for Information Interchange. A character code used by microcomputers.

Asynchronous Communications Server: Enables network workstations to access ASCII applications via switched communications lines.

Automatic Rollback: Under TTS, when a system fails, the database is reconstructed at the point just prior to the transaction during which the failure took place.

Backbone: A high-speed link joining together several network bridges.

Background Tasks: The tasks performed by other network users under PC Network.

Baseband: Single-channel coaxial cable.

Batch File: A file containing commands that can cause several different programs to execute automatically.

Beacon: A special network signal indicating the address of a node immediately upstream from a defective node.

BIOS: Basic Input/Output System. ROM software.

Bit Stuffing: The insertion of a 0-bit to ensure that no data contains more than five straight 0s.

BRI: Basic-Rate Interface. Used under ISDN to service small-capacity devices such as terminals.

Bridge: A connection between two networks that takes place at the data link layer.

Broadband: Coaxial cable that can carry several signals simultaneously on different channels.

Broadcast Messages: Messages sent to all computers on a network.

BSC: Binary Synchronous Communication. A synchronous protocol used on many older IBM mainframe computers.

Bus: A data highway. This term is also used to designate a simple linear-shaped local area network.

Callback Modem: A modem designed to call back a remote caller to verify identity for security purposes.

CCITT: Consultative Committee for International Telephone and Telegraph.

CCITT X.3: A protocol for the Packet Assembly/Disassembly Facility in a public data network.

CCITT X.25: A standard for data packets sent to public switched networks. This standard corresponds to the OSI model's first three layers.

CCITT X.28: A protocol for DTE/DCE interface for a start-stop DTE accessing the Packet Assembly/Disassembly Facility (PAD) on a public data network situated in the same country.

CCITT X.75: A protocol for the terminal and transmit control procedures and data transfer system on international circuits between packet-switched networks.

CCITT X.400: A set of protocols governing electronic mail.

CCITT X.500: A set of protocols governing worldwide directories for electronic mail.

Centralized file server: A single file server that serves a local area network.

Cladding: A layer of glass that surrounds optic fibers in fiber-optic cables.

Contention Network: A network in which workstations compete for the right to send a message.

CSMA/CD: Carrier Sense Multiple Access with Collision Detection. A method of avoiding data collisions on a local area network.

DCE: Data communications equipment. This term generally refers to modems.

Dedicated File Server: A file server that performs only that function and no computing functions.

Directory Hashing: File-server software that maps all directory files and keeps this information in RAM.

Disk Caching: A process in which the file server keeps often-requested files in RAM for rapid response to workstation requests.

Disk Server: A hard disk used to share files with several users. (Most programs are single-user, which means that only one person may use them at a time.)

Distributed File Serving: Distributed data processing to several computers rather than to one central computer.

Domain Controller: A file server controlling security for a set of resources under the Extended Services option of the IBM PC LAN Program.

DTE: Data Terminal Equipment. This generally consists of terminals or computers.

Duplexed Drives: A system fault tolerant technique in which virtually all hardware is duplicated, including disk controller, interface, and power supply.

EBCDIC: The Extended Binary Coded Decimal Interchange Code. A character code used by IBM's larger computers.

Elevator Seeking: A process in which a file server determines the order for executing file requests based on the current location of the disk drive heads.

FAT: File Allocation Table. A table that helps a disk server or file server keep track of where particular files are located.

FDDI: The fiber data distributed interface of fiber-optic cabling. A standard for 100-mbps network transmission speed.

File Locking: The ability to lock a file so that only one user may use it at a time.

File Server: A hard disk with software that permits it to maintain its own FAT and provide files to nodes while appearing transparent to these users.

Foreground Task: A task a user performs on his or her own machine while using the IBM PC LAN Program.

FSK: Frequency Shift Keying. A technique to modulate ones and zeroes and speed up transmission by shifting between two close frequencies.

Gateway PC: A PC containing gateway hardware and software that is used as a LAN gateway to another machine, often a mainframe computer.

HDLC: High-Level Data Link Control procedure. This protocol defines standards for linking a DTE and a DCE.

IEEE: The Institute for Electrical and Electronic Engineers.

IEEE 802.3: The industry standard for a bus local area network using CSMA/CD.

IEEE 802.4: The industry standard for a token bus local area network.

IEEE 802.5: The industry standard for a token ring local area network.

IEEE 802.6: The industry standard for metropolitan area networks.

Inbound Band: Carries data from a LAN node to the head end.

ISDN: Integrated Services Digital Network. A CCITT model for the eventual integration of voice and data and a universal interface for networks.

ISN: Information Systems Network. AT&T's high-speed network featuring integrated voice and data transmission.

ISO: International Standards Organization.

Jam: A signal sent through a network indicating that there has been a data collision.

LAN Manager: OS/2's network operating system.

LLC: The logical link sublayer of the OSI model.

Local Printer: A printer attached to a microcomputer that prints only this computer's documents and performs no network printing functions.

LocalTalk: The hardware associated with Apple's local area network.

Login Script: A predetermined set of steps performed to customize a network environment whenever a user logs on.

LU: Logical units. These can represent end users, application programs, or other devices. Communication under SNA is among LUs.

LU 6.2: A protocol that will make it possible to have peer-to-peer communications under SNA.

MAC: The media-access control sublayer of the data link layer of the OSI model.

Mirrored Drives: A system fault tolerant technique in which a hard disk mirrors everything on the file server.

MSAU: Multistation Access Unit. A wiring concentrator linking several network workstations to an IBM Token Ring Network.

MTBF: Mean time before failure. A standard used to evaluate a product's reliability.

Multimode Fiber: Fiber-optic cabling consisting of several fibers.

NAK: A negative acknowledgement signal.

NAU: Network-addressable unit. Logical units, physical units, and system services control points under SNA.

Network Adapter Card: Circuit card required in the expansion bus of a workstation under IBM's PC Network.

Network Layer: The layer of the OSI LAN model that establishes protocols for packets, message priorities, and network traffic control.

Node: An individual local area network workstation.

Nondedicated File Server: A file server that also functions as an independent microcomputer.

NRM: Normal Response Mode. When a central computer sends a poll bit to a station that wishes to transmit.

OSI Model: Open Systems Interconnection protocols for establishing a local area network.

Outbound Band: Carries data from the head end to LAN nodes.

Partitioning: Dividing a hard disk into several user volumes or areas.

Path Control Network: Responsible under SNA for identifying addresses of devices that wish to converse and then establishing a network path for them.

PBX: Private Branch Exchange. A sophisticated telephone system.

Physical Layer: The layer of the OSI LAN model that establishes protocols for voltage, data transmission timing, and rules for "handshaking."

PMD: The physical media-dependent layer of the fiber data distributed interface found in fiber-optic cabling.

Presentation Layer: The layer of the OSI model concerned with protocols for network security, file transfers, and format functions.

PRI: Primary-Rate Interface. Used under ISDN to service large-capacity devices such as PBXs.

Print Spooler: Software that creates a buffer where files to be printed can be stored while they wait their turn.

Protocol: A set of rules or procedures commonly agreed on by industrywide committees such as the IEEE.

PU: A physical unit. This represents something tangible under SNA such as a terminal or intelligent controller.

Public Volume: An area of a hard disk that contains information that may be shared by several users.

Read-Only: Files that can be read but not changed.

Record Locking: Software that locks a record so that several users can share the same file but cannot share the same record.

Repeaters: Devices on local area networks that rebroadcast a signal to prevent its degradation.

RFP: A request for proposals.

RJE: Remote job entry. The sending of information in batch form from a remote site often unattended by a user to an IBM mainframe.

Rollforward Recovery: Under TTS, a complete log is kept of all transactions to ensure that everything can be recovered.

SCSI: Small-Computer System Interface. An interface used to connect additional disk drives or tape backup units to a local area network.

SDLC: Synchronous Data Link Control. A subset of the HDLC protocol used by IBM computers running under SNA.

Semaphore: A flag that is set in order to make a file local and prevent two users from using the file simultaneously, thereby destroying it.

Session: A logical and physical path under SNA that connects two NAUs for data transmission.

Session Layer: The layer of the OSI model concerned with network management functions including passwords and network monitoring and reporting.

Site Licensing: The licensing software to be used only at a particular location.

SMDR: station message detail reporting.

SNA: Systems Network Architecture. The architecture used by IBM's minicomputers and mainframe computers.

Split Seeks: With duplexed drives the system checks to see which disk drive can respond more quickly.

Splitter: A device that divides a signal into two different paths.

SRPI: Under SNA, the Server/Requester Programming Interface allows PC applications to request services from IBM mainframes.

SSCP: System services control point. An SNA network manager for a single SNA domain.

Star: A network topology physically resembling a star. This network built around a central computer fails completely if the main computer fails.

StreetTalk: The distributed database serving as a network naming service for the VINES local area network.

Synchronous Transmission: The sending of information continuously in packet form rather than one byte at a time.

System Fault Tolerance: The duplication of hardware and data to ensure that failure of part of a network will not result in network downtime.

10baseT: A new IEEE standard for a 10-mbps twisted-pair transmission network.

Token: A data packet used to transmit information on a token ring network.

Topology: The physical arrangement or shape of a network.

Transient Error: A "soft" network transmission error that is often intermittent and easily corrected by retransmission.

Transport Layer: The layer of the OSI model concerned with protocols for error recognition and recovery as well as regulation of information flow.

TSI: Time Slice Intervals. The way a file server divides its time.

TTS: Transaction Tracking System. A way to ensure data integrity on multiuser databases.

Twisted-Pair Wire: Two insulated wires twisted together so that each wire faces the same amount of interference from the environment.

Wire Center: Connections that enable network administrators to add and remove network workstations without disrupting network operations.

Workstation: A network node. Often such nodes do not contain disk drives.

Bibliography

An Introduction to Local Area Networks. IBM Publication GC 20-8203-1.

Apple Computer Corporation. *AppleTalk Network System Overview.* Addison-Wesley Publishing Company, 1989.

AT&T STARLAN Network Custom Guide. AT&T Information Systems Publication 999-350-00115.

Bartee, Thomas C., editor, *Data Communications, Networks, and Systems,* Howard W. Sams, 1985.

Dixon, R.C., Strole, N.C. and Markov, J.D., "A Token Ring Network for Local Data Communications," *IBM Systems Journal,* Vol. 22, Nos. 1&2 (1983), pp. 47–62.

IBM PC Network Program User's Guide. IBM Publication 6361559.

IBM Token Ring Network: A Functional Perspective. IBM Publication G520-6062-1.

IBM Token Ring Network Decision. IBM Publication G320-9438-1.

IBM Token Ring Network PC Products Description and Installation. IBM Publication GG 24-173900.

Introduction to Information Systems Network (ISN). AT&T Information Systems Publication 999-740-1011S.

Menu Utilities. Novell Publication 100-000323-001.

O'Brien, Bill, "Network Management: Tips & Traps," *PC World,* September 1986, pp. 228–237.

Stamper, David. *Business Data Communications.* Benjamin/Cummings, 1986.

Schatt, Stan. *Microcomputers in Business & Society.* Charles Merrill Publishing Company, *1989.*

Schatt, Stan. *Understanding NetWare.* Howard W. Sams, *1989.*

STARLAN Network Application Programmer's Reference Manual. AT&T Information Systems Publication 999-802-215IS.

STARLAN Network Design Guide. AT&T Information Systems Publication 999-809-101IS.

STARLAN Network Introduction. AT&T Information Systems Publication 999-809-100IS.

STARLAN Network Technical Reference Manual. AT&T Information Systems Publication 999-300-208IS.

Strole, Normal C. "A Local Communications Network Based on Interconnected Token-Access Rings: A Tutorial," *IBM Journal of Research Development*, Vol. 27, No. 5 (September 1983), pp. 481–496.

Supervisor's Guide. Novell Publication 100-000425-001.

10Net Software Reference Manual. 10Net Communications (DCA) Publication 001908.

3+ Administrator Guide for Macintosh. 3Com Publication 3283-8145.

3+Backup User Guide. 3Com Publication 1912-00.

3+Mail for Macintosh User Guide. 3Com Publication 4576-01.

3+Mail User Guide. 3Com Publication 1911-00.

3+ Open MS OS/2 LAN Manager User Guide. 3Com Publication 4699-01.

3+Share User Guide. 3Com Publication 1694-00.

TOPS DOS Version 2.1. Sun Microsystems TOPS Division. 1988.

VINES Administrator's Reference. Banyan Systems Publication 092047-000.

VINES User's Guide. Banyan Systems Publication 092002-002.

Answers to Quizzes

Chapter 1

1. a
2. b
3. a
4. b
5. d
6. a
7. c
8. b

Chapter 2

1. c
2. c
3. b
4. b
5. b
6. b
7. d
8. a
9. b
10. c
11. a
12. c
13. a
14. b
15. c
16. b
17. b
18. b
19. d
20. a

Chapter 3

1. b
2. b
3. d
4. c
5. b
6. c
7. a
8. c
9. d
10. c
11. c
12. b
13. b
14. c
15. b
16. b
17. d
18. a
19. a
20. a

Chapter 4

1. b
2. b
3. b
4. a
5. b
6. b
7. a
8. c
9. a
10. b
11. c
12. c
13. b
14. a
15. c
16. b
17. a
18. c

Chapter 5

1. c
2. b
3. d
4. a
5. b
6. a
7. a
8. b
9. b
10. c
11. a
12. c
13. b
14. d
15. b
16. b
17. a
18. d

Chapter 6

1. a
2. c
3. c
4. c
5. d
6. c
7. d
8. d
9. a
10. b
11. b
12. a
13. a
14. b
15. d
16. a
17. b
18. a
19. d
20. b

Chapter 7

1. d
2. b
3. c
4. d
5. a
6. b
7. c
8. d
9. b
10. b
11. a
12. b
13. b
14. d
15. b
16. a
17. b
18. c
19. a
20. d

Chapter 8

1. b
2. c
3. a
4. b
5. a
6. d
7. c
8. d
9. a
10. b
11. b
12. a
13. a
14. b
15. c
16. b
17. a
18. a
19. b
20. b

Chapter 9

1. a
2. b
3. d
4. c
5. a
6. b
7. b
8. c
9. c
10. b
11. a
12. c
13. d
14. c
15. a

Chapter 10

1. c
2. a
3. b
4. b
5. c
6. a
7. c
8. c
9. d
10. c
11. c
12. a
13. c
14. d
15. b
16. a
17. a
18. c
19. d
20. a

Chapter 11

1. c
2. d
3. a
4. c
5. b
6. b
7. d
8. b

Chapter 12

1. a
2. c
3. b
4. d
5. d
6. a
7. c
8. d
9. a
10. a

Index